PELICAN BOOKS

A386

THE AESTHETIC ADVENTURE

WILLIAM GAUNT

*William Gaunt*

# THE AESTHETIC
# ADVENTURE

PENGUIN BOOKS

Penguin Books Ltd, Harmondsworth, Middlesex
CANADA: Penguin Books (Canada) Ltd, 178 Norseman Street,
Toronto 18, Ontario
AUSTRALIA: Penguin Books Pty Ltd, 762 Whitehorse Road,
Mitcham, Victoria

—

First Published by Jonathan Cape January 1945
Published in Pelican Books 1957

Made and printed in Great Britain
by C. Nicholls & Company Ltd

TO
MARY CATHERINE

# CONTENTS

# LIST OF PLATES

# I

# A CONTINENTAL STATE OF MIND

I

A LONG and exhausting war was over. The bloody tide of conquest had flowed across Europe, ebbed and left behind the stagnant flats of anti-climax. A ruined dictator had died, of cancer in the stomach, in the little island to which he had been exiled, far out in the Atlantic. A sick continent, shivering in the rags of ancient finery, amid the remnants of destroyed institutions, looked with gloomy surmise on the future.

This was the state of affairs when the Napoleonic campaigns were ended, and the Emperor, with dramatic finality, had disappeared from the scene. The following stages of mental reaction were spread over many years. First came a mood of depression, which affected many countries but was most strongly marked in France. The cause of that depression was to a large extent physical. France had been bled white, by the wholesale slaughter accompanying those two events of historical brilliance, the Revolution and the First Empire. When the terror had killed off the aristocracy and Napoleon had continued the work of the guillotine by squandering in battle a very large number of young and vigorous lives, the cream of the nation was twice skimmed. The unfit and the disillusioned remained, together with a middle-class, a *bourgeoisie,* staid, prudent, small-minded, tight-fisted, of traders and peasants who had profited by the catastrophes of the evolutionary process and become the backbone of society.

Fifteen years after the battle of Waterloo, among those who were intelligent enough to feel an emotion, despair was widespread. The splendid era which war seemed to promise while it was still in progress had not matured. The idealist found himself in a world from which ideals were conspicuously absent. The republican, after all his trouble, was mortified by the spectacle of a restored monarchy whose unreal forms and spurious titles parodied the Old Régime; and as the heads of those who would have been his patrons were cut off, the man of genius received neither sympathy nor support in this grim, post-war existence.

The names of those who did away with themselves or sank into an early grave, in or about the year 1830, make a distinguished list. Those who did not commit suicide or give up all hope became defiant. Defiance was at once a product of and an antidote to despair. If an idealistic revolution had come to a dull end it was still possible to express contempt for dullness and to flout the society in which it was enshrined. The ardent spirits of 1830 thus became romantic outlaws and outlawry in due course a fashion. The intellectuals of Paris wore the steeple-crowned hats and sinister cloaks of Italian brigands and cultivated disdain for the law-abiding citizen.

The law-abiding citizen was, of course, moral; in, as it appeared to the ardent spirits, a dull, small, hateful way. If only through the necessity of opposition, it was incumbent on them, therefore, to be the propagandists of immorality or, at least, amorality on a generous, a magnificent scale: and in 1835 there was published a book animated by precisely this purpose. It was a novel, called *Mademoiselle de Maupin*. It was written by an audacious young man, who hailed from Tarbes in the Pyrenees, Théophile Gautier.

Gautier was born in 1811 (when Napoleon was planning his attack upon Russia) and was just at the right age to experience the full force of the romantic decade. He wrote, with the fervour of youth, to shock: and he attached to his novel a special preface so that none should overlook the fact that it was meant to be a deliberate onslaught on the propriety of the bourgeois.

*Mademoiselle de Maupin* was impudently pagan. It described with enthusiasm the amorous adventures of a not very specific, gay, cavalier time, in which was plain to be seen the nostalgia of the young nineteenth century for the aristocratic order that had gone. It made much of the piquant and ambiguous position of a young woman masquerading in man's clothes. Its hero, d'Albert, praised the vicious Caesars and irresponsible pleasure seekers of the ancient world. All ecstasies and all excesses were justified in the search for sensation and the delight in beauty which, the author implied, was a law unto itself.

A class was growing up to which this latter proposition was an article of faith. Its name, a place-name without locality, was Bohemia. The word is still used to refer in a vague way to any place where there are young, poor artists struggling with their environment and dreaming of greatness, but, in France, Bohemia was, like the middle class itself, a by-product of the Revolution and its radical displacement of the social order.

Cloud-cuckoo-land was the result of the operation of economic laws. Painters, writers, musicians, no longer had a niche in society, because no class existed which felt any need for their productions or identified itself with their interests. Thus the Bohemian was a sort of anarchist. He must contrive to live without wage or settled income and therefore was unpractical and imprudent from necessity. The bourgeois was his enemy not simply because he was, as the great Daumier was representing him in his lithographs for *Le Charivari*, a creature of greed and craft, of physical and mental ugliness, but still more because the bourgeois had an objection to the arts, and to artists, as performing no useful function he could understand. Such an attitude constituted, for the artist, a release from social obligations. He lived careless of law and landlords, and he began to adopt a defensive attitude of gay mockery. In fact it seemed as if the French character after the Revolution and the Empire split into two. The traditional verve, the light, laughing-loving spirit was now the property of the Bohemian and strongly contrasted with the dourness of the philistines who ruled the land and held the money bags.

So it appeared to Henri Murger, a lawyer's clerk who took

to letters and the happy-go-lucky existence of the Latin Quarter. His famous account of student life, *Scènes de la Vie de Bohème*, shows how the conspiracy of the artist against the rest of the world had grown by 1845. In succession to the mood of despair and defiance came the comparative happiness of irresponsibility. Murger, the renegade bourgeois, represented disorder sentimentally and even as a kind of heroism. The most ineffective of artists was a hero, and the most admirable of bankers, if not a villain, was at least an idiot. Ineffectiveness in itself assumed a charm. Thus Schaunard, the musician, planning the symphony (which, of course, he would never complete), *The Influence of Blue on the Arts*, constantly struck, with a symbolic effort of failure, the cracked note on his piano (*sacré gredin de ré*). Rodolphe, with his poetry, and Marcel dreaming of his masterpiece (in prospect) *The Crossing of the Red Sea*, were kindred spirits, whose charm was make-believe. The work-girls of Paris who strayed within the circle were transformed into docile handmaidens of the arts. When the heroes of Murger wanted to eat, they obtained their supper by some ingenious trick from the proprietor of the Café Momus, and when Bohemians had contrived to sup all the difficulties of life were at an end. They refused to believe in to-morrow. They were great practical jokers and serious and respectable people were their natural butts. At the same time it was implied that their poverty and (possible) genius made them superior and a privileged caste.

This caste feeling was bound up with a rectitude of principle which accompanied frivolity and dissipation. Bohemians had one law, one morality, one devotion, and that was – Art. It had to be so, for it was their sole justification. They were responsible for it, as, in the previous century, noble patrons had been. They must, now that so few others were interested, preserve it like a sacred mystery.

Thus the artists were gradually forced by circumstances into the position of an aristocracy. The squalor of Bohemianism was an accident. The upkeep of standards apart from and above those of the mass was the essential and this created a special kind of fastidiousness. With contempt for those who did not understand there grew up the feeling that art was necessarily divorced from the common affairs of men.

This development was defined in the meeting and intercourse of two remarkable people, the author of *Mademoiselle de Maupin*, in his mature years, and a younger man, the poet Charles Baudelaire.

2

Vividly, through the mists of time, appears the scene of the first conference of these poets in Paris in the year 1849.

The setting, at the Hôtel Pimodan, seemed in itself to remove them far from the everyday world and to create a peculiar enchantment, an air heavy with a mysterious suggestion of luxury. It was a salon decorated in the Louis XIV style, on whose great marble mantel stood a clock in the form of a gilded elephant, round whose walls ran panels, the work of some long defunct court painter depicting the merry pagan chase of satyrs after nymphs. On the fauteuils, tapestried with hunting scenes by Oudry, favourite artist of the fifteenth Louis, or Desportes, once commissioned to record the rare and curious animals of a royal menagerie, there reclined beautiful women. They were celebrated models, who, by dint of much posing for artists, had acquired, like the room in which they sat, an air of dignified detachment. There was the 'snake woman' – original of the sculptor Clésinger's *Femme au Serpent* – who, fresh from the swimming bath, exhaled the moist fragrance of a naiad: and Maryx, who had inspired the *Mignon* of Ary Scheffer, dressed in white, oddly starred with spots of red. In a posture of professional and habitual grace and slowly passing the rings on her left hand to her right hand she listened without change of expression on her mask-like oriental features to the outrageous speculations, the daring paradoxes of the men.

On Théophile Gautier this interior made a strong impression. It was like the court of some fantastic prince in a tale of Boccaccio, both isolated and intimate, into which time could not intrude, where poets, painters, and beautiful women might unite themselves in an eternity of leisure to talk of art, of literature and love.

No less strong was the impression made on him by Charles Baudelaire, the fantastic prince himself.

A neat, delicate little man of twenty-eight. His hair, cut short, made a sharp triangle on the ivory tower of his brow. His mouth had the voluptuous and ironic contour of a drawing by Leonardo da Vinci. His strongly marked jaws, austerely shaven, showed a bluish pallor, and a delicate and polished coldness of manner concealed the excitable nature of his nervous system.

Together he and Gautier represented the complete expression and final result of thirty decaying years. The man of slogans and romantic enthusiasm. The man of inner mystery, scornfully perverse, hypersensitive, the enemy of the accepted and the commonplace.

The character of Baudelaire was a compound of a natural simplicity which inclined him to hero-worship and a natural subtlety which inclined him to what was difficult and strange. Among his heroes were Eugène Delacroix, the great Romantic painter, and the American writer, Edgar Allan Poe, to whose works he paid the homage of a beautiful translation.

Delacroix represented for him the haughty exclusiveness of the artist and regarding himself as an aristocrat on this new model he cultivated an appropriate manner and dress which he derived from that land where aristocracy survived, the mysterious adjacent island of Britain. He tried to appear (as it had been Delacroix' aim to appear) a *vrai Gentleman*, and fascinated by the dandyism of Beau Brummel he made of that exquisite a sort of philosophical principle. English simplicity was the essence of his costume, as his black coat, brown trousers, and polished pumps bore witness, and he would even use sandpaper in order to remove the vulgar bloom of newness. He avoided that to which the romantic Bohemian was prone – the *chic pittoresque* – that smart picturesqueness which in Gautier somewhat regrettably expressed itself by a flaming red waistcoat. A stickler for conventions, he carried politeness to the verge of affectation, choosing his words with great care and avoiding volubility and gesture like the most phlegmatic of Britons though the satanic epigrams which fell from his lips were not British in the least.

In Edgar Poe he found an inspiring morbidity, a morbidity kindred to that which had lurked in France after its ordeal, but adapted to the purposes of literature. A creature of tragedy and a slave of the bottle he had made poetry out of delirium tremens, and induced strange dreams from which he had evolved masterpieces.

Roderick Usher, in Poe's weird story, the *Fall of the House of Usher*, had shown a perverted connoisseurship in books, scents, and liquors which reflected the author's sense of values to be discovered in what was not normal and natural. And this was balanced, it seemed to Baudelaire, by a cool and calculating appreciation of artistic values like his own. Thus to attain a refinement of sensation by taking a hard way through the bog and quicksand of life presented itself to him almost as a duty. In this way the artist could signify the exacting nature of his own code and plunge into what people called evil from austere motives and with a single-minded devotion to his art. Had not Delacroix perceived the splendour of misery? Was not his painting a great and pitiful hymn rising from scenes of ferocious carnage and barbarism? The voyage of aesthetic discovery could be pressed further, towards stranger ends. What was gross and vile as well as what was savage and barbarous might be made to yield its quota of beauty: and any means were justified in achieving that result. There was even a sort of religious exaltation in choosing the necessary martyrdom of vice, a saintly courage in exploring sin, a religious belief implicit in the defiance of religious rule.

These strange notions revolved behind the noble forehead of Charles Baudelaire, and though he was the younger of the two, he exercised a great influence on Gautier. The latter was not so intense, so introvert, but he acquired, through their friendship, some of Baudelaire's refinement as Baudelaire acquired some of his audacity. Together they crystallized the exclusive position of the artist and his separation from the middle-class world. Gautier, the man of slogans, put it in a phrase – *L'Art pour l'Art* – or, as it may be written in English, Art for Art's Sake.

*L'Art pour l'Art.* The phrase had a clarion sound – apart from what it meant – the sound which would rally the faint-hearted on the battlefield and send impetuous cavalrymen dashing forward in heroic frenzy. It is by the reckless im-provization of such general ideas that Frenchmen have egged themselves on to perform deeds of glory or create works of beauty; and what the phrase meant was what Gautier had expressed in *Maupin* and what Baudelaire had learnt from Poe: that moral purpose, deep thought, sage and prudent reflexions, all the worn and respectable trappings of the creative spirit were irrelevant to its free exercise; positively hampered it, in fact.

Gautier defined himself – and the words have the effect of an emphatic slap on a red waistcoat – as *un homme pour qui le monde extérieur existe*. 'A man for whom the visible world exists . . . '

A world of sensation. Forms, colours, feeling were meant to provide the refined pleasure and enjoyment of the man for whom it existed and he must turn them into art without restraint, scruple or concern as to whether this satisfied the policeman, pleased the minister of religion or elevated the shopkeeper.

The word 'aesthetic' which Gautier inevitably used in his exposition of the nature of beauty in art, was not of course a French invention. It came from that matrix of general ideas, ancient Greece: in its original form it made a sharp distinction between thought and feeling – αἰσθητικός, meaning of or pertaining to αἰσθητά – things perceptible by the senses, things material (as opposed to νοητά, things thinkable or immaterial).

The source of aesthetic theory is in certain dialogues of the greatest of philosophers, Plato. Plato, in brilliant phrases, with the most profound depth of suggestion, had outlined the independent existence of beauty, independent, that is to say, of truth, edification or usefulness. In succession to him,

Aristotle (his pupil) and Longinus (an unknown author of the first century A.D.) provided modifications of this idea of beauty without altering its essential purport. In this respect, as in so many others, the germ of modern thought was to be found in the ancient world.

The inquiry into the nature of beauty had been resumed most actively in Germany. The German philosophers of the eighteenth century looking wistfully back to the clear light of civilization in which they sought to illumine the obscure longings of the Teutonic soul; piling up mountainous definitions, logical profundities; retrieved and handled anew the word 'aesthetic'. Alexander Gottlieb Baumgarten (1714–1762) is notable for having first applied it to the 'criticism of taste' considered as a science or philosophy. Immanuel Kant, his greater contemporary, applied it more strictly in the ancient definition as 'the science which treats of the conditions of sensuous perception'. Others, Schelling, Hegel, Schopenhauer, added to the edifice of words. Early in the nineteenth century, 'Aesthetics' was looked on as German property. Thus the *Penny Cyclopaedia*, in 1832, calls it 'the designation given by German writers to a branch of philosophical inquiry, the object of which is a philosophic theory of the beautiful'. It was also regarded with some contempt. Gwilt's *Encyclopaedia of Architecture* criticizes 'a silly pedantic term under the name of Aesthetics ... one of the metaphysical and useless additions to nomenclature in the arts in which the German writers abound'.

The wild humour of De Quincey had first turned the solemn disputations of the theorists to creative account. Art, according to the philosophers (with whom he and Coleridge were so familiar), was distinct from morality. What, therefore, if one were to trace the possible effects of this freedom? In murder, now, for instance. 'It may also be treated aesthetically as the Germans call it – that is, in relation to good taste.' The famous essay, *Murder considered as one of the Fine Arts* (1839), was the result. It was a humorous fantasy, and somewhat morbidly so: though it would be fair enough to say that morbidity and art were connected in De Quincey's mind, inasmuch as the imaginative flights of his prose were stimulated – like the poetry of his friend, Coleridge – by indulgence in opium. There is some significance in the fact that De Quincey was also one of Baudelaire's idols.

It remained for the Frenchmen to turn the scientific anguish, the agony of difficult explanation in which the German philosophers were absorbed, into something more definite and more fruitful. They did so, like De Quincey, as artists rather than scholars. They romanticized a classic principle. A theory was to them an inspiration. Its only value was to assist in the production of works of art.

The beauty in words independent of ideas, the gem-like quality which later was so much to be sought after and imitated, was the object of Gautier's collection of poems, the *Émaux et Camées* of 1852. 'The title' (Enamels and Cameos), said the author, 'expresses the aim of treating little subjects within restricted limits of form as if they were a surface of gold or copper with the bright hues of enamel: or like using the wheel of the engraver of precious stones on agate, cornelian or onyx.' He had been a painter before he took to writing and was for that reason inclined to think that literature could make use in words of the same methods as the painter, the sculptor, and the engraver with their pigments and marble and incised metal. The name of a precious stone, beryl or chrysoprase, was like a rich hue on a palette – a patch of sensuous beauty in the verbal mosaic and its meaning was secondary to the impression which the sound evoked.

Baudelaire said much the same thing. 'Poetry has no other end but itself: it cannot have any other: and no poem is so great, so noble, so entirely worthy of the name as that which has been written simply for the pleasure of writing a poem. If a poet has followed a moral end he has diminished his poetic force and the result is most likely to be bad.'

In a sense this might be called the doctrine of a severe professionalism or at least specialization. It *defined* the artist as such. It distinguished him from the great or creative man (even though the latter was not necessarily distinct). Thus Balzac, supreme genius as he was, was not in this strict meaning an 'artist', lacking as he did the overmastering passion for form and style. At the same time it had its disturbing aspect. De Quincey, as a whim, or even a reduction to an absurdity, had indicated the sinister possibilities of an outlook untrammelled by a regard for any other than purely aesthetic laws. Plato, himself, had not gone thus far. His strong political sense had caused him to reject that which was not – in the highest sense – profitable – even though he had dissociated art from utility. The imitation of what was ugly was not in the Greek canon: and yet somehow in this nineteenth century, in an exhausted society, itself so far removed from perfection, there was a need to escape from idealism to say things no one had dared to say, to embrace reality even in the guise of ugliness: and, though conduct was not the same thing as art – still even in his conduct the artist must, if needs be, undergo these experiences which contributed to create some desired state of mind. There was no knowing where the search for sensation might lead. With Baudelaire it led to orgy. In his own disdainful and at the same time conscientious manner he applied his admirable qualities to 'satanism'. A devoted son, a loyal friend, a scrupulous and sympathetic critic, he did his best to be bad. In avoiding 'a moral end' he pursued vice, that is to say sensation for sensation's sake, with a profound seriousness never disturbed by anything so middle-class as a sense of humour. The smoke of hashish rose in a blue cloud and hung over the decorative furniture of the Hôtel Pimodan and the court of the fantastic prince became a sort of opium den. In the sensual negress and the sexually aberrated he found, more inspiring to him than ideal beauty, the baneful attraction of the vampire, and the studies he pursued greatly to the detriment of his health and fortune resulted in the famous *Les Fleurs du Mal* of 1857.

These 'flowers of evil', poems exquisite in form, were to become the bible of 'decadence' – a word somewhat indiscriminately applied to the following of Baudelaire to describe either their perverse outlook or artificial style. The sensuous disquiet of the *Fleurs du Mal* was to haunt the minds of poets for many years afterwards, not only in France but in England.

Poetry, the supreme breaker of restrictions, entered on forbidden ground in the name of an unlawful or anyway unrecognized authority – Art.

## 3

The craving for sensation, the fastidious and patrician research for strange refinement, the jealous cultivation of art as a thing removed from the common affairs of men constituted the prevailing atmosphere of the 'brilliant' period which was now beginning – the Second Empire. By a series of republican (and even Bohemian) revolutions, assisted that is to say by 'vagabonds, disbanded soldiers, discharged prisoners, fugitives from the galleys, sharpers, jugglers, professional beggars, pickpockets, conjurers, gamesters, pimps, brothel keepers, porters, men of letters, organ grinders, rag pickers, knife grinders, and tinkers', Charles Louis Napoleon Bonaparte, third son of the King of Holland, made himself Emperor of the French. The description of his helpers is that of Karl Marx who, it will be seen, places 'men of letters' somewhere between porters and organ grinders; who further described French Bohemia as 'the scum, offal, and detritus of society'.

The social structure might be imperfect. Nevertheless, it was in the Second Empire that France won back a dominance over the culture of the world not unlike that she had possessed in the days of Louis XIV. The rebuilding of Paris in itself turned all eyes on the capital. In the same year as he married his Spanish countess, Eugénie de Montijo, the Emperor chose Georges Eugène Haussmann, a Paris-born financier of German origin, to carry out a magnificent series of public works, designed to win support from the working class for whom they provided employment. The first fruit of this programme which was to turn the city into the most superb of modern capitals, to widen streets, lay out boulevards and parks, was the great exhibition in 1855, rivalling and surpassing those that had been held in England a short while before.

From this time onwards the flow of visitors to Paris steadily increased, an interest abroad in things French grew more pronounced and the capital, by its beauty as well as the creative genius to be found there, took the place which Rome had previously occupied as art centre of the world. Painting, as well as literature, helped to establish this position. The rediscovery of the visible world was even more the painter's business than the writer's. His separation, economically, from the rest of society was more pronounced. He could, with more justification still, apply to himself the guiding principle of Art for Art's sake.

The new ideas, passing from one original mind to another and from one art to another in a symphonic movement, changing and yet preserving the influences from which they had sprung, gained an added power and importance by being set against a showy imperial background. But that, with its parade of activity and progress, made no other difference. Amid its slightly satirical and derisive splendour the arts pursued a destiny already laid down. It was by the theory and practice of art for art's sake, intertwined with a variously interpreted 'decadence', that the culture of France was to have influence abroad and, in particular, to affect the opposed and island culture of Britain ...

4

Britain, in this same period, with all her wealth and power, in spite of the fact that her possessions stretched round the globe, was, in mind, a hermit. When the Napoleonic wars were over she withdrew herself from interest in continental affairs. France, as far as she was concerned, was a back number. The future lay in mechanical industry.

Britain had arrived at a way of living previously unknown in the history of the world, and as yet unique. Never before had so many inventions been turned to practical advantage and made to produce riches. Never before had the life of a people been made to depend on machines. This novel development in itself made Britain isolated. She was alone in the Industrial Revolution. Unlike France she was concerned, not with the moods of defeat and decay, but the problems and anxieties of success.

The result was that Britain, absorbed and energetic in her own business, looked on the Continent as a different, an inferior world. The discipline of industry had led not to the loosening but to the affirmation of moral principle. That one Englishman was equal to six of any other nationality was an idea firmly implanted by Trafalgar and Waterloo. Great wealth, hard work and a strict régime combined to increase this feeling of superiority. A Frenchman was an undersized, frivolous, vapouring creature left behind in the magnificent competition of Progress; and the only continental sympathy of Britain, in the first half of the nineteenth century, was that with Germany. Germanic morality and discipline were in keeping with the strenuous life of the nation. Historians dated all the national virtues from the arrival of the Angles and Saxons. For the monumental work which he devoted to that least prepossessing of rulers, Frederick the 'Great', Thomas Carlyle was decorated by the Prussian Government. Goodness was incarnated in the person of the Prince Consort.

Hence the strong moral tone of the arts. Progress and the general welfare were their concern. Social, economic and religious questions were of paramount importance, and even a movement of artists, like that of the Pre-Raphaelites, which began in the forties, was profoundly coloured by these issues. The idea of 'Art for Art's sake' was entirely foreign to Victorian England. That Art might go contrary to moral principles or leave them out of account seemed utterly outrageous – the distinction between sensuous perception and sensual indulgence dangerously slight.

It is strange to reflect on, difficult to exaggerate, the mutual absence of understanding between Britain and her nearest neighbours. To the intelligent Frenchman, the demoniac activity of the island (combined with its fogs), the puzzling contrast of prudishness and rigid morality with a wild and abandoned night-life, created a sort of admiring horror. The intelligent Englishman, ironically enough, returned the feeling.

Used to the fog and the activity, blunted by habit to the poverty and ugliness which surrounded him, he saw himself on a pedestal of respectability at an unquestionably higher level than the rest of mankind. The lurid descriptions of London by Taine in his *History of English Literature* or by Dostoevsky in his *Bourgeois of Paris* would have seemed quite absurd to the islander of the sixties, well accustomed as he might be to the scenes of which these foreign observers wrote. At the same time when he went abroad he became acutely aware of the instability of foreign society, he everywhere scented iniquity and instinctively shut his mind to modes of thought which might threaten his most cherished principles and were contrary to the hygienic soundness, as it seemed to him, on which his life was based; and in consequence he steered clear or remained ignorant of the intellectual life whose discovery was often the ostensible purpose of his visit. The protective spirit of isolation was common to the writer, the painter, and the man of worldly affairs.

Yet the barriers, in the latter half of the nineteenth century, were to be broken down. The 'moat' of the Channel, powerful against 'infection and the hand of war', was less so against the onslaught of ideas. Books, pictures and thoughts crossed the narrow sea. Gautier and Baudelaire were spoken of in London. A few propagandists went to and fro spreading the gospel of Art for Art's sake. A hybrid movement called 'aesthetic' came into being. Decadence became a watchword. Opposition was aroused. Offensive was launched and counteroffensive, in the course of which two sensational and remarkable trials were fought out in the Law Courts. The conflict to which the inroad of foreign ideas and uncongenial aims gave rise shocked, astonished and fascinated Britain. It is the theme of the pages which follow.

## II

# MUSTER OF FORCES

I

## Shirts and No Shirts

'CAN'T you get the concierge to do that sort of thing for you?'

The scene was a set of rooms in Paris, in the rue Notre Dame des Champs. The time, the year 1856. The speaker was a young American, James Abbott McNeill Whistler. The occasion of his remark was the spectacle of his English friends, fellow art students, going through various healthful exercises. One was swinging on a trapeze. Another was vigorously twirling a pair of Indian clubs. The place was full of the properties of sport. Ropes to climb hung from a beam in the ceiling. Foils and boxing gloves lay about among the easels and portfolios; and to Whistler all this was very strange and rather irritating.

Hence the remark, one of the first of many witticisms which its author was to level against the 'islanders'. It was witty rather than funny; it implied ridicule without appreciation. It was a neat reduction to absurdity. Evidently, one did not come to Paris to develop the muscles. Any fool could tire himself out, anywhere, at any time. The concierge could do it.

There were four of these insular sportsmen: George Louis Palmella Busson du Maurier, the future *Punch* draughtsman and author of *Trilby*, was their leader. He was of French origin, the grandson of émigrés who came to England at the time of the Revolution. But he had become more English than the English themselves. As a boy he went to a day school near Passy where he had acquired a great dislike of French schoolboys and their ways. '*Le vrai chic anglais*' – English modes and manners – was his ideal and he brought from London, where he had studied at University College to be an analytical chemist, the fashionable 'Noah's Ark' coat in order to impress the Latin Quarter. A little, sensitive man, with weak eyes, he adored music, drawing and big Englishmen. Snatches of French song with gay and absurd refrains, *flarifla* and *zing-tra-la* trilled spontaneously from his lips and, accompanied by a Greek musician Sotiri, he would play on the hired piano such favourite ballads as *Le vin à Quatre Sous*.

> Fi! de ces vins d'Espagne,
> Ils ne sont pas faits pour nous,
> C'est le vin à quatre sous
> Qui nous sert de Champagne.

Then there was Edward John Poynter, famous president-to-be of the Royal Academy. He was an earnest, bearded young man, the son of an architect. His mother was a granddaughter of the sculptor, Thomas Banks, first in England, according to Sir Joshua Reynolds, to produce 'works of classic grace'. Educated at Westminster School, he was sent to Italy at the age of seventeen because of his delicate health. He met another future president of the Academy in Rome – Frederick Leighton, handsome, twenty-three and already the deuce of a swell, convinced, indeed, that only by being a deuce of a swell could an artist hope to win success. Awed and admiring young Poynter had watched the progress of Leighton's first sensational painting – *Cimabue's Madonna carried through the streets of Florence*. He had determined to rival him in this 'classic' style of painting. Dreaming of fame he would sit, tapping out on the communal piano airs from the popular *Il Trovatore*. Thomas Lamont and Thomas Armstrong completed the group. The former was an affable Scotsman with side-whiskers ('The Laird' in *Trilby*). Armstrong came from Manchester and in later life was to become a meritorious official of the Victoria and Albert Museum and a Commander of the Bath.

Theirs was a very simple and even homely bohemianism.

In the morning they went to draw at the *atelier* of the painter Charles Gleyre. This was a large and dirty room with a grimy north light, its bare walls covered with charcoal scribblings of many mischievous hands and the colourful scrapings of many palettes. It was a sort of half-way house between the personal workshop and the school of art.

Once upon a time master painters found it needful, when they became prosperous, to take on an apprentice 'or apprentices, with whom their relation for a while was almost that of father and son. But this, in 1856, already belonged to the past. Gleyre's studio was not his own place of work but was personal in name only. It was open to a swarm of would-be artists who came and went as they pleased. Order was kept by a *massier* – a senior student usher. Together with some thirty or forty French *rapins* (or 'daubers' as the students were called), close-cropped, blue-bloused, astraddle low stools, the *Angliches*, distinguished from the rest by their size, the peculiar cut of their whiskers and the air of gravity which was the Victorian hallmark, drew for some hours from the nude male or female model. Gleyre himself, a Swiss disciple of the great Ingres, who had inherited the studio from Delaroche, paid a state visit once a week to give a perfunctory look at the work that was being done. The upholder of a cold and dead classicism he was not in himself an inspiring master. A few, like Poynter, might admire and imitate him: for the rest his atelier was a convenience for working and meeting with congenial spirits.

When the morning session was over – it lasted in summer from six to eleven – the students dispersed for more work or play as they pleased. Many a poor French lad, son of a tradesman or well-to-do peasant who with much misgiving had allowed his offspring to take up an occupation for which, evidently, there was no place in the scheme of things, went on to bread and butter work. He might eke out the grudged pittance from home by painting church pictures of a crude sort. There were shops in the rue Bonaparte and the rue des Saints Pères where canvases were supplied with a ready printed outline of a composition for one of the Stations of the Cross. Some thirty feet of canvas had to be covered with oil paint to win the hungry artist the sum of seven francs, this being the standard rate for each picture.

But this hard, badly paid labour was for the very poor: and the *Angliches* were not so poor as that. They could do what they liked – box, swing on ropes or be otherwise leisured. When it came to eating, their insular prejudice was still strong. They cooked chops for themselves and drank bottled beer and gin. Their chosen restaurant when they dined out was a little place in the rue Royale, patronized by the racing crowd, where it was possible to get roast beef and boiled mutton. The Christmas dinner of the crazy English was '*Gigot Bouilli – Dieu de Dieu.*' 'One must,' said the concierge, 'be English to eat a dish like that.'

With these tastes, they kept somewhat aloof from the other students. They were aloof from Paris itself.

Those who seek for some explanation of what art was all about in the late fifties of the nineteenth century will look in vain in the pages of *Trilby* which describe the student life of these admirable and respectable young men. There is a vague impression that something exciting was going on: but what it was is not very clear and though it is true that *Trilby* was not intended to be the vehicle for serious information it is open to doubt if the author or the friends he portrayed had in fact any but the haziest notions of what was stirring in the attractive city of Paris. To them it was an incidental stage of a tour. Antwerp or Düsseldorf would have done as well; and, in fact, du Maurier and Armstrong went on to complete their education at these alternative centres. The group of friends paid a visit to Barbizon, the famous haunt of landscape painters, which struck them as a mean and untidy-looking village. Millet, the painter of peasants and peasant life, was there, an amiable burly man like a farmer, though it was not until a considerable time afterwards that they realized he was of any importance. The 'Barbizon School' to them was represented by a painter called d'Aligny, who treated his pupils like a drill sergeant and, taking out his watch and marshalling his squad in the early morning, gave the word of command, 'At the poplars with your brushes! It is six o'clock and chrome yellow is back in nature.'

In most respects, du Maurier, Poynter, Armstrong and Lamont were the complete opposite of young James Abbott McNeill Whistler. Paris to him was home. It was so partly because all his childhood associations were concerned with continental Europe. From the age of nine to the age of fourteen he had lived like a little prince in St Petersburg. The decision of the Emperor Nicholas I to build a railway from St Petersburg to Moscow, and his choice for that task of Major-General George Washington Whistler, civil engineer, United States officer, and the father of James Abbott, brought the future artist to the Russian city. He had skated on the Neva, learnt French, studied drawing at the Petersburg Academy of Fine Arts and almost became a page at the Imperial Court. Then in 1848 Mrs Whistler's fear of the effect another Russian winter might have on his health caused her to transfer him to England. This hovering between the old world and the new, of which England remained the focus, had been a traditional part of the family history. The line of fighting men and clergymen who were the ancestors of Whistler on his father's side had their origins in Ireland and England. The names of seventeenth-century Whistlers are recorded in the church at Goring-on-Thames. Dr Daniel Whistler, in the time of Samuel Pepys, was described as 'the most facetious man in nature' – a term which would have well suited his more famous descendant. James Abbott McNeill's grandfather had been a private in the British army. His elopement with the daughter of Sir Edward Bishop had led to their migrating to America, to his becoming an officer in the service of the United States on its pioneer western frontiers. Whistler's father, born in the wild west and destined for the army, had, in adopting the subsidiary profession of railroad engineer, resumed contact with England. Thence came the main supply of locomotives for the new age of steam and in 1828 George Whistler had crossed the Atlantic to survey the English railway system.

The family of Whistler's mother (his father's second wife)

had closer connexions still with the 'old home'. The McNeills of North Carolina had been Stuart supporters who went to America from the island of Barra, in 1746, after the battle of Culloden. The father of Anna McNeill had been born in Scotland. She, herself, had 'crossed the brook' before the Russian enterprise to see remaining relatives, had confidently entrusted Deborah, daughter of Major Whistler by his first wife, to Aunt Eliza at Preston. Thus it was natural enough that Jamie should live in London. He stayed at 62 Sloane Street for about a year, with his half-sister Deborah who had married an English doctor, Seymour Haden, a fashionable and even, it was said, a brilliant man who knew Dickens, had met Browning and nodded to Carlyle. The stay was too short, however, to give Jamie a thorough acquaintance with English life and on the death of Major-General Whistler in 1849 the family returned to America.

But America offered no attractions. Three years were wasted in the United States Military Academy at West Point from which, in 1855, Whistler was dismissed for failure in a chemistry examination. 'Had silicon been a gas,' he said later, 'I should have been a major-general.' If silicon had been a gas he would no doubt have fought in the Civil War. He then spent some months in the Coast Survey. He worked in Washington, was considered something of a wit, drew random sketches of his own on the copper plates intended for severe geographical outlines. Getting tired of this he persuaded his mother to let him become an artist. An artist was out of his element in pioneer America, so in 1855 he crossed the Atlantic again fortified by an annual allowance of three hundred and fifty dollars.

This early wandering experience had several effects. It sharpened his intelligence while it prevented him from acquiring any very great learning. It enabled him to understand and sympathize with the European mind while it kept him from looking on any one country as his own or having a preference for Anglo-Saxon modes of thought and living. Paris was far less strange than Lowell, Massachusetts, where, in a demurely attractive Puritan house, he had first seen the light of day. 'I do not choose to be born at Lowell,' he was to say to an American who claimed him as fellow-townsman. He elected to go to Paris (to which only few American visitors yet came) mainly because he had read Henri Murger's book *Scènes de la Vie de Bohème*. Devouring that sentimental fairy-tale at an impressionable age, Whistler came to the conclusion that the ideal existence was that of the Bohemian.

From the first he adopted a Bohemian programme. When he landed at Boulogne and took train for Paris he got into conversation at once with a young Irishman, in the casual fashion which Murger would have prescribed. John O'Leary was going to walk the hospitals. O'Leary knew no French. Neither of them knew where to stay. It was in the spirit of *la Bohème* that they should agree to share rooms. 'Drive to the Latin Quarter,' said Whistler to a cabman who intelligently deposited them at the Hôtel Corneille. This was a large, dingy apartment house near the Odéon Theatre, inhabited by some eighty rowdy lodgers – students of law, medicine and art. The rickety wooden box tied up with rope, which contained the Irishman's belonging, came to bits on the way up the stairs and the sovereigns carefully wrapped in his clothes came rolling out in a golden trickle. 'If it's been leaking like that all the way, it's few that will be left for me,' said the owner.

This to Whistler was an admirable beginning. Thus and in no other way should two Murgeresque students meet. He mimicked, joyously, O'Leary's accent. The scantiness of the latter's wardrobe was, in itself, both amusing and correct and poverty was the greatest joke in the world, to one, of course, who could count on that small but reliable sum of three hundred and fifty dollars a year.

So Whistler gradually surrounded himself with what he called his 'no-shirt' friends. These were penniless students and amusing characters of the Quarter. They lived in empty rooms and drew their furniture on the wall in charcoal with skilful effects of light and shade. Idle and unkempt, they would lean out of top windows, absorbed in the pastime of fishing for their landlady's goldfish in a bowl on a balcony underneath, with a hook let down on the end of a piece of string. They used the bath for any other purpose than that for which it was intended. They ate off the bottom of a plate when the right side was dirty and had a gift for breaking crockery and furniture. Whistler was thrilled. One 'no-shirt' in particular, Ernest Delannoy with his ancient straw hat, gaping shoes, and amiable futility, was a never failing source of entertainment. It was necessary to be like such a man, to create situations of financial difficulty and comic hardship in order to savour to the full the insolent happiness of Bohemian life.

'I have just eaten my washstand.'

With these words Whistler gaily addressed the American friend of the family who came in search of him with letters from home and the usual remittance. He was in a small room in a back street up ten flights of stairs. The furniture consisted of an easel, a bed, and a chair on which wash-basin and water pitcher stood. He had, he explained, been living for some months on his wardrobe and retreating skywards to a smaller and cheaper room as his funds dwindled, 'though I seldom get as high as this before the draft comes.'

A legend grew up round him. It was he who pawned his coat to buy a drink and spent the three following days in shirt sleeves; who left his only mattress at the Mont de Piété when they would not advance any money on it and went off saying he would send a man to collect it; who chose a pair of shoes in which to go to Mr Thackeray's evening dress party from those left outside the doors in an hotel, returning them in the small hours. He shared rooms for a while with a French bank clerk. As a prudent measure they obtained thirty pillboxes and put in each a sum for one particular set of expenses. After the first fortnight all thirty were, and remained, empty.

He it was on whom a model lavished a tigerish affection so intense that it induced her to tear up all his drawings. This was Héloise, a little sallow-faced girl, who carried about a basket of crochet work and a volume of de Musset's poems and sang a pretty song about the artistic way in which artists loved.

> Ils aiment si artistement
> Ils sont de si artistes gens.

Héloise was possibly the original of Trilby herself; though it is a fact of some interest that Poynter, when commending the faithfulness of du Maurier's description of their student life, added firmly that there was no Trilby in it. No doubt Whistler thought of Héloise as the Mimi or the Musette of his admired Murger. Nature was already beginning to imitate art.

In Paris, even among Bohemians he was considered unusual. *'Personnage étrange, le Whistler, au chapeau bizarre.'*

A strange fellow, Whistler, with his queer hat. It was of straw with a low crown and an extremely broad brim, with a ribbon dangling over the edge. Beneath the hat was a small man in a white duck suit, with dark, sparkling eyes, a head of luxuriant black curls in which there was a curious white streak, and an air of sauntering through a world with which he was very well satisfied.

With the French he was at home; but with the English it was a different matter. The English students had shirts; and they were not Bohemian in his way. At Gleyre's they kept apart from the greasy fellows Whistler knew. Poynter, especially, was scandalized by the company Whistler kept, by the practical jokes he played. All of them were quite sure he never did any work. They tolerated him and laughed when he held his stick like a banjo and sang a negro song from his native America. Nevertheless, from a serious point of view he was merely an 'idle apprentice'. The description du Maurier wrote of Joe Sibley (Whistler) in *Trilby* shows the impression he made – 'The King of Bohemia ... always in debt ... vain, witty, eccentric in attire ... the most irresistible friend in the world as long as his friendship lasted' – which was not for ever. He would try to punch his ex-friend's head but 'he was better with his tongue than with his fists'.

Whistler's attitude was equally uncomprehending. These fellows seemed to miss a lot of the fun of Paris, with their chops and boiled mutton and bottles of imported beer. He,

Whistler, preferred to dine in the civilized French style at Lalouettes' where you could get a bottle of Burgundy fit for an epicure and costing one franc. Working at Gleyre's and doing gymnastics was very praiseworthy, but the real way to learn was to keep one's eyes and ears open, to use one's head. That was what he did, even when he seemed to be idling. Gleyre taught you to mix your tints on the palette, so that they could be applied to the canvas without further mixing or alteration. All right as far as it went, but you wanted more than this – an inspiring contact with a man like Courbet who had thrown overboard all the old stage properties of painting and was doing something new and real. When that massive and revolutionary genius said '*Il a du talent, le petit Whistler*' – that meant something. To meet a man like that, a man like the poet Charles Baudelaire, was to get a new understanding of art, a sense of something original and creative that was just beginning. There was a man called Lecoq de Boisbaudran who had some very interesting ideas about training the visual memory. You discussed in these circles this amazing art of the Far East, a brand new discovery as exciting almost as the discovery of America itself must have been. To move amongst such people was to drink in the spirit of Paris. That was worth a great number of hours, he thought, of plodding labour: it was exactly what his standoffish English acquaintances were missing.

# Yankee at the Court of King Arthur

AT the end of his student days, Whistler came to England.

It was the obvious place to go. His relatives were there. There, also, was great wealth, and a middle class which, unlike the French middle class, bought pictures and paid large sums of money for them.

He came with a gay confidence born of the Latin Quarter; and brought a couple of 'no-shirt' friends with him. Their names were Fantin-Latour and Legros. These followers, if they be called Bohemians, were so from necessity and not from choice. They did not have that delight in poverty which is fortified by an allowance of three hundred and fifty dollars a year. They were poor and picturesque because they could not help it.

Ignace Henri Jean Théodore Fantin-Latour was a lean, shabby young man with high, famished, Slavonic cheekbones, desperately copying Veronese's *Marriage at Cana* when Whistler first came across him in the Louvre. He was the son of a Russian mother and a half-French, half-Italian father, who had come from Grenoble to try his luck in Paris. They got talking. They began to meet in the Café Molière, one of the places where artists foregathered; and acquaintance became a close friendship.

Fantin introduced Whistler to another friend, a prodigy of M. de Boisbaudran's memory classes, who could look at a picture once and copy it shape for shape with uncanny accuracy and without looking again. This was Alphonse Legros. He was a Burgundian. He had worked as a house-painter in the provinces. He was too serious to be really Bohemian. Oppressed by the hard struggle for existence he remained serious throughout his life and has left only one recorded witticism. This was when somebody asked him why he became a naturalized Englishman. 'So that I can claim to have won the battle of Waterloo, *parbleu,*' he replied.

The destitution of these sombre figures fascinated the American. Legros was in such a mess that 'it needed God or a lesser person to get him out of it'. In winter Fantin used to draw in bed, because of the cold. Shivering, mournful, persistent, he sat there one day, in a threadbare overcoat, a top hat over his eyes and a scarf round his mouth, balancing a candle on the edge of his drawing board and sketching with numbed, gloved hand. Whistler sat by his side, laughing and talking, his own pencil busy. 'Fantin in bed, pursuing his studies under difficulties', he wrote under the portrait. This was droll (droller of course to him than to Fantin). Another situation from Murger, and one in which Rodolphe might well have found himself. It was a drollery which might be continued in England, that strange country of which Whistler himself knew very little except that it rolled in wealth. It was typical of him that he should decide to introduce to his relatives in London, not the respectable English acquaintances that he had made in Paris but two needy Frenchmen. Clearly, Seymour Haden his opulent brother-in-law was the man to appreciate and help them. So Whistler sang to him Fantin's praises and in 1859 engineered an invitation to Sloane Street which became also the means of introducing Legros and even Delannoy.

62 Sloane Street was a revelation to the Frenchmen of the luxury of English middle-class life. To them the comfort was like nothing they had known, its heavy Victorian appurtenances of an incredible splendour, its lavishness in food and drink breath-taking. Delannoy was awed by the bathroom and the 'Niagara' which resulted when the shower was turned on. The champagne at dinner flowed like water and Whistler himself remarked on the pleasure of drinking a glass of brandy without having to pay for the *consommation*. In the music-room in the evening when Deborah in her crinoline knitted by the light of a heavy table lamp and Seymour, settled squarely in his chair, cast a dignified eye over *The Times*, it seemed very secure and reassuring to Fantin-Latour. Conventional by nature he scraped enough money together to appear in correct evening dress.

Considering all things the introduction was successful, though the servants had their doubts about Delannoy, the eccentric foreign guest, who shambled about the house in slippers so as not to exhibit the distressing condition of his shoes. Whistler went to a great deal of trouble on Fantin-Latour's behalf. He introduced him to Alexander Ionides, a Paris friend, one of the wealthy Greek colony in London, which included generous collectors of the work of promising but unknown young men. He took him to visit his friends the Potters, who lived in a big house near Manchester. Everything about the Potters was big, the house, the dinners, the number of visitors and children, the butler. This was as daunting as Sloane Street, though a commission to paint Mrs Potter steeled Fantin for the ordeal. Finally he met, through Whistler, a lawyer called Edwards and his wife, who virtually adopted him, bought his pictures and made others buy them. Fantin always remembered with gratitude *les jolies journées chez Edwards à Sunbury* and he painted a portrait of his patrons, now in the National Gallery in London, which brings them before the eyes with a photographic vividness.

The exchange of benefits was not one-sided. Fantin had been the means of introducing Whistler to the 'movement'. Through him he had met Courbet, the opponent of 'imaginative' art – who believed in painting things as they really were – had so far come under his influence as virtually to be his pupil. Through him he was to retain a connexion with Paris: for one thing became clear – much as Fantin-Latour appreciated the support he received nothing would induce him to remain in England. To Paris he belonged and to Paris back he must go.

It was now that the disturbing question presented itself to Whistler – where did he himself belong? He was in the position of being on the fringe of something whereas he wished to be in the centre; but where was the centre? It was not, apparently, anywhere near Sloane Street. Soon that discrepancy between his own and his brother-in-law's views which was eventually to become a real enmity, showed itself

- in small but unmistakable signs. For example, in what Whistler called 'the brother-in-law's crime'.

This incident concerned Legros. Haden bought from him a little picture called *The Angelus*. It was a quiet, grey church interior with women kneeling in prayer. The owner contemplated it often, and as he looked he became convinced that something was wrong. Yes, surely, the perspective of the floor. It worried him.

Now the doctor was also an artist. His real enthusiasm was not his surgery but was reserved for the copper plates, the baths of acid, the needle, and the printing press which go with the craft of etching. These materials were kept at the top of the house where he would shut himself up and become absorbed in the production of his prints.

So now he felt a great temptation to alter Legros' picture himself. One day he took it down from the wall, removed it from the frame and bore it off to the room at the top of the house. And there, behind a locked door, the deed was done. He altered the offending floor, putting on some brighter colour at the same time, and the operation over, returned *The Angelus* to its usual place.

Shortly afterwards Legros and Whistler were dining in Sloane Street in the absence of its owner. Their eyes went to the picture. Legros admired the frame. That was how a work of art should be treated. He looked closer. Something was different. Admiration gave way to rage. A scoundrel had altered it, painted over it. Could it be? – there could after all be no doubt, the scoundrel must be Haden.

Whistler, too, was angry; and anger with him showed itself in two ways; first in an urge to prompt action, in which he was entirely American. Secondly, in the urge to play a practical joke which his reading of Murger must certainly have encouraged. He took charge. They must make off with the picture and restore it to its original condition. That was the necessary action. Then they would put the picture back without saying anything and enjoy the embarrassment of its owner. That was the joke. They went off in a cab with the canvas to Whistler's studio. They had scraped and wiped it and repainting was in progress when Haden appeared in hot pursuit. The situation was quite as good an anything in *Scènes de la Vie de Bohème* and Whistler appreciated it to the full. This was the proper Discomfiture of the Interfering and Pretentious Bourgeois. Mastering his annoyance, Haden said, 'So you have wiped it all out. Well, do it better.'

Legros was always a man of few words. He replied simply: '*Oui!*'

So the incident passed over. It was not in itself very important, not, that is, unless you considered a painting a very important thing and any infringement of its individual being as rather like sticking a knife into a man's back. But Whistler did so look upon it. The brother-in-law's crime was a real crime to him. Among *confrères*, one's fellow artists, a word which to him was equivalent in dignity and in its suggestion of a scrupulous code of behaviour to the word *gentleman*, such things were not done. It seemed as if the word *confrère* was not a term very well understood on this side of the channel.

There was a gulf. It was strange to be among people who talked the same or pretty much the same language as yourself, and yet whose minds worked in a different way, a way that you could not understand at all. In the old days in the rue Notre Dame des Champs you did not notice it so much; but in London it was very obvious that you couldn't remain in sympathy with the English students who had evidently acquired nothing from their student days. So Whistler may have thought when as a young man of twenty-four he was working on his etchings of the Thames. It is true he shared rooms with du Maurier for a while. They went together to the East End, where with firm strokes and an enthusiasm for detail soon to disappear from his work Whistler drew the barges and warehouses and where, in the riverside pubs of Limehouse and Wapping, somewhat incongruously they sang the old gay songs of the Latin Quarter. But this did not last. Whistler was not English enough for du Maurier. He was not respectable enough for Poynter. Whistler remained a Bohemian and the others looked on all that as an episode which now, in the necessity of making a serious career, must be put behind them. The links were severed and they went their several ways.

Painting in England at the beginning of the sixties was indeed a serious business. It was also very profitable. Unlike the French bourgeoisie the English middle class were picture-buyers; and, unlike the French painters, the English found a steady demand for a particular kind of picture. They were a recognized and esteemed type of professional, ranking equally with such other esteemed professionals as barristers and doctors. They were, likewise, conservative and conventional as well-to-do people thoroughly identified with the society in which they live, must be.

The subject picture was the source of their fortune. Therefore they attached great importance to the subject. It was a thing to be jealously guarded and concealed from possible imitators until, shortly before the day of public exhibition at the Royal Academy, it was safe to expose it to the view of a chosen circle of admirers. This necessity of concealment created at least the appearance of unfriendliness; and Whistler, accustomed to a free interchange of ideas, was keenly aware of it. He described, sarcastically, the way in which artists locked themselves up in their studios, the prevailing air of mystery and suspicion. 'And at last on Varnishing Day there was the subject in all its glory – wonderful! The British Subject! Like a flash the inspiration came – the Inventor! – and in the Academy there you saw him: the familiar model – the soldier or the Italian – and there he sat, hands on knees, head bent, brows knit, eyes staring; in a corner angels and cogwheels and things; close to him his wife, cold, ragged, the baby in her arms – he had failed! The story was told – it was clear as day – amazing! – the British subject.' The style of this description (reminiscent of Mr Jingle) is that of Whistler's maturity – but the view was one that he formed at an early date.

It was not that his own reception was really so bad: seeing that his painting *Au Piano* (inspired by Courbet) was hung in the Academy and on the whole quite favourably noticed;

it was the uneasy feeling he had of being out of the running, of missing something that was no concern of the staid Academy at all, that now sent him voyaging to and fro, restlessly, between London and Paris. How different in the latter place was the sharing of discovery, the keenness of excitement over values that had nothing to do with the soldier or the Italian. One discovery in particular impressed the young man – that of the art of the Far East.

2

When Commodore Perry sailed with a squadron of the United States fleet into Yokohama harbour in 1854 to enforce a trading arrangement he little realized he was opening an epoch of art as well as of trade. Since Japan had expelled the Portuguese merchants in the seventeenth century hers had remained a secret culture unknown to and uninfluenced by the rest of the world. When the Western Powers put an end to this isolation (and since trade they must) the Japanese began to send overseas the produce of their skill – pottery and small ornaments and, for packing, the popular woodcuts which had little more value than a newspaper. In 1856 the eye of Félix Bracquemond, painter and etcher, was caught by a print of queer design wrapped round some imported oriental china. He looked at it with excitement, as well he might, for it was by one of the great artists of the world, the Japanese Hokusai, 'the old man mad about drawing' as he described himself, who had died seven years before the date of Bracquemond's find. This unknown greatness was eagerly discussed. Other prints came to light in the same chance fashion and a vogue began.

In these works of what appeared to the Westerner an almost uncanny delicacy, as strange and detached from everyday life as if they had dropped from the moon, was a confirmation, to the men of the Second Empire, of their theories and longings. Here was an example of that difficult refinement, that aristocratic aloofness in art which Baudelaire had sought. Here surely was art for art's sake, living intensely

42

in and for itself exactly as Gautier had imagined it in his poetic enamels and cameos. There was no subject, or at least no subject you could understand or need bother about (which came to much the same thing). There was no vulgar imitation of nature (how vulgar by comparison appeared the oil painting of the salon). But on the contrary a fastidious, a deliberate selection of line, shape and colour, made, beyond question, with the purpose of imparting a pure aesthetic satisfaction. The black-haired dolls, posed inactive and expressionless in empty box-like rooms, meant as little in themselves, had the same remoteness, as the models whose dumb beauty ornamented the rooms in which Gautier and Baudelaire conversed. The wisdom of the Far East had been conveyed across the sea at the most opportune moment possible.

A shop for the sale of oriental objects of art, established in the rue de Rivoli by a Madame Desoyes in 1862, was frequented both by painters and men of letters. Here came Baudelaire (who now had only five more years to live), the artist brothers Edmond and Jules de Goncourt, who took to the realization in words of their hyper-acuteness of feeling and found in the art of Japan the same delicacy as in that of eighteenth-century France; the painter Manet, handsome, elegant, thirty years of age – and among others Whistler and Fantin-Latour. It was Whistler's great experience. He felt himself at last to be in the centre of things. In the newly discovered art was the secret he had lacked, by whose knowledge he might henceforward excel.

3

Again through the introduction of Fantin-Latour, it was about this time that he met, in Paris, the poet Algernon Charles Swinburne. This extraordinary young man, with a shock of flaming red hair and pale green eyes, a pale face, a chin that receded to nothing, and shoulders that sloped abruptly down, was of Whistler's own age – and despite the peculiarities of his appearance a man whom Whistler found he could get on with, an Englishman who talked to some extent at least his own language. For one thing the little red-haired poet loved France.

It has been supposed that this attachment began with a prize Swinburne won at Eton – a gorgeously bound edition of Victor Hugo's *Notre Dame de Paris* with illustrations by Tony Johannot. It is certain he had acquired a veneration for Hugo and with it a republican sentiment which produced a passionate hatred of Napoleon III, whom he always alluded to as 'le Beauharnais' or 'Buonaparte the Bastard'. Convinced that he himself was really half-French, he was an ardent supporter of the new French writers in whom he saw his own revolt against convention. He had read Baudelaire's *Les Fleurs du Mal* in the expurgated edition of 1861 and written an enthusiastic letter to the author who replied, after an extremely long interval, that he had not expected such sympathetic appreciation of the French idea of beauty from an English writer ( *je n'aurais jamais cru qu'un littérateur anglais pût si bien pénétrer la beauté française, les intentions de la prosodie française*). The gospel of art for art's sake was one that made a great appeal to Swinburne. 'If any reader', he said, 'could extract from any poem a positive spiritual medicine – if he could swallow a sonnet like a moral prescription – then clearly the poet supplying these intellectual drugs would be a bad artist.' He praised the good sense of M. Baudelaire who 'ventures to profess that the art of poetry has absolutely nothing to do with didactic matter at all'.

All this or as much as transpired seemed on the right lines to Whistler. No one can possibly represent him as a student of letters or a well-read man. Indeed some of that hatred he always felt for writers had already crept out in his comment on Baudelaire's appreciative criticism in *Le Boulevard* of the Thames etchings. The expression of an immense city's poetry – *poésie profonde et compliquée d'une vaste capitale*. That was how the great man described them. All very well, thought Whistler, but beside the point: and with a foretaste of a later and increasing acidity he had remarked: They do better articles in London – *on fit encore mieux les articles à Londres*. However,

Baudelaire was undeniably an artist – and Whistler admired Swinburne for his admirations and the result of their meeting was that, when they were both back in London, Swinburne introduced him to Dante Gabriel Rossetti.

'You must meet Gabriel,' one can imagine the little man chattering, his green eyes lighting up with fervour, and hopping about in gleeful excitement. The wonderful, the adored Gabriel – the prince of poets and painters. Thus it was that the Yankee entered the 'Court of King Arthur'.

4

That peculiar household of Dante Gabriel Rossetti has been described elsewhere.* His wife had recently died. He was installed at Tudor House in Cheyne Walk. A portly bearded man in the thirties, he had begun to paint industriously – idealized, romantic women – and his recreations were the collecting of curiosities – animals, craftsmanship, human beings. His amazing personal magnetism, his power of kindling enthusiasm surrounded him with friends, worshippers, and hangers-on, and through him and those who had felt the magic of his influence the celebrated Pre-Raphaelite movement which he was largely instrumental in starting lived on and was a power in the land. His later disciples William Morris and Edward Burne-Jones were still in close and friendly contact with him and were busily engaged in the attempt to transform the decoration and furnishing of the country on the model of an imaginary ancient past.

With this remarkable man Whistler remained on very intimate terms, seeing him almost daily for some ten years.

Both were lovers of curious combinations. Their own friendship was such. Indeed how these two contrasting personalities remained so long in harmony is very surprising.

Perhaps it was that neither took the other very seriously. The outlook of Whistler as of most Americans was strictly contemporary. He liked the latest thing. He had no particular

*See *The Pre-Raphaelite Tragedy* by W. Gaunt.

use for history and the attempt to live in or recreate the atmosphere and surroundings of the Middle Ages, as Rossetti did, was something he was quite incapable of appreciating. And Rossetti's views on and methods of painting seemed, to his cosmopolitan mind, absurd. 'No artist, you know, but charming and a gentleman.' To one habituated to the cleverness of Parisian cafés, who was passing from realism to the still more exacting cultivation of form as understood by the Japanese, the practice of painting elaborate costume pictures and subjects from Dante was nonsense. That sort of thing might be poetry but poetry was poetry and painting was painting. Whistler's implacable hostility to the alien form of expression appears in his celebrated remark 'Why not frame the sonnet', when Rossetti was considering in what frame to put a picture which he had accompanied, as he frequently did, by a poem.

Nor did Rossetti take any great notice of Whistler's enthusiasms beyond approving them *as* enthusiasm. Paris was a different world to him, without the slightest attraction. Whistler introduced him to Fantin-Latour, thinking that he would share his admiration for the French artist and the circle to which he belonged. He was mistaken. Rossetti did Fantin some kindness and Fantin was sufficiently grateful to wish to include him in a large portrait-group, *Homage to Delacroix*. It was his habit to reward his friends by assembling them on canvas; but to Rossetti it was a most embarrassing invitation. He had no particular wish to be represented as paying homage to Delacroix, nor did he think a great deal of Fantin's abilities. In consequence he did not sit. Whistler did, of course. It identified him with the 'movement'. He occupies, in this well-known picture, a most commanding position in the middle of a bearded group, with Baudelaire sitting somewhat uncomfortably on the outer edge. To Rossetti the effect was that of 'a great slovenly scrawl, like all the rest of this incredible new school'. About Manet's *Déjeuner sur L'Herbe*, shown among the refused pictures of the Salon at the same time as Whistler's *Little White Girl*, Rossetti was moved to a criticism unusually violent for one so good humoured. It was, he said, 'simple putrescence and decomposition'.

So on questions of art they agreed to differ. But otherwise they got on, because Rossetti liked to be amused and Whistler with his sharp sayings and restless vitality was undeniably amusing. Affectionately Rossetti recorded his pugnacity (as was his habit) in a limerick:

> There's a combative artist named Whistler
> Who is like his own hog-hairs a bristler.
> A tube of white lead and a punch on the head
> Offer varied attractions to Whistler.

The limerick was inspired by the regrettable fact that Whistler had pushed his respectable brother-in-law through a plate glass window in Paris.

Rossetti's life was after all a kind of Bohemianism, though not of the French kind. The freedom of such a life was essential to him. Mid-Victorian propriety irked him. His estrangement from the middle-class Haden was growing. One cause of dispute was Whistler's model, an Irish girl with beautiful red-gold hair, called Joanna Heffernan – whose father referred to Whistler as 'me son-in-law'. In Paris she attracted the admiration of Courbet who painted her as *La Belle Irlandaise*. In London she was Whistler's devoted slave. She went with him to Wapping when he was painting the view, was his model and his messenger to the dealers, and was established at the house he took in Lindsey Row in Chelsea. Haden was invited to dine there. He accepted but made the condition that Jo should not appear. Angry words were spoken. At Sloane Street, Haden followed him from the studio at the top of the house to the front door voicing his moral indignation. And at the door Whistler realized that he had left his hat in the studio. 'Must we go through all that again?' he groaned.

It was a relief to go to a circle where the behaviour of an artist was his own affair and where everything and everybody was touched by the spirit of the fantastic. Fantastic to him were Rossetti's Pre-Raphaelite friends with their queer taste for the Middle Ages, which he was unable to share – the

Burne-Joneses, the Morrises, Ford Madox Brown, and the minor poets who revolved around them: fantastic also the hangers-on – Fanny Hughes, vulgar and florid, who dominated Tudor House – and in particular a Portuguese adventurer, Howell, the cause of never-ending amusement to Rossetti, who seemed to Whistler like a swashbuckling, picturesque rogue out of a book. He told the most amazing lies. He dealt in anything and his dealings always became wonderfully complicated and confused so that you scarcely knew whose money and whose property was whose at the end of a transaction. What belonged to others became his in no time. Rossetti's assistant Treffry Dunn relates for instance how they looked through a book which contained a series of Rossetti's drawings and at last among the pencil and chalk sketches of many famous people they came on a beautiful face, delicately drawn and shaded in pencil, with a background of pale gold. 'Howell, with an adroitness which was remarkable, shifted it from the book into his own pocket and neither I nor Rossetti ever saw it again.' It is interesting that Rossetti caused Howell with his long, irregular, and slightly sinister features to sit to him for a head of St George. 'Criminally speaking', said Whistler looking back on their acquaintance, 'the Portugee was an artist.'

Howell might be described as a general factotum. He was always ready to amuse or to arrange amusements. In particular he had awakened Rossetti's interest in collecting. Rossetti collected romantically, indiscriminately, things that were old or diverting. Draping his antique four-poster bed, hung thick heavy curtains with seventeenth-century crewel work, in a pattern of fruit and flowers. Around the house were littered brass *repoussé* bowls, curiously wrought candlesticks, mandolines, lutes, and dulcimers, antique chests, filled with necklaces, crystals, old costumes, and a hundred miscellaneous things, which satisfied his passion for what was ancient. Whistler gave a new direction to this haphazard interest – the taste for oriental things which he had acquired in Paris. To him it was still a matter of artistic discovery. To Rossetti it was a further excursion in the 'quaint'. To

Howell it was a chance to display his truly amazing gift for buying and selling.

They collected Japanese screens, fans, prints, and above all Oriental pottery. The latter was known to them as 'Blue' or 'Blue and White'. This was the Chinese porcelain of the seventeenth and eighteenth centuries, of the K'ang Hsi (1622–1722), Yung Cheng (1723–35), and Ch'ien Lung (1736–95) periods: though to Rossetti at least 'Blue' was a perfectly sufficient description. They acquired ginger jars decorated with the blossom of prunus and hawthorn, and the tall vases which Whistler facetiously styled 'Long Elizas' from their Dutch name 'Lange Lysen'. Farmer and Rogers's oriental warehouse in Regent Street was one of their main sources of supply. Rossetti introduced Whistler to the manager, Lazenby Liberty, who was later to launch a famous shop of his own on the crest of the aesthetic wave. An intelligent dealer called Murray Marks advised them. His business card, a gorgeous affair printed in colours from a great many wood blocks and adorned with a ginger jar on a patterned gold ground, and peacock feathers (copied doubtless from feathers of the peacock in Rossetti's private menagerie) is supposed to have been the joint work of Rossetti, Whistler, and William Morris.

And Howell was tireless. He encouraged his friends to bid one against the other. He scoured the shops and made a collection of his own in which pieces bought by others would insist on turning up. Many are the stories told of that juggling with property for which he had a kind of natural talent. The most striking case is, perhaps, that of an oriental cabinet he arranged to sell. First he took the lid of the cabinet to a pawnbroker and obtained money for the whole, promising to send the body of the cabinet a day or two later. Next he explained to the prospective buyer that the lid had been broken and sent for repair. Subsequently he told the pawnbroker that the cabinet had been damaged – and he kept this situation going until at length Whistler redeemed the cabinet. On another occasion he persuaded a friend to borrow, in his own name, a tiara, on the plea that he, Howell, very much wanted another friend of his to wear it at a fancy dress ball. The delay, the silence which followed, roused the suspicions of the friend who had been induced to borrow the jewel. He made insistent inquiries and was lucky enough to intercept it just as it was about to be dispatched to America. The same plan was applied to his oriental discoveries. He sold a collection of excellent pieces to a pawnbroker, who demurred that he was not an expert. 'I insist', said Howell, 'on having them valued at Christie's.' The valuation was more than Howell's own estimate and the lot were sold. Howell produced a second collection. This time no valuation was considered necessary; and this time the pieces proved to be worthless and modern. On one occasion the ownership of forty blue pots became the subject of legal proceedings and it was ordered that they be produced in court. Howell made a sensational appearance at the head of forty four-wheelers (he loved cabs), each containing a single choice pot. In court his persuasive fluency won him the case and he was awarded pots, damages, and the cost of the forty four-wheelers.

The fluency that could prevail with a judge was still more powerful with the ordinary unsuspicious citizen. A diamond merchant called Paddon fell under his spell and to him Howell described how he had seen some black Chinese ware of the utmost rarity – expensive, it is true, but a triumph for the collector who could obtain it. Paddon bought the rarity – but later he noticed some exactly similar black pots in the window of a shop in Oxford Street. 'May I have those?' he asked. 'With pleasure, and as many more as you like,' said the shopman indicating a pile of them. They were a cheap line produced in large quantities.

Nevertheless, Rossetti and Whistler, between them and with Howell's help, acquired amazing things, for though in the eighteenth century there had been some vogue for 'chinoiseries', now in the 1860's they had the field practically to themselves.

Rossetti's finds contributed to swell the picturesque disorder of his house. Whistler, on the contrary, in the arrangement of his treasures, evinced that quality of which he had almost too much – good taste. The pots were arranged at exquisitely proportioned intervals. The fans whose silken tissue was covered with dim, graceful shapes were set in exact level lines. The Japanese prints hung in a harmony with their surroundings governed by a geometrical progression as nicely calculated as that which the artist himself had shown within the limits of the picture. The world of difference between the two men appears very clearly even in this.

But whatever the differences in their personal taste the main fact remains that together they had set a movement going. Others, like Sir Henry Thompson the surgeon and Francis Leyland the famous Pre-Raphaelite patron, collected on the advice of Rossetti. The fashion spread. In the 1870's most of the treasures of Rossetti and Whistler went back to the dealers and were resold, the former being broken in health and the latter declared bankrupt. This dispersal helped to increase the circle of admirers of 'Blue'. From being the private sport of a few collectors, the art of China and Japan became a cult: and twenty years after it had first made its appearance in Paris it became absorbed into that strange rapture called English 'aestheticism'.

## Poet in Frenzy

MEANWHILE Algernon Charles Swinburne was running riot.

He divided his time between the feverish composition of poems, wild, brilliant, rebellious talk, and a dissipation so unsuited to his physique that it assumed the appearance of an extravagant burlesque.

He could hold neither liquor nor words; and both had a devastating effect on his frail form, producing an almost epileptic condition. Thus one day he stood before a sofa in Whistler's studio, reciting some work that had aroused his enthusiasm, his little arms and legs jerking like those of a marionette and skipping up and backwards on to the sofa and down again as he read. The words went to his head, his excitement grew, his voice rose to an hysterical screech and then suddenly he stiffened, became silent, fell down rigid and unconscious. Mrs Whistler nursed him back to health. The painter's mother had a great affection for Algernon. His frailty and helplessness awoke a tender and protective instinct in her.

His revolt against Victorian convention was sometimes farcical, as on the celebrated occasion when he was expelled from the Arts Club. A special meeting of the committee was in progress when Swinburne arrived with a friend and the cloak-room was full of silk hats. They decided to destroy these emblems of respectability. They placed the hats in two rows on the floor and each, with the left ankle clasped in the left hand, hopped from one hat to the next crushing them in turn. The attendant came in to find the poet and his friend dancing in wild excitement among the ruins. The committee was informed and expelled them both on the spot.

In the same way, and giving curiously the impression of a naughty child determined to show how naughty it could be, Swinburne did not so much indulge in vice as talk about it, and make a parade of libertinage which he had got out of books. It was fun to be shocking like the Marquis de Sade, exciting to strike a blow with all the force of his tiny hand and all the resources of his florid vocabulary against the heavy smugness of the middle class, as Baudelaire, his admired Baudelaire, had done.

Howell encouraged him. He was always greatly interested in the failings and excesses of his famous friends. He was for a long time, in the phrase of Sir Edmund Gosse, 'all that Atticus was to Cicero', though this comparison may be unfair to the literary associate of the ancient Roman. The puerile indecencies of Swinburne and his desire to be, in writing, 'as offensive and objectionable as possible' made excellent matter for anecdote. At a later date Swinburne complained, in a typical sentence, of Howell's practice of 'habitually amusing mixed companies of total strangers by obscene false anecdotes about my private eccentricities of indecent indulgence as exhibited in real or imaginary lupanaria'. Still, Howell lent him his somewhat alarming assistance and when Moxon, the publisher of Swinburne's *Poems and Ballads*, took fright at the storm it aroused and suppressed the book it was Howell who acted as agent in transferring it to a publisher of 'the curious' called John Camden Hotten.

The *Poems and Ballads* which outraged Britain in 1866 were the first literary symptom of the advent of 'Art for Art's Sake'. With Whistler as its solitary (and as yet unvocal) advocate the movement had arrived as a question of style in painting and the arts that were meant to be seen. The pleasurable sensation to be derived from looking at a ginger jar was one into which neither morality nor immorality entered. But with literature (and with Swinburne) it was different. However much he might appreciate the severity of style of his French masters he was quite incapable of reproducing it in his own language and in his own poems. In them it was the rich spate of words, quite beyond his control, which was remarkable, a buoyant rush and sweep as of a Northumbrian stream. Borne along in this cloudy torrent, exhilarating mainly by its emphatic motion, was all the driftwood of decadence. By sheer emphasis the poet almost converted the pessimism of Baudelaire into optimism. It is only by the closest possible shave that he did not make it actually comic. Nevertheless the defiant aspect of Art for Art's Sake, its determination at all costs to break the bounds of morality, plainly appears. Swinburne shook his small trembling fist at Christianity in his *Hymn to Proserpine*.

Wilt thou yet take all, Galilean? but these thou shalt not take,
The laurel, the palms and the paean, the breasts of the nymphs in the brake.

In *Dolores*, inspired by Adah Menken, the female Mazeppa of Astley's Theatre, he wrote in ecstatic praise of the 'noble and nude and antique'. In *Faustine*, which Ruskin, strangely enough, found 'glorious' – 'All hot like pies with the Devil's fingers in them' – he wrote of the sapphic love which had so much fascination for the author of *Les Fleurs du Mal*. The romanticization of sin, the prospect of 'new passions for daytime and night', thus came openly for the first time to the appalled but interested ears of the British public.

The effect was tremendous. The poems were promptly stamped as a danger to public morals. To talk appreciatively of 'lithe limbs' in an age so suspicious of limbs as to drape the legs of a piano was bad enough; but to write with equal appreciation of 'strange great sins', that was positively menacing. There must have been many innocent souls who wondered what these sins 'seventy times seven' could possibly be – many others to whom they appeared all the more horrifying because they were unknown. On the other hand those who were impatient of restraints, and especially the young, welcomed the *Poems and Ballads* as a form or a herald of social revolution – and young men at the universities marched arm in arm round their quadrangles, chanting

Could you hurt me, sweet lips, though I hurt you?
Men touch them and change in a trice
The lilies and languors of virtue
For the roses and raptures of vice.

just as students abroad, singing political songs in unison,

made themselves ready for the overthrow of a government and a new era of freedom.

But *The Times* was reported to be about to discharge a blast. The *Saturday Review*, snarling and terrified, said we were 'in the midst of fire and serpents, wine and ashes, blood and foam and a hundred lurid horrors'. Bertram Payne of Moxon's bowed to the storm and withdrew the book: 'My friend Mr Howell' acted as agent in the transfer to John Camden Hotten, publisher of the *History of the Rod*. Hotten published a brochure in defence of *Poems and Ballads* by William Michael Rossetti who spontaneously offered to write it and later Swinburne made his own defence, reasserting 'When England has again such a school of poetry, so headed and so followed, as she has had at least twice before, or as France has now; when all higher forms of the various arts are included within the larger limits of a stronger race; then, if such a day should ever rise or return upon us, it will be once more remembered that the office of adult art is not that of the cloister or the harem; that all things are good in its sight, out of which good work may be produced.'

This unfortunately did not settle the matter. The British 'Philistine' might meekly acquiesce when he was exhorted, as indeed he had been by Matthew Arnold, to look to France for Culture. He was not so agreeable when Culture presented itself as an absence of moral restraint; and the upshot was a long running battle which reached a crisis when in 1871 Robert Buchanan launched his famous attack on the 'Fleshly School of Poetry' in the *Contemporary Review*. With a confusion that has since persisted the Pre-Raphaelite friends of Swinburne, Morris, and Rossetti, were dragged in; and Rossetti became the chief victim of a wordy set-to, which in fact scarcely concerned him at all.

2

There was another, a minor victim it is true, but still a victim – a victim, not so much of this particular controversy as of the whole trend and association of ideas which Swinburne had introduced. The first type to appear in Britain of those post-Baudelairean figures who, with a sort of deliberate renunciation, let themselves slide into misery and squalor, becoming from some obscure sentiment of protest an artistic enemy of society, was a Jewish painter called Simeon Solomon. He took the course which in other circumstances Swinburne himself might have taken. In some ways he was not dissimilar to the French poet, Paul Verlaine, though he lacked his genius and his capacity to extract from a squalid life the vindicating fragment of beauty. Simeon Solomon, one of a clever family, was born in 1841 at 3 Sandys Street, Bishopsgate Without. His father, an importer of Italian-made hats, was the first Jew to become a Freeman of the City of London. Simeon's sister Rebecca and his brother Abraham were both painters – in fact on one occasion the three Solomons all figured in a Royal Academy Exhibition together. Simeon was taught by his elder brother and sister, but the prevailing Pre-Raphaelite style made a strong impression on him and in due time he became a disciple of Rossetti and one of the distinguished band of illustrators of the sixties.

Then he met Swinburne. His bohemian sister Rebecca had previously had a flirtation with the poet but it was Burne-Jones who introduced him; and before long they were fast friends.

The painter was handsome in a way that was Jewish and yet with its well-cut profile almost classical. He looked, one might imagine, like the true pagan of an archaic time, with something of Greek delicacy and something of oriental richness in his appearance, and this appealed to a poet whose most impassioned lines were written in praise of exactly this antique and pagan combination. His talk also had a certain interest. He revealed a mysticism, that is to say a sense of meaning in things which went deeper than the surface value, though this too was pagan and not Christian. He 'twisted ideas' and in his play upon words, light and humorous, his habit of turning a thought upside down, there was a facility which might pass for wisdom. He was sensitive, touchy, impressionable, imaginative. His art was highly esteemed though it seems a more dubious quantity to-day than it did in his own time. It was esteemed because it was 'strange'. The yearning and dolorous beauty of the Pre-Raphaelite, with him acquired a less pure, a vaguely though not explicitly sensual character, a mannerism of style which was not Pre-Raphaelite at all, but hinted on the contrary at 'decadence'. A woman's head by Rossetti had the mysticism of medieval Christianity. The soul was at war with the flesh. A head by Solomon was mystic rather in its replacement of the Christian soul by some enigmatic daemon, whose disquieting influence was not reduced by the comparative feebleness of drawing.

But to Swinburne, the fair little Hebrew was a living exemplar of the golden age. When Solomon posed in ancient Greek costume, with a laurel wreath round his russet locks, sandals on his feet, a lyre in his hand, his much admired profile displaying a classic raptness, he seemed like Apollo himself come back among mortals of a singular drabness and vulgarity to shame them with his beauty. It was a marvellous game to Algernon, this playing at being pagan. It was to the intense bewilderment and discomfort of Rossetti that he saw them scampering naked in wild glee through Tudor House, Swinburne like the thin white stalk of a mushroom with a vivid red top and Solomon scurrying behind, though less classical as to the legs than the head for he was rather bandy. To Solomon unfortunately the game was to be not altogether a game. He made that dangerous transposition which was one of the striking features of the age that followed, of the terms of art and life. He began to see himself in fact as the product of some exotic other world rather than the product of Bishopsgate Without. When Swinburne drew forth a paper from his pocket and skipped round the painter's shabby rooms in John Street, Bedford Row, vehemently beating the rhythm of a defiant hymn to the old gods, Solomon was carried away by it. The books in Swinburne's library, erotic and unusual books, had their effect on his impressionable temperament. The admiration of Swinburne's literary friends went to his head, and an interest both in what was literary and what was perverse had a deteriorating influence. He and Swinburne skirted, with a fascinating nearness, the territory of actual vice as well as its literary sublimation. They showed an uncommon interest in a famous case of the time, the Queen versus Boulton and others (1870), which painfully exposed the fatuity of a man, with more classical education than sense, who had conceived a maudlin affection for two effeminate youths who were in the habit of dressing up as women and whom he was pleased to regard as 'Lais and Antinous in one'. It is possible, and the verdict of the court was certainly given in that sense, that there was no more in this than pure folly and a taste for amateur theatricals: but the 'Lais and Antinous' of Evans's coffee rooms in Covent Garden made a sufficiently ridiculous appearance at Bow Street in low necked evening dress and with an incipient whisker. In the cold clear light of British justice the hermaphroditism which Gautier had so entertainingly described and which inspired Swinburne, on a visit to the Louvre, to write a poem before its symbol in statuary, became only a melancholy weakness. Yet it is indicative of the trend of Solomon's thoughts that, after being taken by defendant's counsel to the trial, he should write to Swinburne 'B . . . is remarkable – he is not quite beautiful but supremely pretty . . .'

3

Thus it came about that Solomon, to quote a reference made to him in a newspaper obituary of 1905 (the year in which he died in St Giles's workhouse of chronic alcoholism) 'stepped back into the riotous pages of Petronius'.

Before calamity came, he enjoyed a brief flash of fame and the censure which accompanies it. Swinburne in these years went often to Oxford, particularly to see his friend Dr Jowett, the Master of Balliol. Jowett, in spite of the fact that he had delicately intimated at an earlier date that it might be in the interests of Algernon if he did not resume his studies at Balliol (it would not be fair to call so exquisite a communication 'sending down'), had remained on most amicable terms with him. He had respect as well as tenderness for the wayward poet who would often provide so happy an amendment to the translation of a passage in Plato. Through these visits by which Swinburne kept in touch with the world of Oxford, he gave celebrity to his friend. Drawings of Sappho and Antinous by Simeon Solomon began to appear on the walls of the rooms of the more cultured undergraduates and the younger dons. To their innocent enthusiastic minds his drawings constituted him the 'Shelley of Painting'.

In 1870 came the censure which was almost as good as praise – the outburst of Buchanan against the Fleshly School of Poetry. The feeling that something untoward was happening in the Arts, that something was 'up', was the theme of this outburst of morality. By an irony of fate, there was no discrimination in it. The exact source of danger was not yet localized: so entirely innocent figures found themselves in the pillory. William Morris and Dante Gabriel Rossetti, and especially the latter, were main butts with the grievous effect on the latter which is well known: but Swinburne was in it too (though to his satisfaction rather than otherwise) and Solomon had his share. 'English society,' said Robert Buchanan, 'goes into ecstasy over Mr Solomon's pictures – pretty pieces of morality such as Love dying by the Breath of Lust.' He (Solomon) was one of those who 'lend actual genius to worthless subjects and thereby produce monsters'. These strong words had little effect. Indeed the whole controversy which went on for a long time, with Swinburne playing a vigorous and conspicuous part, was very oblique, a mere hint of the direct battles which were still to rage over a more precise issue. But as far as Solomon was concerned, Robert Buchanan might have claimed justification of his thunder some years later. In 1873 the artist got into trouble which, it is to be feared, refers us back to Petronius and landed him in gaol.

The idea of Art for Art's Sake had claimed its first casualty. The effect on Swinburne was temporarily sobering. 'I suppose,' he wrote, to his friend George Powell, 'there is no doubt the poor unhappy little fellow has really been out of his mind and *done* things amenable to law, such as done by a sane man would make it impossible for anyone to keep up his acquaintance and not be cut by the rest of the world as an accomplice? I have been seriously unhappy about it for I had real affection and regard for him – and besides his genius he had such genuinely amicable qualities. It is the simple truth that the distress of it has haunted and broken my sleep. It is hideous to lose a friend by madness of any kind let alone this. Do you – I do not – know of any detail of the matter at first hand? Pater I imagine did.'

## 4

## Hard Gem-like Flame

WALTER HORATIO PATER was one of those younger dons who had taken up Solomon. He had greatly admired a picture by him, a Bacchus which had mystery, a quality of which Pater especially approved. The picture was painted after Solomon had been to Italy with the Cambridge don, Oscar Browning. He was, as a result of this visit, enamoured of the pagan works of the Renaissance masters. The Bacchus, painted under their spell, seemed to Pater a very remarkable interpretation of the Greek wine-god. Here was a head, unfathomable and secret, maybe sensual and cruel, but perfect in form. The face of the Bacchus was such as Pater had imagined to himself when pondering over the legends of classic mythology, the immortal nature spirit in human guise whose abstract malignance was wrapped in beauty.

Solomon was delighted by his praise. He asked in return that he might paint his portrait and this was the prelude to friendly acquaintance, in the course of which Solomon went often to Oxford. To Pater, as to Swinburne, he was the embodiment of Art for Art's Sake and Art for Art's Sake was to Pater a dominant motive in life. How it came to be so may be traced, though somewhat obscurely, in the early development of this enigmatic man.

His father, a doctor in the East End of London, 'a tall grave figure, a little cold and severe', had died when he was a small boy and he was left in the care of mother, grandmother, and aunt. They lived in no very affluent fashion at Enfield until it was decided to send Walter to King's School, Canterbury, when a move was made to Harbledown. At school he was by no means a popular boy. The gentle home existence which had made no demand on him was abruptly replaced by what seemed to his prematurely developed sensibility as mere savagery. His favourite amusement at home had been to dress up in a surplice and preach a sermon to his admiring

Aunt Betty. But, for snowballing in the Mint Yard and round the Norman staircase, between the King's School boys and the town cads, Walter had not stomach. He would not fight. 'I do not seem', he said, 'to want a black eye.' He joined in no sports. Football and cricket were outside his ken, and that part of the school ritual which he liked best was the procession to the Cathedral on a Saint's Day (of which he regretted that the Church of England recognized so few). The rows of white surpliced King's Scholars in that 'melodious, mellow lighted space', beneath 'the reserved grace of the perfect Gothic arch', already suggested to him the beauty implicit in ancient ceremony and quite apart from belief.

He wandered in the cloisters of a past age, finding the emblems of mortality more comforting than the presence of living beings, a plain and dismal boy. He was thin, prematurely whiskered, heavy-jawed, with the deep-set eyes near together and the hunched back which was a family characteristic (being known as 'the Pater Poke'). He made only two friends, McQueen and Dombrain – queer boys like himself who would spend their pocket money on books of devotion and cut games in order to attend a church service. His unpopularity continued and in 1856 he was set on by a group of boys and in the scuffle got a savage kick from which he was laid up for weeks and which left a permanent impediment in his gait. He sent, however, an earnest request from his sick-bed that the affair should be passed over.

At this stage he appeared to suffer almost from an excess of Christianity. He was considered 'a tremendous Ritualist'. He never ate meat in Lent and every night he murmured a Latin prayer. Anxiety was expressed lest Ritualism should lead this young Thomas à Kempis to Rome. The fact was far different. By the time he went up to Oxford, with an Exhibition from King's School in 1858, he had already lost all religious faith. A reading of the doctrines of Christian Socialism as expounded by Maurice and Kingsley which have brought others to belief caused him to doubt. He seemed now to take a malicious delight in shocking his devout friends and in saying sneering and disturbing things out of

character. 'Be boy-like boys,' said Pater in a parting moni-
torial address at the school, looking fixedly at Dombrain –
Pater who had rejoiced in being the most unboy-like of boys.
'Mephistophelian sneers', said the puzzled Rainier McQueen
of his attacks on the Bible in the manner of Voltaire. It was
horrifying to him to think that one of their holy 'triumvirate'
could suggest: 'What fun it would be to be ordained and
not to believe a single word of what you are saying.' Nothing
could be more disconcerting than this demure devilment. It
was not as if Pater had revealed serious doubts which could
be wrestled with in communion with staunch friends – such
wrestlings might in themselves be called a religious exercise
and perfectly proper. No, it was as if a demon had quite
suddenly asserted itself in his mind. 'An enemy,' said this
demon, in Pater's own voice, 'to all Gothic darkness' and
'full of a better taste.' McQueen was horrified, heart-broken.
'Please desist from that kind of talk,' he implored. To which
Pater with quiet savagery replied, 'When I was at Canterbury
I was a contemptible hypocrite.' His heresy was 'the cause
of a rupture which could have come to pass by nothing else'.

Religious experience, shades of religious belief, were then
the main preoccupation of Oxford. There were various
religious sets like so many political parties – the High Church
set who wore their hair plastered very sleekly and close to
the head, and went in for incense at seven shillings and
sixpence a pound, the puritan Anglicans who liked the interior
of St Mary's because it was bare, the Broad Churchmen,
prominent among whom were the Rev. Mark Pattison and
Benjamin Jowett, the Regius Professor of Greek, who with
five collaborators in the *Essays and Reviews* of 1860 had earned
the title of the 'Seven Against Jesus'. Occasionally and to
the sound of tears and sobs, someone would go over to
Rome, with the effect of a wilful child who, reaching too
far for a flower, had tumbled over a cliff.

And about none of these things did the new Pater, the
Mr Hyde Pater, now care in the least. He was indifferent.
As to the painful case of one who had gone over to Rome
he remarked dispassionately: 'In fact, as far as mere comfort

of mind is concerned, I consider conscientious Roman catholics quite enviable.' As for himself he even went to the length of giving away or selling all his religious books, including a copy of *The Christian Year*. Robert McQueen wrote to his brother: 'Pater must be in a very bad state. What particular religion does he profess to belong to?' No one knew, though it seemed that philosophy had replaced religion in his mind from the fact that his favourite reading was Heraclitus, Pythagoras, and Plato, the Germans Schelling and Hegel, and the story was told that he sat up all night reflecting on the absolute (τὸ ὄν).

He profited or at least was affected by certain contemporary influences. He attended Matthew Arnold's lectures on Poetry. He was impressed by his attacks on the Philistine, his crusade for 'sweetness and light', his cosmopolitan attitude to letters. He read the books of John Ruskin. The decorative fluent prose of *Modern Painters*, the insistence on art as the supreme business of life, the reiteration of great names, Titian, Angelico and Tintoretto, with as much reverence as if they were Prophets of the Old Testament, all this undoubtedly turned him to the thought if not to the actual study of art.

So too must those authors whom he cared for enough to translate. He translated Plato and Aristotle. He read passages of Goethe and from him he derived a serene, a meditative approach to the classical perfection of Greece. He imitated Goethe in destroying his own early poems because of their Christian sentiment. By 1860 he was regularly translating a page from Flaubert whose great first book *Madame Bovary* had appeared three years before. The deliberate choice of words, the detachment from the bourgeois world, in which Flaubert is so much akin to his contemporary Baudelaire, could not fail to strike the translator. His view of art, his sense of style, was built on this study of ancient Greeks, modern Germans, and modern French.

Gradually Pater became more inscrutable. It was about this time (1860) that he grew that moustache which completed the mask-like nature of his expressionless features. He was a 'Caliban of letters', was very sensitive about his looks, had been heard to say, 'I would give ten years of my life to be handsome'. Meetings were held among his friends to discuss 'the External Improvement of Pater'. Various suggestions were made. It was agreed that a moustache was the thing if anyone dared try to persuade him. To their surprise Pater took kindly to the idea and shortly there burgeoned on his upper lip that formidable luxuriance which provided him with a distinct character not his own.

This sensitiveness about his own appearance helped to make him interested in ideal beauty. He could not bear ugly people. His friends were good-looking. He admired his brother Willie Pater, a tall, handsome guardsman type, with Dundreary whiskers and a fascination for women, because of his physical well-being and comeliness. Walter Horatio had been known to speak of a boy at school who was uglier even than he in terms of the most utter contempt and with un-relenting sarcasm.

Perhaps through diffidence, a sense of his unattractiveness, or through a naturally sluggish habit, he was no lover. Apart from a mild, a vague, a passing warmth for a cousin he was able to dispense with the tender passion and even his friend-ships were restrained and tepid. He abstained from love as he had abstained from cricket the better to enjoy contempla-tion. Any kind of violence became alien to the rhythm of his life and it was almost a sign of his avoidance of the spec-tacular, of energetic outward display and vulgar excess that he took only Second Class Honours in the Final Classical Schools in 1862. His visits to Heidelberg (to see his sisters who had gone to live there) were, however, supposed to have given him a special equipment in philosophy: he was reputed to have special knowledge of the systems of Schelling and Hegel. Because of this or some perception of an inner and latent merit concealed by his reserve, his abstention from being brilliant, he was fortunate enough to be elected Fellow of Brasenose in 1864.

It is interesting that he should have tried to persist in his diabolical plan of becoming ordained. His friends opposed him (as Rainer McQueen said) for his own sake. Dombrain, the most bigoted of the young triumvirate, shut Pater completely out of mind. McQueen, more sensitive and affectionate but equally religious, sorrowfully 'spoke with him for the last time in this world'. He found it difficult to reconcile the 'ascetic and saintly boy' of his earlier acquaintance with this cold stranger. He wondered 'what the real Pater was'. But a clergyman surely he must not be. 'If you make the attempt I shall do all I can to prevent it,' said his former master the Rev. J. B. Kearney. 'And I shall do so, too,' said McQueen. Both wrote to the Bishop of London imploring him in the best interests of their infidel friend to prevent his taking orders. The veto was upheld. Aunty Betty was deeply grieved but he showed only a passing annoyance and instead settled quietly down to being a writer, in his academic haven.

His mental isolation was singularly complete. He presented to the world an imposing array of negatives. He was no administrator – his attitude to undergraduate manliness being expressed in the remark that they were 'like young tigers at play'. He was no scholar, in the Oxford sense, and got rather quickly at sea in construing Virgil's *Georgics*. He had neither the capacity nor the energy for research and he had extremely few points of contact with his colleagues or with contemporary life at all. He conceived himself as a 'crystal man', a man of taste, that is to say, with a mind adorned by 'the reminiscence of a forgotten culture', but entirely himself, unaffected by the age in which he lived, and cherishing his isolation from it.

His was an inward existence. He was content with the most frugal and monkish of surroundings and equipment. His rooms at Brasenose were small, simple, austere. The little chintz curtains, the stained floorboards that bordered the matting and the Turkey carpet, the few line engravings after Michelangelo, Correggio, and Ingres, in themselves a frugal choice from among the riches of art, spoke of plain and even threadbare living. A bust of Hercules, somewhat out of place in these prim quarters, bore witness to an entirely abstract approval of the force its owner did not possess. 'Hercules, Discobolus, Samson,' apostrophized an admirer, 'these be

thy gods, O Pater.' The only touch of adornment was the
bowl of dried rose leaves which stood on the table. Even his
books were few. A few small shelves held some battered
paper-backed and cheap editions. When Pater wanted to read
he went to the Bodleian or else borrowed a book from a
friend. The adjoining bedroom, which lay along a narrow
passage approached by a low Gothic doorway, was only a few
feet wide and was in fact so cramped that the head of the
bed had to rest, without legs, on a projection in the wall.

In his sitting-room he would settle down in the morning
to wring a few reluctant, anxiously weighed words from his
pen. The table would be covered with small lozenges of
white paper – each bearing a phrase or a word, with here
and there a blue lozenge, this representing a key point.
Such were his 'notes'. There is something in this neat and
precise plan that reminds us of Pater's Dutch ancestry.

Having cast off religion and being without interest either
in scholarship or in practical affairs Pater began to con-
centrate on the subject of Art. That he was much impressed
by Swinburne is certain though he knew him only slightly.
It may have been partly through him that he imbibed the
doctrine of Art for Art's Sake in the emphatic form which
the French writers had given it. He became one of a circle
of young poets and painters whose watchword it was. There
was John Payne, the poet who had set forth Gautier's
doctrine of aesthetic perfection in an essay on *The Poets of the
Neo-Romantic School in France*: Arthur O'Shaughnessy of the
British Museum, and the painters J. T. Nettleship and
Simeon Solomon, in whose studios they often met. There
is no question but that an essay on Leonardo which Swinburne
wrote in 1864 inspired the style and a celebrated passage of
Pater's own later essay on the artist. Here is Swinburne:

Of Leonardo the samples are choice and few: full of that indefinable
grace and grave mystery which belongs to his slightest and wildest
work. Fair strange faces of women full of dim doubt and faint scorn,
touched by the shadows of an obscure fate; eager and weary as it
seems at once, pale and fervent with patience and passion, allure and
perplex the thoughts and eyes of men.

The likeness is close with Pater:

The presence that rose thus so strangely beside the waters is expressive of what in the ways of a thousand years men had come to desire. Hers is the head upon which all 'the ends of the world are come' and the eyelids are a little weary. It is a beauty wrought out from within upon the flesh, the deposit, a little cell by cell, of strange thoughts and fantastic reveries and exquisite passions.

It was a very vague and dreamy conception of ideal beauty, yet with its own tension and quiet ruthlessness. One pursued beauty as Johann Joachim Winckelmann had pursued it with 'a feverish nursing of the one motive in his life'. In that Prussian archaeologist a 'religious profession was only one incident of a culture' in which the moral instinct like the religious or political was merged in the artistic. And great pains had gone into the fashioning of the sentences which set forth this superlative aim. The reserved and cautious man thought it necessary to weigh every word, to restrain the violent and importunate epithet so prone to appear, to bring into the 'passion' which so much coloured the theme that sort of frugality manifest in his own surroundings.

This spartan care for form was something new in English literature. English writers wrote to say something, to serve a moral end; but the series of essays contributed by Pater to the *Fortnightly Review* and published in 1873 as 'The Renaissance: Studies in Art and Poetry' served no such end and seemed to many people very insubstantial in consequence. They seemed to Mrs Mark Pattison an 'air-plant independent of the ordinary sources of nourishment – a sentimental revolution having no relation to the conditions of the actual world'. They were not, as the writings of Ruskin were, an incentive to production, a call to contemporaries to emulate the past. They took no account of the kind of society in which art flourished. They established an attitude, of one attempting to put in words certain tenuous sensations, representing the 'sharp apex of the present moment between two hypothetical eternities'. Pater's writings were concerned with great artists, though the author knew nothing of visual art and as technical criticism his account of their work has little value. Pater sought, following Goethe, for the relation in which a work of art stood to the inner nature of the person contemplating it. To obtain from art as many pulsations as possible, 'to burn always with this hard gem-like flame', was 'success in life'.

In this egoistic vision of ideal beauty there lurked a poison – the same poison as in the poems of Baudelaire, from the study of whom Pater may have imbibed it direct. It was the sense that something vaguely evil was to be found at the very centre of beauty, an evil not to be avoided but to be embraced and enjoyed (intellectually and imaginatively) by the writer. An excitement was given to the quest for the perfection of the gods by the idea that it held some corrupt and diabolic secret. There is a curious passage in Pater's early study of *Aesthetic Poetry* (omitted from the final version of the *Appreciations*) in which he was writing of William Morris, and grafted on to the poetry of Pre-Raphaelitism a sentiment of his own, with little relation to the subject. 'The colouring is intricate and delirious as of "scarlet lilies". The influence of summer is like a poison in the blood,' he wrote. He envisaged 'a strange complex of conditions where, as in some medicated air, exotic flowers of sentiment expand, among people of a remote and unaccustomed beauty, somnambulistic, frail, androgynous, the light almost shining through them'. Here is the spirit of the *Fleurs du Mal*, the sentiment of decay. In later essays, in the *Imaginary Portraits,* Pater elaborated in various ways the idea of some horror or demoniac element haunting peaceful lives and pleasant places, itself concealed beneath some outward fairness of aspect.

Jowett scented danger. The sturdy little Broad Churchman with immense forehead, the cherubic face and the barrel-bodied greatcoat, was a practical man and as such he had little patience with gush about beauty, which was no concern of a scholar and a gentleman. Anyone going in 'for poetry and all that nonsense' aroused his irritation. But here was something more. He could not put a finger on it quite but there was a pernicious feeling in it. Undergraduates might get hold of the wrong idea and be led astray by this overheated, artificial style of thing. The classics should be approached as a straightforward exercise in knowledge and not as a romantic excuse for self-indulgence. He was frankly alarmed at 'the mental and moral attitude' with which Pater was credited, none the less because he had once said to Pater, 'You have a mind that will attain eminence.' He tried by every means to keep him away from Swinburne, on whom he thought Pater would be a most dangerous influence. Seeing that Algernon openly professed to be 'dangerous', and that he and Pater had visited the same source for their inspiration, this seems rather ironical.

Pater went imperturbably on. It was one of his characteristics not to care in the least what was said or thought of him. 'To burn always with this hard gem-like flame is success in life.' It is to be assumed that this illumination burnt in his mind as he bent his head with every mark of the reverence he did not feel in prayers in the college chapel which he so punctiliously attended; or as he waved a hand to a friend when limping along the High Street with a famous gesture, indeterminate, yet indicating in a delicate way that, while he was sensitively and even gratefully aware of the friend's presence, on this occasion he begged that it should be, without the exchange of words, understood that it was quite impossible for him to pause, even for a moment, for the exchange of mundane courtesies. Life became, increasingly, a system of aesthetics. 'But why should we be good, Mr Pater?' an undergraduate is supposed to have asked.

'Because it is so beautiful,' was the reply.

Religion, like virtue, was an aesthetic subdivision. He liked to visit St Alban's, in Holborn, the polychrome creation of the Gothic revivalist, William Butterfield, which was particularly 'High'; and also the principal Roman Catholic chapels, to admire the flowers, arum, jonquil, and narcissus, banked before the altar, the clouds of incense, the splendid robes, the elaborate ceremonies. On the other hand the 'starveling ceremonies of the Low Church are not worth witnessing'.

'It does not matter what is said provided it is said beautifully.'

A languor of manner seemed the necessary accompaniment of this continued and exalted preoccupation with Beauty. In the withdrawal from the stirring and the bustling contacts of the ordinary world, it was desirable to explain that the sensations still retained their acuteness, that they might even be exhausted by their own refinement. Thus Pater, walking one summer evening in Christ Church meadow with a friend, remarked to him, 'Certain flowers affect my imagination so that I cannot smell them with pleasure. The white jonquil, the gardenia, and the syringa actually give me pain. I am partial to the meadow-sweet but on an evening like this there is too much of it. It is the fault of nature in England that she runs too much to excess.'

There are few who suffer to any extent from the smell of meadow-sweet. This is not to say that Pater was not altogether serious. At the same time the attitude appeared uncommonly close to a pose; and the 'flute-like modulations of voice' which he adopted had to some listeners the sound of affectation.

For Oxford it was an entirely new style of behaviour. The remnants of its eighteenth-century tradition, bluff and jovial, mighty eaters and drinkers, had no nonsense of this sort about them, nor had the typical men of the nineteenth century, grave, earnest, wrapped up in questions of religion. Pater opposed to the materialism of the one and the spirituality of the other a new form of self-indulgence.

He was the first of university 'aesthetes'. As such he met with opposition. Jowett took good care that he was not given the disciplinary office of Proctor (worth some £300 a year) and others beside Jowett were heartily contemptuous. Once at a dinner party in the Bradmore Road he began to discourse 'with spring flower sickliness' on the beauty of the Reserved Sacrament in the Roman Church. 'As though,' snorted the Rev. Mandell Creighton, of Merton (who was present), 'he was describing a house in which lay a dead friend.' A sturdy Protestant made a sarcastic remark and a closure had to be applied to the heated discussion which followed. There was a lack of understanding in Oxford which made Pater dislike the place.

His pupils were more impressionable than his fellow dons. Some of them sat at his feet in adoration, but his enemies were careful to point out that these worshippers were not usually very good in their examinations. The burning of the hard gem-like flame did not ensure success in the Final Schools and one young man, it is recorded, who excelled in aesthetic ecstasy 'got only a Fourth'.

## 5

## Intensity in the Drawing-room

It was in the late seventies that the various efforts of Whistler, Swinburne, and Pater to interpret 'Art for Art's Sake' began to make an impression on English society and to be combined, after a muddled fashion typical both of the country and the age, with the influence of the Pre-Raphaelites into a confused whole called 'Aestheticism'. 'Are you intense?'

The scene is 'passionate Brompton'. The question is asked by a soulful lady, in a loose, flowing gown covered with art embroidery, who twists ecstatically on a small and insubstantial chair towards an amiable but not at all soulful looking man. The couple was drawn by George du Maurier and the drawing appeared in *Punch* in 1879.

The man is typical and average, not understanding 'art and that sort of thing, y'know' – a bit of a bore, what! – rather wishes he had gone to the club instead of coming here to have these odd questions fired at him. He knows and likes horses, billiards, sherry and bitters, fine figures of women, and the virile activities and diversions of the army, but, as to being intense – who ever heard of a decent chap being intense? In the evening dress of the period, superlatively ugly though created, no doubt, by a superlative West End tailor and possessing then the allure of the latest fashion which is not now perceptible any longer, he stands, solid and commonplace, beaming agreeably and vaguely: 'Well-er-not really. Can't say I've ever gone in for it, y'know.' He, this amiable figure, is the 'Philistine', one without, in the opinion of those who should be qualified to say, liberal culture. Against him and his Anglo-Saxon obtuseness Mr Matthew Arnold has hurled many a bitter gibe and Mr John Ruskin has angrily thundered: though as he reads very little and would be cheerfully impervious to gibe and thunder even if he did, their scathing criticism and fiery admonition has been hurled in vain.

Not so with the lady. Having all the time on her hands that the womenfolk of the well-to-do have in these days, she reads. The well-stocked shelves of Mudie's library have filled her head with strange yearnings. There is something in life, though she is not sure what it is exactly, which is to be sought outside the everyday round. She is sure, however, that it is very deep and to be interested in it is to be highly refined. Though she may not understand quite what those clever remarks of Mr Arnold meant, she has the feeling of a noble m ssion. What is more she has a position in society to keep up. Other women more powerful than she in the social order have taken to Culture. She must keep pace with them. It would never do to get left behind in the severely competitive business of fashionable living.

So she has adopted a dress and phraseology which seem to her the right, the modish thing, though it is to be feared that this 'aesthetic' lady is almost as vague about what she is really up to as the genial Philistine himself. Still of one thing we may be sure, that she is devoted to Art.

But what is Art? As Mr Ruskin has expounded it, it is a very serious matter, like Religion. And that being so, it would seem that you have to behave like you do when you go to church. You look pious and reverent and speak in a special kind of awed, hushed voice. Art is like a solemn service with its own congregation of worshippers doing their best to shut out of their minds all memory of worldly things.

It is possible that Mr Ruskin alone would not have willingly caused quite this form of worship; but then there was the influence of Mr Pater too. Mr Ruskin was rather strenuous. He urged the necessity of work upon his hearers and of course when he suggested that art had something to do with ordinary daily life, and that it might even be mixed up with such a practical hard-headed business as economics, why then, though his language was beautiful, it became very difficult for many of those hearers to follow him. The great thing about Mr Pater was that as the result of listening to him you did not have to make any effort at all. You simply had to *be* – to admire. He never suggested as Ruskin did that people who were interested in beauty must concern themselves also with such ugly facts as railway trains and factory chimneys and cheap lodging houses. On the contrary he caused these things to disappear by never referring to them at all. None of the vulgarities of existence must be allowed to disturb the state of contemplation in which 'full and perfect experience' was to be found. His habit of picking and choosing words with such precision might make it difficult to know what their real meaning was, but the words were beautiful in themselves and had the secret power of a charm or incantation. His followers were well content to believe that culture was a mystery.

Walter Pater in the seventies was influential enough to be caricatured and the caricature extended his influence still further. It was contained in a witty book, *The New Republic*, by W. H. Mallock, which appeared in 1877. A series of dialogues in the manner of Plato introduced a number of famous Victorians in the thinnest of disguises and speaking in accents so very close to their own that the parody was all the more pointed. Jowett, strenuous and practical, appeared as Dr Jenkinson, scientific Mr Storks was Thomas Henry Huxley, cultured Mr Luke was Matthew Arnold, Mr Herbert (the least satisfactory portrait of the lot) was John Ruskin, Pater completed the collection under the name of Mr Rose. It is interesting because typical of the confusion which existed as to what such a label really meant that Mr Rose was described by the author as 'the Pre-Raphaelite'. Pater had very little of the energetic and self-forgetful spirit of the Pre-Raphaelites and the description of Mr Rose is distinctly not that of one of their number. It gives a picture, on the contrary, of an egotist, of one whose attitude is as carefully considered and cultivated as that of a Regency dandy. He 'always speaks in an undertone and his two topics are self-indulgence and art'. His words float down the table 'in a languid monotone'. His views are so close to those of Pater that they seem almost to be actual quotations. 'I rather look upon life as a chamber which we decorate as we would decorate the chamber of the woman or the youth that we love.' What, Mr Rose asks, does successful life consist in? 'Simply,' he answers in Paterian strain, 'in the consciousness of exquisite living.' The warring of endless doubts was wearisome to him. He took 'a profounder and more exquisite pleasure in the colour of a crocus, the pulsations of a chord of music, or a picture of Botticelli's'. Mr Rose, the author of *The New Republic* conveys, is more than a little odd. He is made to show undue interest in certain books of a curious character, including the *Cultes Secrets des Dames Romaines*, which occupy a locked compartment of his host's bookcase. There is a faint suggestion that his languid enthusiasms are not only sickly but even a bit dubious in morality.

Pater, as always, impervious to the opinions of others, did not object to, even enjoyed the portrait of Mr Rose 'the Pre-Raphaelite'. 'I am pleased,' he said, 'to be called Mr Rose – the rose being the queen of flowers.' The world was welcome, if it liked, to call him 'self-indulgent'. Though he was once moved to a mild protest at a popular conception of him, it was rather concerning the correct definition of a word than for purely personal reasons. 'I wish,' he said, 'they would not call me a hedonist. It gives such a wrong impression to those who do not know Greek.' But if there was a slight twist of misrepresentation in the *New Republic*, it established all the more effectively a plausible image of Pater in the mind of the upper middle class and it did more than this – it provided, as clearly as any book of etiquette, a formula of 'aesthetic' behaviour.

Such part of the middle class as was in revolt against itself was equipped with a suitable deportment. Those who had, or thought they had, souls, moved in imagination 'to the sound of flutes', became languid, crooned in low adoring tones and tried to succeed in life by developing exquisite sensations.

Women displayed all their remarkable gift for physical adaptation. Nature began, in earnest, to creep up to art. Art was important enough now to be confused with fashion. What kind of art was a matter of choice.

Some women became like Pre-Raphaelite pictures. They imitated the composite ideal which Dante Gabriel Rossetti had evolved from Elizabeth Siddal and Jane Morris, sad eyed, brooding with passionate melancholy, with full drooping lips and a long columnar neck. On the other hand for those who were not medievally minded there was another type which seemed to derive from the highest art – the classic. There was the stately beauty depicted by Frederick Leighton and Edward Poynter, the aristocratic Romans of Alma-Tadema, the ladies painted by Albert Moore who sat on marble benches, in flowing draperies, doing nothing in particular. It was not hard for an English girl to adopt the straight nose and clear-cut features which these artists had rendered more attractive than had Phidias or Praxiteles; to look as aloof and unapproachable as the caryatid of a temple on the Acropolis. Thus it came about that the Beatrice of Dante was reincarnated in Kensington and the ballrooms in the London season were full of eligible Dianas and stately Minervas.

Dress was affected similarly. The long medieval folds with which the Pre-Raphaelites had delighted to clothe their Belle Iseults, their Marianas, the severe classic draperies in which the rival school specialized, became necessary properties of the aesthetic life. Hence the shapeless flowing creation in which the lady drawn by du Maurier was dressed.

Decoration was naturally allied to garb. The stage must be properly set if the actor, and more particularly the actress, were to achieve the intended effect. And again the Pre-Raphaelite influence came to the fore. William Morris was now making furniture, textiles, wallpapers, designed and patterned on medieval principles; so that if you were in the movement you sat on a Morris chair as du Maurier's lady did, surrounded by the intricacies of Morris ornament. And then, what? You adored Beauty. Adoration was the keynote of the whole performance. That, at least, was how the middle class interpreted the admonishings of its various mentors; and the prime object of adoration was the new and strange art which came from the East. Beauty, it seemed, was concentrated in oriental vases with blue designs on a white ground; and in this way the enthusiasm which Whistler brought over from Paris took root. Early in the seventies Rossetti had collapsed from the effect of chloral and mental strain. His collection had been dispersed and bought by other collectors. The minor poets had begun to take their inspiration from the vogue for pottery – Andrew Lang with his *Ballades in Blue China* of 1873, Austin Dobson with his *Proverbs in Porcelain* of 1877. A special view of Sir Henry Thompson's collection was held in 1878. An increasing number of Japanese prints appeared on the walls, of fans over the mantelpieces and objects of bamboo in unfilled corners. With the normal jumble of things in a Victorian room they made a strange mixture; but to the British public they were less to be seen than to be venerated as the symbols of culture, they were a form of mysticism. 'Can we live up to it?' gravely inquired the young married couple standing hand in hand before the vase which they had bought.

On the whole the Aesthetic Movement was a comedy of errors. 'You want us to be cultured?' said the middle class in effect, 'This then is what you mean?' throwing itself into a posture which was both serious and ridiculous. And no one was much advantaged or satisfied. To the average Briton it was all vaguely effeminate and unhealthy. To Whistler it was a barbarous mockery of severe and exacting artistic principles. To William Morris and his associates it was the opposite of their energetic creed in which the mere appreciation of art had no place.

The first perceptible effect of the new art-consciousness was to create a fad and farce.

## 6

## Café Society

MEANWHILE, in France, a very different, a creative movement, was on foot. It was precise and purposeful. It was limited to a number of talented, hard working men in deadly earnest. It grew, not in the frivolous atmosphere of salons and drawing-rooms but in the professional and ideological discussion of the cafés.

The café was of peculiar importance. It represented Liberty, Equality, and Fraternity. It was open to everyone without distinction. It imposed no conventions. Its character was that of those who chose to frequent it. It allowed either of quiet contemplation or of animated and intimate talk. It encouraged, by virtue of being both a species of club and a public resort, the exchange of ideas and the sparkle of wit. It was therefore especially frequented by writers and painters.

A friendly group would meet in one favoured café. The exchange of ideas made a link between them. Painting and literature entered into partnership. The painters planned to show their work together. The presence of the writers helped to clarify the theories of the painters. In due course it became necessary to provide them with a name. Thus the café became the birthplace of a movement in art. The number and diversity of the café groups has helped to create the corresponding large number of modern art movements.

In this way the so-called 'Impressionists' came together.

They had, of course, no such name to begin with. It was provided for them later by a journalist enemy.

The studio of Gleyre, where Whistler and du Maurier went at the end of the fifties, produced some of them. By 1862 its student friendships constituted a bond between Claude Oscar Monet, Alfred Sisley, and Pierre Auguste Renoir. They were offshoots, poor or otherwise, as chance decreed, of the philistine bourgeoisie. In them, the divorce of art from social meaning, already declared as a phrase or intention, was producing a distinct outlook and character. They were painters not for a public (they had none) but for their own satisfaction. The precision which they gave to their programme was typically French. The 'story' was entirely laid aside. For them, as for Gautier, the visible world existed. They were not interested in 'compositions' whether of the old Romantic or the old classical kind. They simply painted what they liked, in the way it looked to them.

Monet was born in Paris but, his father being a merchant at Le Havre, he spent most of his youth at the port and was inspired to paint by the local genius, Boudin, a native of Honfleur, with the sea salt in his blood, who excelled in shipping and harbour scenes. To the horror of his parents Monet decided to take to art. They promised to buy him off military service if he would give up this desperate idea. Refusing, he had gone with his regiment to Algiers.

Sisley was born in Paris of English parents. His father was a well-to-do man of business with a profitable South American trade. Alfred was intended for commerce and when eighteen was sent to England but he gravitated back to France, and, as an amateur, attended Gleyre's famous school.

Renoir was born at Limoges. His father was a tailor who came to work in Paris. Pierre Auguste began earning his living by decorating porcelain. He took to painting because he was thrown out of work by machine production.

As young students they had an admiration in common – for the brilliant and popular man who was now eclipsing Courbet as the light of a realistic new generation – Édouard Manet. Popular, that is to say, among 'confrères' – though the object of furious attack by others, which were a source of great disturbance and anxiety to him for Manet most earnestly desired to be thought respectable.

Great offence was given by his celebrated picture *Le Déjeuner sur l'Herbe*, in which a girl model, without clothes, is sitting on the grass at an open air picnic with a party of correctly, even heavily, dressed gentlemen with black coats and peg-top trousers. It was exhibited in the collection of pictures refused by the Annual Salon in 1863 – a collection made at the suggestion of Emperor Napoleon himself.

It is significant of the unsocial nature of nineteenth-century art that rejection should become, among those who knew, a diploma of merit and the Salon des Réfusés an honoured event. It implied that good painting was not understood either by the average layman or by the official practitioner. Whistler was delighted to identify himself with the noble outcasts by sending his *Little White Girl*.

The hatred with which these pictures were received was the instinctive reaction of a class which scented revolution in the works of those who so obviously did not conform to bourgeois standards. This at least is the only rational explanation of the howls, the hisses, the impassioned mockery which arose from the philistine visitors, who were, after all, under no compulsion to go and who could not be said to suffer in any material particular from the existence of some small pieces of coloured canvas. The novelist, Émile Zola, witness of the scenes which took place when Paris came to scoff, later devoted, in *L'Œuvre* (his attempt to portray the life of the artist), many pages to the crescendo of fury which arose and the phases through which it passed from an uneasy titter to blustering storm.

Outspoken in defence of Manet were the admiring pupils of M. Gleyre. They mustered in the Café Guerbois, at the beginning of the avenue de Clichy, which was near the house in the rue de Saint-Pétersbourg where Manet lived with his wife and mother, and was consequently patronized by the great man. One would find him there, probably with his friend, Edgar Degas, a painter of about his own age, a sharp-tongued, sharp-featured fellow with a genius and character as distinct and impressive as that of Manet himself. There was an outer circle of satellites, such as Astruc, the sculptor and poet, and Duranty, the novelist and critic. But letters took second place to painting, which of all the arts was held in the highest esteem. When the painters came in, the scribblers, poets, and journalists stood up in their places as a mark of respect.

So, a group was formed and from its discussions there emerged an idea. The exciting thing about *Le Déjeuner sur l'Herbe* was not the presence of a naked model. It was the fact that the figure was painted in the open air. It was, moreover, painted with a new liveliness of colour, a method of breaking it and causing it to sparkle which Manet had learnt from Velasquez and Delacroix (who in his turn had acquired it from Constable and Turner). Painting in the open air, it seemed, was full of alluring and delightful possibilities and by developing the method which Manet had used, the actual sensation of the changing moods of the atmosphere could be magically transposed into paint; though it was an obvious condition that you no longer shut yourself up in a studio to work according to set rules but must go out and pursue the transient effects of nature as they passed.

This radical conclusion appealed more to his followers than to Manet himself, who had found the new path almost by accident; but for some years the meetings and fruitful discussions continued and the group, as yet nameless, expanded. A youth from Provence, mad about art, and absorbed in heavy, awkward efforts to paint, Paul Cézanne, persuaded his school friend, Zola, who was already making a name with his pen, to champion Manet. Urged on by Cézanne, Zola wrote in 1866 an article in *L'Evènement* in Manet's defence, and was co-opted into the circle of friends. Manet brought in Camille Pissarro, a French Jew, born in the Antilles, who had come to Paris at the age of twenty-five to take up painting. They were all in process of finding themselves when, in 1870, came the complete dislocation of all such self-regarding activity.

In July of that year the boulevards rang with the cry 'To Berlin'. 'By an unheard of presumption,' telegraphed the King of Prussia to the King of Bavaria, 'we have been driven from the most profound peace into war.' The Emperor Napoleon 'placed himself at the head of his valiant army'. But the German state of profound peace soon appeared to have comprised a well-designed plan of hostilities. Rumours began to fly that all was not well. The Empress Eugénie, in the absence of her husband, called on the citizens of Paris to maintain order. Sedan came in September. Victor Hugo arrived in Paris 'for the purpose,' he said, 'of defending the capital of civilization'. Camille Pissarro suddenly found that he was within range of the guns. He was forced to decamp hurriedly from his house at Louveciennes which was occupied by the enemy troops. The Prussians turned it into a slaughter-house and the canvases were spattered with the blood of beasts. No further trace was seen of the pictures he left behind.

The painters acted each according to his temperament. Degas served in a battery of artillery. Manet stayed in Paris as an officer in the National Guard. Pissarro crossed the Channel to England. Monet went to Holland first and then joined Pissarro in London. Cézanne stayed at home in the south, painting. When asked what he did during the war he explained '*je travaillais sur le motif*'. 'I was working on a design.'

And so in the year 1871 you might have seen two foreigners of distinguished appearance, both wearing the profuse beard of the period and carrying the traps proper to a painter on a sketching expedition, haunting the stretch of the Thames around Westminster and Charing Cross.

Decidedly, this was a strange city to which only the freak of war would have brought them. It was less a city, like the beautiful Paris which Haussmann had planned, than a vast shapeless mass of organic life – 'an accumulation of toil'. In 1871 a wave of new building was swirling round the remnants of a more stately and ordered past; round the churches of Wren and the squares of the eighteenth century. The new buildings were largely a fantastic imitation of the Middle Ages. A queer conscience implanted in the manufacturers and architects, largely by the writings and exhortations of Ruskin, had caused the factory chimneys to be adorned with Gothic detail and streets of small houses to repeat endlessly the ornate porch style of Venetian palaces. Pissarro and Manet looked with astonishment at the works of two eminent living architects – Sir Charles Barry's Houses of Parliament, now twelve years old, Sir Gilbert Scott's St Pancras Station, whose dreaming pinnacles were brand new.

They were fascinated by this extraordinary city, not because of its design nor its mode of life but by the heavy coloured atmosphere through which there loomed ghostly and delicate outlines. It seemed to be created not so much by men as by the misty smoke-laden air which broke the light into a whole prism and flattened, softened and made poetic the grotesque and irregular buildings. Monet had in his eye a picture, *La Tamise à Londres*: soft and vague, with Big Ben faint in the distance, the dim shapes of tugs on the river whose banks were lost in a fleece of fog, a landing stage in the foreground, sharply defined and rescuing the whole from blue-grey chaos.

They went to the National Gallery and looked at the works, new to them, strange to them as the city itself, of British painters. They were probably impressed on this occasion by the forerunners of Impressionism, Turner and Constable. Pissarro certainly was, although Monet is reported to have been disappointed. 'This brown thing – is this your Turner?' They soon became homesick. 'I am only going to stay here a short while', wrote Pissarro to the critic, Théodore Duret. 'I shall not remain here and look forward to returning to France as soon as possible. Only when abroad do you realize how beautiful, great, and hospitable France is. What a difference here! Here one is treated with dislike, indifference, even with rudeness (*grossièreté*); among fellow artists (*confrères*) jealousy and the most selfish mistrust. Here there is no art at all, everything is commerce.' This bad impression was heightened, may even have been created, by a failure to sell anything. 'As far as selling is concerned I have done nothing except with Durand-Ruel who has bought two small pictures from me.'

Durand-Ruel was the French picture dealer – a small, energetic, dark-eyed man whose father had made a fortune out of art during the earlier romantic epoch. An instinct for what was good led him to acquire works from Manet, Renoir, Pissarro, and Monet when they were otherwise ignored. The war had brought him to England and his stock of unwanted masterpieces came with him. He held exhibitions in Bond Street. In fact the Society of French Artists continued there, to the great dissatisfaction of the native academicians, until 1877.

It was a slight contact between two cultures. Monet and Pissarro went back to France when the war was over, having made no perceptible impression on England but gaining some slight stimulus from its atmosphere. Things were different in Paris now. The meetings at the Café Guerbois were finished. The painters were badly hit by the war. There was no Salon in 1871 and less encouragement for experiments than ever. Those who never had much money were near to destitution. (Sisley's father lost everything and Alfred, no longer a wealthy amateur, had to paint in real earnest. He was never without money troubles until the end of his life.) Many were dispersed in cheap country retreats where they worked quietly at landscape – Pissarro at Pontoise, Monet at Argenteuil, Sisley at Voisins, Cézanne at Auvers.

Desperation caused them in 1874 to hold an exhibition – cheaply, in a suite of rooms occupied by the photographer Nadar in the boulevard des Capucines. Monet, Pissarro, Sisley, Boudin, Renoir, Degas, Cézanne, and Berthe Morisot (a friend of Manet) were principal exhibitors. It was now that they acquired a name. Monet contributed a little picture of the sun rising over water which he called *Impression*. The Parisian journalists seized on the word 'the Impressionists'. *Le Charivari* described them thus and the term stuck.

The Impressionists were as unpopular as Manet had been. They were accused of communism, incompetence, and feigning insanity. Evidently all you had to do to be a painter of this sort, said Albert Wolff in the *Figaro*, was to throw colours haphazardly on the canvas and then sign it. Cézanne excited as much horror as if he had been an ogre.

The public showing of Impressionist pictures which followed almost yearly until 1886 amounted to little more than auctions at absurdly low prices. Thus in 1875, at the Hôtel Drouot, Monet got between 165 and 325 francs for a picture, or between £6 and £12; Sisley between 50 and 300 francs (£2 to £12). Renoir got about £4 apiece for twenty pictures. When Cézanne went back to Aix in 1879 he left piles of canvases with Father Tanguy, the old colour merchant and artists' friend. The small canvases were priced at 40 francs, large ones at 100.

At the same time the prestige of the Impressionists was growing. At a new centre, the Café de la Nouvelle Athènes in Montmartre near the Place Pigalle, Manet and Degas received a positive veneration, and here came everyone with pretensions in letters and art. But the spirit of the place was exclusive. The years of neglect and difficulty had had their effect. The Café de la Nouvelle Athènes was a place of secret understanding among those who had gone through the mill together. As for the true intimates, the secret was by this time so well understood that they could, as it were, talk in a private language one with another; and as for the rest – so much the worse for them, they were beyond the pale.

It was at some time in the late seventies that there pushed, through the glass door which scraped on the sanded floor of this famous resort, a young Irishman, who, like the American Whistler twenty years before, was captivated by the brilliant life of Paris and was destined to return like a missionary bearing wonderful tidings to the island of Britain. He was of curious appearance – in some ways not unlike Swinburne. He had bright yellow hair, the colour of a daffodil, a white bulging brow, blue bulging eyes with a rather blank expression and pale cheeks. His chin receded into a long neck on which his head was set like a bulb and the shoulders fell away at a steep angle. His name was George Augustus Moore.

Rarely could anyone with pretensions to culture have come to a great capital more completely devoid of acquired learning. George Moore was like a new sponge about to be dipped in water for the first time.

He had grown up as a young savage in the Homeric circle of an Irish country house. He had ridden, shot, and fished as a boy with his brothers at Moore Hall, the family house, built in the late eighteenth century by a merchant ancestor on the slope called Muckloon, overlooking reedy, dangerous

Lough Carra in County Mayo. This healthy and spacious life did not make him take kindly to school. He hated Oscott, the Roman Catholic college near Birmingham to which he was sent and where, whether passively or wilfully, he resisted all efforts to teach him anything. His headmaster complained that among other heinous mistakes he habitually spelt *Jesus* as *Jeasus*. When he left the school his mind was a complete blank, whose blankness some years spent in Alfred Place, South Kensington, did little to correct.

On the other hand he had the quick Irish intelligence and a liberal curiosity which prevented him from being unduly hampered by an absence of knowledge. He hankered after new horizons. He felt little enthusiasm for settling either in his own country or in England and when his father died, leaving him a property of 12,500 acres representing nominally an income of nearly £4,000 a year (though with the various impediments usual to an income derived from Irish land it was probably much nearer £500) he determined to go to Paris. Without French, and even with very rudimentary English, but with an Irish valet at his back, the young, barbarous landowner arrived at the capital in 1873 in order to study art, for which, it may be added, he had no talent and of which, as of so many other things, he knew nothing.

But the primitiveness of George Moore's mental equipment was only matched by the ease with which he took to sophistication. In a very short while he found out what were the right books, the right matters to discuss, who were the people who counted. He became suddenly knowledgeable about European literature. A memory at once excellent and inaccurate stood him in good stead. He began to write home in confident, idiomatic, ungrammatical, and misspelt French although when he first arrived he was not able to express his wish to become a pupil of the painter Cabanel and remained for some weeks in idleness except for the acquisition of a few basic words.

At first, his enthusiasms were of an uneducated kind. He admired the conventional artists of the Salon, notably the pretty and vapid pictures of Bouguereau, which excited then, as they have done since, the mirth or anger of the serious. But Moore soon realized the sort of esteem in which Bouguereau was held. He acquired good taste and slang with equal speed. He showed a curious mixture of conceit, imitativeness, and discernment and became, as he thought, almost a Frenchman. He bought a copy of *Les Fleurs du Mal* which inspired him to produce an *Ode to a Dead Body*. His collection of early poems, *Flowers of Passion*, with a skull and cross bones and a lyre stamped on the cover, won him the gratifying epithet of 'bestial bard' from the vigorous, moralistic journalist, Edmund Yates of *The World*.

For a while Moore studied at the Académie Julian; a crowded cosmopolitan place where Bouguereau taught. It furnished the Irishman with material for an extremely amusing description and convinced him that he would never be a painter. He read the modern French poets and found to his ingenuous surprise that language had a beauty of its own. He claimed in the *Confessions of a Young Man* to have kept a pet python in his rooms, though this may well have been an invention suggested by a book published two years before the *Confessions* – Huysmans' *A Rebours*. It was inevitable that he should sooner or later find his way to the café of the great men.

It is easy to understand how much the inner intimacy of the Nouvelle Athènes appealed to Moore. The aloofness, the aristocratic disdain with which the Impressionist circle defended themselves against the jeers of the mob and brushed aside the criticism of the ignoramuses appealed to the country gentleman and the snob in him. The fact that they were arrayed against or had arrayed against them certain powerful organized forces was attractive to him as an Irishman. The way they had of talking of art in their own special language aroused his inquisitiveness. Manet, to him, was godlike, with his fine open features, his square shoulders, his manifest genius; Degas was, if formidable, fascinating, and who more truly a poet than Villiers de l'Isle Adam, of the long hair, the slender feminine hands and the enchanting stories? That there was a certain discipline in the Café de la Nouvelle

Athènes – the necessity that is to say of behaving as an artist should or of paying the due reverence to the accepted objects of worship added an additional savour to its freedoms.

This discipline was strictly upheld by Degas.

Among painters, that remarkable man most nearly sums up the artist type which conditions in nineteenth-century France had tended to produce. He was the creative aristocrat as Baudelaire had conceived the part. He had an immense contempt for the mass of the people. A crusted Tory, he was the enemy of popular enthusiasms and the supporter of ruling cliques. In the famous Dreyfus case, his attitude was what would now be known as 'fascist'. As the son of a wealthy banker he had no need to sell his work or to take trouble to interest others in it and this was fortunate, for he professed a strong disbelief in work supposed to help or to be for the benefit of humanity. So far was he from thinking that his own art might come under this head that the idea of a public exhibition was distasteful to him. In a characteristic phrase he said '*Laissez-moi donc tranquille. Est-ce que c'est fait pour être vu, la peinture? dites!*' Don't bother me! Is painting meant to be looked at?

Painting, he asserted, was private life. You practised it for two or three living friends and 'some who were dead'. The others knew nothing about it and never would know anything and consequently you did not care what they thought. The only competent critics were those few who were also painters and whom you respected. Writers, with the superficial vanity of their own (lesser) art were especially to be dreaded and avoided. When in the fullness of time George Moore wrote an article about him, a garrulous impertinent entertaining article, Degas was very angry indeed and refused any longer to admit him to his house.

This fastidiousness was all the more impressive seeing that no one could deny his superlative ability. His eye and hand were so wonderfully exact and sure. He knew his job, in a way which Cézanne, the plodding, oafish disciple of the Impressionists did not and never would know it. True to his principles Degas disliked and despised Cézanne. He disliked equally his enthusiasm, his earnestness, and what seemed to him his incompetence. To desire to draw and paint and yet not to be able to do it consummately well was unforgivable. It was an attitude which to the English Pre-Raphaelites, with their love of the amateur, their regard for enthusiasm rather than perfect execution, would have seemed cruel and narrow. So indeed it was, though it was a sign also of a serious and exclusive devotion.

As art was for Degas the one thing that existed, religion, morality, and other serious concerns had no meaning for him and he was at some pains to dissociate art itself from any taint of idealism. ('Art is a vice. One doesn't marry it legitimately, one rapes it.' – 'Art is dishonest and cruel.') His strictly aesthetic devotion caused him to worship in the theatres and dance halls where the shifting lights and colours, the varied postures of the dancers inspired him not with profound thoughts but with the delight of vision. So, when he was asked what honour the state could bestow on him, he answered, 'You wish to decorate me – that is please me. Well then, give me a free pass for life to the Opéra'.

With such terse, dry phrases he expressed his philosophy or rather his fanaticism. A great many of his recorded remarks are personal and wounding. A kindly and nervous man, he had a deftness and economy in words which made his comments all the more cutting. Of the woman painter Berthe Morisot he said, 'She paints pictures as she would make hats'. Of Gustave Moreau, 'He is a hermit who knows the times of all the trains'. Of a picture by Meissonier, 'Everything is metal – *except* the breast-plates'. Of the painter Besnard, 'He is a man who tries to dance with leaden soles'. Each of many other such comments ingeniously exposed a weakness of his contemporaries.

The Nouvelle Athènes admired his art and feared his tongue. George Moore in his twenties and Whistler in his forties (for Whistler still endeavoured to keep in the movement) both showed a deference which it was little in the nature of either to display. Whistler was the more subdued of the two. He felt himself at a disadvantage in technical skill for he had never subjected himself to the vigorous apprenticeship which Degas had undergone and felt he was no match for him as an artist. In the matter of wit, also, he deferred to the stronger personality. When the man in the pepper and salt suit, with his brows shaped in quizzical remark like a circumflex accent, said concisely 'Whistler, you behave as if you had no talent', the latter accepted the rebuke with a meekness he would certainly not have shown if some Royal Academician had used the same words in London. This, of course, was not lost on Moore. 'In sarcasm', he said later, 'Mr Whistler is to Degas what Theodore Hook was to Swift and when Degas is present Mr Whistler's conversation is distinguished by brilliant flashes of Silence.'

Moore's skin was a harder tegument. With cheerful impertinence he airily assumed a position of equality in the circle. No doubt at first the Nouvelle Athènes looked curiously on this new arrival, this 'Englishman' which, though he was Irish, was the natural description for any visitor from across the Channel. There was some laughter at the mistakes he made when he began to vie with the others in artistic discussion; but in course of time he was tolerated and accepted as all people are who take intimacy for granted and he began to preen himself on being the possessor of inside information and even an active participant in a great pioneer effort.

When the revenues of Moore Hall arrived at one of the strange confusions which sometimes overtake the revenues of Irish landowners and George Moore came back to London to earn his living he felt like those who having supped with the gods become like gods themselves when they return to human society. In the role of art critic he was happy to explain to the English the nature of the wonderful company of which he, in glorious and immortal hours spent at marble-topped tables, had been one, positively, as he came to be convinced, one of importance. France had become his property. Having known Manet he was evidently the destined prophet of French Impressionism – just as having read Flaubert's *Madame Bovary*, he considered himself to be the

discoverer of the literary value of adultery. The revelation
of style had flooded his naïf and uncouth mind. To communi-
cate the nature of this find to the island where it was unknown
was a pleasure strongly fortifying to the vanity, and one to
which from 1880 he devoted himself with glee. And to him,
as to the men from whom he had learnt, art was style. It
might be style in words, or style in shapes and colours; but
the distinction between words and shapes was less important
than the distinction between work, in whatever medium, that
had style and work that had not. His experience of two arts
had led him to divine a secret link between them, the link
which bound them also to the abstract rhythms of music.

# III

# BATTLE

## I

### *The Trials of a Prophet*

WHILE the forces of aestheticism were mustering; while Swinburne was mouthing defiance; while Pater was declaring that 'all the arts aspire to the conditions of music' and Whistler and Moore were worshipping gods as yet unknown in Britain, there sat enthroned in that island a prophet with a greater, a louder voice than any of these, upholding the direct opposite of what they upheld. This was John Ruskin, at the height of his influence and fame.

He had stormed at the British people, preached at them, bewitched them with golden and fiery words until they had accepted him as the sole arbiter in all questions concerning art and culture. He had lectured all over the country and these lectures were published in tall slim volumes with covers of dull, olive green, under titles which were fanciful but suggested some deep and hidden meaning – *Sesame and Lilies*, *The Crown of Wild Olive* and *Ethics of the Dust*. When, in 1868, the antiquary and collector Felix Slade left the sum of £35,000 to be divided between the universities of Oxford, Cambridge and London for the endowment of professorships in the Fine Arts, it was almost inevitable that Ruskin, famed 'Oxford Graduate' of *Modern Painters*, the virtual dictator of taste, should be elected at his own university. He embarked, then, on a fresh triumphal progress. His lectures were the most popular that had ever been given. His inaugural address in 1870 attracted such a large audience that it was necessary to hold it in the Sheldonian Theatre.

There was no doubt about the sway he had over his hearers, his instinctive command over all the devices of the oracle. His abrupt changes of subject kept interest alive. His comparisons were so novel and stimulating, as when he compared the workmanship of a Greek gem with that of a drawing from *Punch* by Charles Keene; and his humour and indignation both flashed out in a way that never failed to jerk back the flagging attention to a lively interest.

But the main secret of the popularity of his lectures was their humanity. Art to him was not, as it was to Pater, a thing of strange dim charm existing in a mysterious vacuum, but of fiercely insistent contemporary questions. If he spoke of a beautiful city of the past it was to demand with mounting anger what evil spirit hampered us from making such another beautiful city here and now. Constantly he presented a problem and a challenge – a problem not only for the age but for the individual, a challenge to the energy of each one of his listeners. He tried to induce them not to dream but to act.

He himself was more active than ever before. Though he established his headquarters at Brantwood, Coniston Lake, in 1871 (he was then fifty-two), this was no retirement. As well as his lectures he wrote frequent letters to the Press; had an enormous private mail, which he dealt with regardless of time or the importance of the subject; published a mass of miscellaneous writings and constantly busied himself with the schemes for social improvement which constituted the central core of his ideas. At Oxford he took congenial quarters with his old friend Sir Henry Acland, the Regius Professor of Medicine. The friendly, domestic atmosphere suited him and he had a room looking out on a blank brick wall where he found he could write more freely than anywhere else.

The question of how the people could most satisfactorily find happiness in work was his obsession. In 1871 he established a sort of magazine, or monthly pamphlet, called in the fantastic style of his other works *Fors Clavigera*, which may be translated as *Chance, the Club-Bearer*, though even when translated its meaning remains obscure. It was published for him by George Allen, an engraver and ex-pupil at the Working Men's College, who had shown uncommon skill in engraving the plates in Ruskin's earlier books. The Professor had fallen out, characteristically, with his former publishers (Smith, Elder & Co.) because they gave a discount to booksellers. He considered that the bookseller, being a middleman, had no right to exist; and when Smith, Elder refused to alter the usual practice, Ruskin took his books away from them and turned to his trusted assistant to publish them for him. *Fors Clavigera* was the first publication issued under this new arrangement. The price per part was sevenpence, post free, if ordered direct. No discount was given to booksellers. The retail price over the counter was, however, fixed at tenpence, in order to discourage the public from buying in the bookshops.

*Fors Clavigera* was written in the author's discursive lecturing style, now amiably confidential, now ecstatic, now harsh and stern with righteous ferocity. It served as the basis and propaganda for Ruskin's pet scheme of 'practical' improvement, the St George's Guild.

The Guild, which came into being in 1875, was intended to restore the most attractive features of the Middle Ages, bring about the reform, on medieval lines, at which the Pre-Raphaelite movement had aimed. It was a blow against capitalism, demonstrating Ruskin's principle that 'There is no Wealth but Life'. Town life was to be avoided and country life encouraged. Honest work was to be done under benevolent guidance, machine-labour excluded. Ruskin himself was the 'Master', the 'tyrant' (but not the 'despot') of a chivalrous system of government in which there were several main departments. There were *Comites Ministrantes* or administrative companions of the order, *Comites Militantes* who did the manual labour, and *Comites Consilii* who went on with their own jobs but assigned a tenth of their income to the Guild. All alike shared in the common property.

The Master drew up a creed of eight articles to which members of the Guild must subscribe. It restated the teaching of the Sermon on the Mount. It also included a typically Ruskinian order to obey the laws of the country as long as you agreed with them. The state of Christian anarchy was to be regulated by a system like that of the Italian Free Cities of the thirteenth century. A special coinage was designed (of pure gold and silver, without alloy). Newspapers were not to be allowed to members, until they could have one of their own, but Ruskin drew up a list of specially recommended books. He inscribed the Roll of the Guild on the blank leaves of an eleventh-century manuscript of the Gospels.

The Utopian plan failed. The prospective *Comites Consilii* displayed a reluctance to part with a tithe of their income. Few contributions were made from outside, although in 1872 thirty pounds came from a stranger in Wells and some acres of rocky ground little suited for agriculture were presented. A museum near Sheffield (from whose industrial operatives came the only sign of real interest) was the sole material result. Yet somehow on the preliminaries and incidental expenses the Master himself contrived to dispose of the sum of ten thousand pounds.

His disappointment was great, not on account of the money expended, for that to him was immaterial, but because of his desperate anxiety to put into practice what he preached, to create a real alternative to the industrial system he hated. But each practical step seemed so small in result, so beset with difficulties. As part of his Back to the Land campaign he undertook in 1874 to mend a bad patch of road at Hinksey. Among the undergraduates who came to his lectures were many landowners, or landowners-to-be, with a duty to their tenants. What better way of teaching them their duty than to give them a taste of honest work? The Hinksey Road was bad. He and they should mend it. The Slade Professor took lessons in wielding the pick. Downes the gardener from his house at Denmark Hill was pressed into service. A party of undergraduates (some of whom arrived, with their navvies' tools, in cabs) set to work and to the scandalization of the conventionally minded, the piece of road was mended, not very well, perhaps, but still mended it was. The outcry against this innocent performance was loud; not that this affected the Professor; yet he fretted that the effort seemed to lead nowhere. He did not care much whether it was called freak of fancy or a noble gesture. What really worried him was that no further roads were mended in like fashion. The problem was baffling. It was difficult to induce intelligent people to work with their hands, nor was hand work as easy as it looked. At the Oxford Museum he built one of the brick pillars himself. The workmen had to take it down again and rebuild it.

The excitement and frustration incidental to making a Utopia were not good for Ruskin. The strain of lecturing, in itself was considerable. The sense of failure preyed on his mind. He had also an intimate reason for agitation, an unfortunate love affair.

Rose La Touche, the object of Ruskin's affections at this time, was Irish, of Huguenot descent. She was one of three children to whom he had been asked to give drawing lessons. While still a little girl she was his favourite and she addressed him by the nickname of 'Crumpet', a term of endearment which later, because of his philanthropy, became 'St Crumpet'.

After a long interval Ruskin visited the family in Dublin. Rose was now a young woman of eighteen. He fell in love. He carried about one of her letters cased in plates of fine gold, and in 1873 when she came of age he made a proposal of marriage. She refused him – on religious grounds. She had become severely evangelical, was the author, at the age of twenty-one, of a devotional work called *Clouds of Light*. Ruskin's openly avowed disbelief was an impassable barrier to their union.

This was the climax of a series of disappointments in love. Ruskin was seized with a fever that affected his brain, in the sacristan's cell at Assisi where he had taken refuge. And worse was to come. The young evangelist was failing in health. In 1875 she died.

Ruskin was badly shaken. The thought of her haunted him. He attended séances in the hope of communicating with her. He became obsessed with the idea of her saintliness. He had always had a particular reverence for Carpaccio's painting *The Vision of St Ursula*. In a dangerous renewal of his illness it seemed to his disordered mind that Rose La Touche *was* St Ursula. So constantly had he thought of each that the two images became one.

In view of all this distress, toil and illness it is not to be wondered at if his lectures were more and more starred with sudden attacks on some objects of dislike, if the tone of *Fors Clavigera* became increasingly querulous and erratic. The object of attack might be Darwin or the industrialist or science in general. In 1878 it was James Abbott McNeill Whistler.

So preoccupied was Ruskin with the virtues of the Middle Ages and the greatness of the early Italian masters that it had scarcely occurred to him that changes might be taking place in art without his especial sanction and blessing. He was accustomed to hector contemporary painters as if they were sinners who had fallen away from the true path and must be guided back to it in a state of humble repentance. He considered his own time to be a wilderness, and the artist a poor creature lost and groping in it without such guidance as he himself could give. Thus his own preferences assumed an absolute value. When he stayed in Paris at the Hôtel Meurice he was probably unaware of the existence of the brilliant group at the Nouvelle Athènes; but if by chance he met someone he liked whose work happened to take his fancy then that person loomed large in fancied importance. If he met Kate Greenaway and liked her and her charming little drawings of children (liking them because he liked children) then Kate Greenaway was, for the time being at least, to be numbered among the best artists living. It is possible that if, as Swinburne had tried to arrange, he had met Whistler in person, that if Burne-Jones had succeeded in getting him to visit Whistler's studio, all would have been well – or comparatively well, for it is not easy to imagine their finding many subjects on which they could agree. But these projected meetings had not taken place. There was no prior circumstance to incline Ruskin favourably to the

American painter. He went one day in 1877 to the Grosvenor Gallery, Sir Coutts Lindsay's new enterprise, and there he saw an unusual picture, a picture that filled him with horror and dismay, a picture that must be properly and solemnly flayed together with its author in the very next number of *Fors Clavigera*. It was one of Whistler's Nocturnes. It was not the first time that Ruskin had seen a Whistler. Some time previously he had been moved to a fretful note of criticism. But this was an important occasion – an exhibition demanding a close and careful inspection.

The Grosvenor Gallery was starting off with great *éclat* and modernity. The paintings hung on its walls of gold and green included *The Days of Creation* by Edward Burne-Jones, the soulful allegory of G. F. Watts, *Love and Death*, the *Bath* by Alma-Tadema, portraits by Sir John Millais, in fact an acceptable mixture of academic and not so academic art. And yet Sir Coutts Lindsay in his modern zeal had admitted an outrageous interloper. A man who had the impertinent affectation to call a portrait of Irving as Philip of Spain, *Arrangement in Black No. 111*. A man who put down a mere smudge of colour and borrowed a musical term to give it a fictitious value. Nocturne! Nocturne in Blue and Silver! Nocturne in Black and Gold – the Falling Rocket! This would never do. Off went Ruskin and wrote those celebrated lines which were duly published in his magazine:

For Mr Whistler's own sake, no less than for the protection of the purchaser, Sir Coutts Lindsay ought not to have admitted works into the gallery in which the ill-educated conceit of the artist so nearly approached the aspect of wilful imposture. I have seen and heard much of Cockney impudence before now but never expected to hear a coxcomb ask two hundred guineas for flinging a pot of paint in the public's face.

Thus was the challenge flung down. It was not to go unregarded.

## Butterfly in the Box

If you had walked along the Chelsea foreshore in those early seventies when Ruskin was dreaming of his Utopia you might well have chanced to see a small dandified man stepping briskly along with a friend at his side and stopping every now and then to gaze intently across the river Thames. The time at which you would have been most likely to see them was in the evening, when as night advanced the water and the buildings shed the steel-grey grimness of day and softened into a smoky blue. The behaviour of the two pedestrians was unusual. The little man, having stared for a while over the wall of the embankment, would face about and say, like one reciting a lesson: 'The sky is lighter than the water, the houses darkest, there are eight houses, the second is the lowest, the fifth the highest. The tone of all is the same. The first has two lighted windows one above the other, the second four.'

'Wrong', said his companion, who was checking these details.

The little man turned sharply round. Once again he devoted his attention to the landscape, looked away, gave his recitation. At length he got it right. He wasted no time then. With a sharp good-night, he swung on his heel and went home, the blue silhouettes of bridge, buildings and stream being impressed on his mind. It was Whistler, and this was his way of preparing to paint what he termed a 'nocturne'. He saw there, though expressing it with a different technique, that vibration of atmosphere which Monet and Pissarro had seen.

Sometimes he had himself rowed on the river by a couple of boatmen. They were his faithful servitors these two. They were called Greaves. 'The boat-people, a sort of Peggotty family', Whistler described them. The Greaveses, like most of their trade, had a long tradition. Their father had known the great Turner when he lodged in Chelsea with an old Scotswoman, Mrs Booth, had rowed him around as the sons rowed Whistler.

The young men taught Whistler what he called the 'waterman's jerk'. In return he taught them to paint. Walter Greaves, then in his twenties, dreamed of being an artist like 'the Master', whom he and his brother followed about in a humble, adoring way. They copied his mannerisms and attitudes so much that it seemed as if Whistler was accompanied by two caricatures of himself.

They went on the river at all hours: sometimes in the morning as early as five o'clock. They might eventually get as far as Putney – where Whistler would have breakfast with his friend Charles Augustus Howell. Thus Whistler took pains to capture the spirit of the river and back in his studio he sought to recall it by a few exquisite outlines on a ground of soft blue, remembered and yet consciously selected and arranged.

He called these pictures 'Nocturnes' – partly because they were of night, partly, or perhaps even mainly, because the word was famous as the description of a form of musical composition. As such, it had already an estimable lineage, having been used by Haydn, the Irishman John Field and the French Pole Chopin. It may have been suggested to Whistler by Francis Leyland, 'the Liverpool Medici' to whom Rossetti had introduced him. That munificent patron was also a keen piano player, a lover of music. But however arrived at, the word most effectively proclaimed a gospel – that painting, as Pater implied, aspired to be music, that it was above all a rhythmic exercise, and that its importance had nothing to do with subject matter. For these reasons his use of the word 'nocturne' seemed a startling novelty and even an affectation.

In these years Whistler was doing his best work. The nocturnes must be put in that category. The two world-famous pictures, of his mother and of Thomas Carlyle, had been painted. The *Mother* was called severely *Arrangement in Grey and Black,* though there were some obstinate people who

chose to regard it as a work of filial affection and an interpretation of the calm and sweetness of motherhood. But
both portraits were ample cause for satisfaction. Whether
Whistler was really satisfied with himself is another question.
Outwardly he was gay, self-confident. Yet he did not feel
himself at ease. With artists in England his relations became
worse rather than better. His witticisms fell on unsympathetic
ears; and the tenor of his talk shocked many. 'It was not,'
said Holman Hunt, with heavy distaste, 'of the kind which
transfixes truth by a subtle shaft but amuses for the moment –
like a conjurer's trick confusing common sense.' And this
momentary amusement was of a very dubious kind. An
admiring lady had said to him, 'I am sorry to hear you are
in difficulties'. Whistler had retorted in his Murgeresque vein,
'Oh, don't pity me. Pity the poor devils that won't get their
money.' Hunt was horrified. 'This levity of nature could
not but affect his otherwise maturer art.'

His association with Rossetti was at an end and there
seemed to be no one else (save Howell) who could amuse or
understand him. At the same time, even if inspired, he was
not especially elated by his visits to Paris. Possibly they made
him realize his shortcomings, increased his gnawing doubts
of himself, the timidity which underlay his assertiveness, and
appears in the fragile delicacy of his paintings. He had a
feeling even in Paris that he was out of the running. With
Impressionism as a method he had no sympathy. The creation
of atmospheric effect by placing touches of pure colour side
by side was quite different from his practice of mixing the
exact tint required on the palette. And as for working from
nature – Nature 'put him out'.

He did not belong anywhere. The process of merging, of
transforming his identity which had brought him across the
Atlantic was incomplete. It was possibly an attempt to reverse
the process that took him back on a mysterious voyage to
Valparaiso; but if this was a further experiment in trans-
plantation, it also was unsuccessful.

These circumstances made him increasingly sensitive to
criticism and the criticism of Ruskin in *Fors Clavigera* was

the last straw. The anger of this artist in words was very unpleasant. There was a sort of instinct in the placing of the barb and, hastily as Ruskin had written and without personal knowledge of his victim, he had somehow contrived to give a portrait with a certain distorted likeness. 'Ill-educated conceit.' (Whistler was not well-educated either in the general or a specifically technical sense and he was conceited.) 'A Cockney.' (He was nothing else.) And a 'coxcomb'. (The archaic word does suggest that little, dapper, strutting, arrogant figure.) As for 'flinging a pot of paint in the public's face', it was true enough at least that Whistler detested the public.

But of course it was very unfair; very unfair, indeed. The picture buying vogue of the late Victorian age was now at its peak, and two hundred guineas were nothing when compared with the sums which insignificant academicians of whom Ruskin disapproved as much as he did of Whistler were in the habit of receiving. It was almost like taking a crust out of a poor man's mouth, especially in view of the weight which attached to the Slade Professor's pronouncements. Picture buyers, however opulent and prodigal, were a nervous and fickle tribe. They would spend a great deal of money on the right thing but a hint that a thing was wrong would quickly deter them and a word from Ruskin (always so much more than a hint) was the strongest of deterrents.

Whistler might well say, therefore, that he, an unoffending painter, had been singled out for wanton attack, while pursuing his profession, by a man of great power, holding a public and responsible position; that this attack would gravely endanger his chance of earning a living.

But questions of more general importance were involved in the famous trial for libel which followed – one of the most interesting episodes of the nineteenth century. At last the foreign doctrine which had crept so far quietly and insidiously into Britain was openly challenged. In the person of Ruskin, the social idealism of Britain was in arms against the cynicism of the continent represented by Whistler. On the continent the artist minded his own business and he left social reform to those others whose business it was.

Imbued with Degas' disdain for any attempt to mix art with the affairs of ordinary life, it was impossible for Whistler to understand a thing like the St George's Guild. The welfare of the country, if this was an effort to improve the welfare of the country, was not his affair. Politicians could say and do what they liked about the status of the workman, but according to artists who were proud of being artists, workmen should work and there interest in them finished. Ruskin encouraged stonemasons to exercise their imagination by carving gargoyles to their own fancy round the Oxford Museum; but Whistler had such contempt for the manual workers that he would not even let them mix the paint for the decoration of a room. They could apply it when it had been mixed for them. That was all. Their function was simple and unintelligent, controlled by the master mind of that superior being, the artist.

The artist was not a teacher and he resented any effort others might make to teach him. He was not a reformer and he did not want to be reformed. He was a being apart, cultivating with a candid selfishness his own rare gift, and indifferent to its effect upon the understanding of the masses.

This appeared perfectly reasonable to Whistler and abominable to the British mind. William Morris, with scathing inflection, denounced 'an art cultivated professedly by a few and for a few, who would consider it necessary – a duty if they could admit duties – to despise the common herd, to hold themselves aloof from all that the world has been struggling for from the first, to guard carefully every approach to their palace of art. It would be a pity to waste many words on the prospect of such a school of art as this, which does in a way, theoretically at least, exist at present, and has for its watchword a piece of slang that does not mean the harmless thing it seems to mean – art for art's sake. Its foredoomed end must be that art at last will seem too delicate a thing even for the hands of the initiated to touch.'

The prolixity of ornament springing from the undisciplined

1. *Déjeuner sur l'herbe* from the painting by Édouard Manet

2. *Blue China* (*Whistler and Carlyle*) from a drawing by Max Beerbohm

3. *Algernon Charles Swinburne* from a painting by Dante Gabriel Rossetti

**REFINEMENTS OF MODERN SPEECH.**

Scene—*A Drawing-room in " Passionate Brompton."*

*Fair Æsthetic (suddenly, and in deepest tones, to Smith, who has just been introduced to take her in to Dinner).* " ARE YOU INTENSE ! "

4. '*Refinements of Modern Speech*' from a drawing by George du Maurier

efforts of many hands was repugnant to Whistler. The co-operative enterprise of William Morris which encouraged it was wrong from start to finish. When shown a specimen of lustre-ware made by William de Morgan, Morris's potter associate, Whistler made this curious remark:

'Can one forgive a plate for a peculiar shine?'

There was a sort of malignance in this remark and also jealousy. How dare a mere craftsman set up to be an artist as well? All that Whistler had learnt from Degas made him champion his own exclusive caste and challenge the right of any public criticism at all.

It might be said Ruskin was unbalanced and that Whistler was logical and clear, but it was true that Ruskin's was a noble madness. He was responsible even in irresponsibility. And Whistler's was a narrow and selfish sanity. If you agreed with Ruskin it meant that you saw a purpose in art, you admitted that pictures were painted for the benefit of those who were not painters. If on the other hand you agreed with Whistler you accepted the view that art was divorced from life – that the artist was his own judge and the laws he obeyed were peculiar to himself. This was the underlying issue. The famous Ruskin *versus* Whistler trial was the trial of Art for Art's Sake.

With what dreadful joy, what unappeasable malevolence can one imagine Whistler reading through *Fors Clavigera*. Having been attacked, he was in no mood to spare his attacker. If he knew of Ruskin's psychological difficulties, of his unfortunate love for Rose La Touche, these could only be the object of derision. Whistler was devoid of sympathy, and his fiendish laugh – the celebrated Ha! ha! – so blood-curdling in sound that Irving imitated it for some of his most dramatic effects, must have rung loud and long. What was this twaddle about a 'St George's Company'? So Ruskin was to be a despot, and forbid the use of steam and machinery, decide what books the members should read and what dresses the women were to wear, and provide his tenants with a religion? So he charged tenpence for these twenty-four widely printed pages of stuff addressed to the workmen and labourers of Great Britain when there wasn't a workman or labourer in Great Britain who could afford to pay that much. What did Ruskin mean by calling Goldwin Smith a goose? mixing him up with the adulteration of butter and the nice girl waitress who described to him the adulteration of honey with carrots. And here he was attacking Sir Henry Cole, 'who has reduced art teaching in England to a state of abortion and falsehood from which it will take twenty years to recover'. It was, in one of Whistler's favourite expressions, 'Amazing'.

All this was duly put down in the Brief over which Mr Anderson Rose, Whistler's solicitor, laboured long, his client making many amendments and corrections. It had solemn touches here and there as of a dignified solicitor properly aware of the reverence due to the law and the seriousness to be expected from a legal document, and then it suddenly acquired a nasal twang and a vivid and cutting turn of phrase. 'If Salvator Rosa had lived, even in extreme old age, to the present day he might give his critic cause to remember that knives have edges.' Whistler was not unmindful of the fact that knuckles could still cause black eyes. Though somewhat submerged by the witticisms, a main point was made. 'Mr Ruskin's opinions are accepted as gospel in matters of art and there can be no doubt that his expressed opinion in *Fors Clavigera* is calculated to do Mr Whistler great pecuniary harm.' This of course was the material strength of his case. Ruskin could turn off the stream of gold from any artist he wished as surely as water could be turned off by a tap. That was why artists did not oppose him and why, when it came to the point, Whistler found it extremely difficult to get anybody to give evidence on his side, discovered in fact that there was a considerable opposition to him among artists who suspected all that he stood for. 'They all hoped they could drive me out of the country or kill me! And if I hadn't had the constitution of a government mule they would.'

Who would give evidence for Whistler? Certainly not Holman Hunt, the most conscientious follower of the original Pre-Raphaelitism, who thought Whistler showed at the

Grosvenor Gallery 'a defiant slovenliness of work which he could not have intended to be taken seriously'.

Millais regarded him from a correct academic standpoint as one who had never come up to the examiner's standard. As a man 'who has never learnt the grammar of his art! Clever, yes,' but 'all too clever'.

Edward John Poynter, who became a Royal Academician in this year (1877), was opposed to him. Since those days when they had been entertained in the rue Notre Dame des Champs by the negro songs of the amusing American he had remained convinced with a conviction that the years only strengthened that Whistler was an idle and impudent fellow.

So in the matter of allies Whistler was at a loss. He approached Charles Keene, the *Punch* draughtsman, that sensitive and solitary man, whose gifts were genuine and great, and whom Whistler himself ranked as an artist with Hogarth. Keene disappointed him. He was not at all anxious to give evidence and begged Whistler to do without him if he could. Nor did he take the matter as seriously as he should have done. 'A lark' was his anticipation of the matter. 'If the evidence is adduced it will be the greatest "lark" that has been known for a long time in the courts.' Frederick Leighton (who had never been sympathetic to the ideas for which Ruskin stood or the artists he had at various times supported) promised to appear; but refused at the last because he was going to be knighted on the day for which the trial was fixed. Dante Gabriel Rossetti would, no doubt, have stood up for Whistler, but Dante Gabriel was a sick man; though his brother William Michael Rossetti, in spite of his friendly relations with Ruskin, did actually appear for Whistler. In the long run only two painters appeared on his side. They were not of the most important. One was Albert Moore. The other was the Irishman, William Gorman Wills, a playwright and minor portrait painter.

A bigger gun altogether would have been someone like Edward Burne-Jones. That artist had exhibited side by side with Whistler at the Grosvenor Galleries. He was, he had been a friend of Whistler's. He had expressed a liking for his art. His word would undoubtedly carry weight in a court of law. Burne-Jones, alas, was one of Whistler's bitterest disappointments. He gave evidence on the other side, for Ruskin.

It was all very uncomfortable for Burne-Jones. He had the greatest distaste for arguments, quarrels, and public scenes. He didn't really want to appear for anybody – but just to go quietly along with his pictures of beautiful old legends and things happily far away. And now here was this unpleasant dilemma. Whatever he did he had to offend somebody: to offend his patron Ruskin, who had been generous and indeed lavish in his support, or to endure the contempt of a fellow artist fighting single-handed against the whole weight of a people's prejudice. No doubt Burne-Jones winced when he thought of this and of the withering quality which Whistler was able to inject into his contempt.

But Ruskin was insistent. There was no chance of temporizing. He had to be on one side or the other and painfully therefore he was constrained to support his patron and the principles of Pre-Raphaelitism. His patron was looking forward to the case. It was, as he said, in one of his fantastic phrases, 'nuts and nectar' to him to answer for himself in court. He looked forward to asserting 'some principles of art economy' which would be read all over the world in the newspaper reports. Neither of the litigants was deficient in courage. Both Ruskin and Whistler looked forward to a personal encounter. This, however, was not to be. Ruskin was overtaken by one of the brainstorms, or mental lapses from which he was to suffer at intervals for the rest of his life. He was supposed to have recovered, to have made some efforts to appear, but his doctor would not allow it.

The preliminaries excited as much attention as the progress reports of two heavy-weight boxers in training, and when the case began, on 25th November, in the Court of Exchequer Division, the court was crowded and people stood in the corridors; and there began an episode unique in legal history. John Walter Huddleston, last baron of the Exchequer, presided. Mr Sergeant Parry appeared for the plaintiff; the

Attorney-General, Sir John Holker, for the defendant. Gingerly, even nervously, the legal luminaries handled this mysterious matter of art, so much more mysterious and difficult than a divorce or a murder. The tone of Mr Sergeant Parry in opening the case for Whistler was almost apologetic and noticeably deferential to Mr Ruskin, 'a gentleman well known to all of us and holding perhaps the highest position in Europe or America as an Art critic. Some of his works are destined to immortality . . . ' It was, however, so much the more surprising, said Sergeant Parry, that a gentleman in such a position could traduce another as Mr Ruskin had done. The attack was 'unfair and ungentlemanly' and was calculated to do, and had done (Whistler), considerable injury.

Whistler was the first witness called. He stepped briskly and precisely into the box. He looked round jauntily, superbly self-confident in his powers of repartee, his fingers daintily posed in an attitude of nervous elegance, his dark eyes flashing and his monocle ready for effective adjustment, his moustache and chin beard suggestive of the 'southern gentleman'. He spoke in a drawl which clearly indicated America, and an intense vitality was evident in his bearing and even in the precision of his gesture and clothing. He began by saying that he had been born in St Petersburg (which was not so). He had studied in Paris with Du Maurier, Poynter, Armstrong. He had been invited to exhibit at the Grosvenor Galleries. The Nocturne which Ruskin had attacked was for sale and since the attack he had not been able to sell a Nocturne at the same price as before.

Sir John Holker, the Attorney-General, this preliminary canter being over, rose to cross-examine.

What, he asked, was a Nocturne?

Whistler explained that this was a word he applied to his night pieces. These were primarily arrangements of line, form, and colour and he meant that they were to be looked on as such and not because of any outside interest.

There followed a little comic 'business'. *The Falling Rocket*, the Nocturne in question, was brought in upside down. Laughter in court.

*The Falling Rocket*, Whistler said, represented the fire-works at Cremorne.

Attorney-General: 'Not a view of Cremorne?'

Whistler: 'If it were called a view of Cremorne, it would certainly bring about nothing but disappointment on the part of the beholders, (Laughter.) 'It is an artistic arrangement.'

This did not seem to get very far. The Attorney-General tried another opening. 'Why,' he asked, 'do you call Mr Irving an Arrangement in Black?' (Laughter.)

It was palpably a deliberate confusion. The judge here interposed, though not perhaps without a realization that further laughter would follow, to point out that the picture, and not the actor, was the Arrangement.

The great Irving liked this picture. It was to hang in the Beef-Steak room of the Lyceum Theatre, keeping its ghostly eye on many a jovial Saturday supper. 'It is accounted a fine portrait of me in the part,' said the great actor in the style of language proper to the drama of the period. 'Indeed, I so account it; but – I forget [Whistler was present and it was necessary to exercise the insulting wit of the period] who painted it.'

They reverted in court to Cremorne. A 'stiffish price', suggested the Attorney-General, 'two hundred guineas' and, with a sneer, 'How soon did you *knock it off?*' (Laughter).

In the report of the trial, Whistler answered, with what deprecation of the phrase one must imagine: 'I *knocked it off* possibly in a couple of days.' In his own account, in *The Gentle Art of Making Enemies*, he improved somewhat on this. 'I beg your pardon,' he represented himself as answering and the implied sarcasm, contempt, reproof for the vulgar phrase, is stressed by the accompanying bracket of (Laughter).

Attorney-General: 'I am afraid I am using a term that applies rather to my own work.'

Whistler, self-possessed, disdainful, condescended. 'Oh, no! permit me, I am too greatly flattered to think that you apply to a work of mine any term that you are in the habit of using with reference to your own.'

'Let us say, then, how long did I take to' – he went

through the pantomime of recalling and forcing himself to utter the curious and distasteful jargon of the lawyer, and paused – 'how long did I take to *knock off* (I think that is it) – to *knock off*,' he repeated, 'that Nocturne? Well . . .' It was a moment for a deliberate trailing of the coat. Perhaps he had already prepared in his quick mind the trap in which the lawyer might be caught by his own astuteness. 'As well as I remember, about a day . . . I may still have put a few more touches to it the next day if the painting were not dry. I had better say, then, that I was two days at work on it.'

It almost seemed as if Whistler were giving his case away in thus complacently emphasizing and elaborating upon the short space of time which the picture had occupied.

The lawyer rushed upon the point, triumphant. 'The labour of two days then is that for which you ask two hundred guineas?'

Then came the lunge. Whistler had got Sir John just where he wanted him. He produced the brilliant riposte: 'No; I ask it for the knowledge of a lifetime.'

A hum went round the court, the laughter, which was beginning again, checked, merged into a gradually mounting applause. That was clever. Something in it too. The slowest of wits could scarcely fail to draw a comparison here. After all, for what else did a barrister receive his very large fees but for such long experience used in a brief encounter. One can see the monocle in action as Whistler gazed upon the court, as if he figuratively wiped the stain of blood from his rapier with a cambric handkerchief, the Attorney-General flushing darkly and staggering from the thrust.

They passed on to the question of criticism.

'You don't approve of criticism.'

This produced a further *tu quoque*. 'I should not disapprove,' said Whistler, 'of technical criticism by a man whose life is passed in the practice of the science which he criticizes; but for the opinion of a man whose life is not so passed, I would have as little regard as you would if he expressed an opinion upon law.' It was one of Whistler's main contentions and a very significant one indeed.

The *Nocturne in Blue and Silver* was then produced. It was not the picture to which Ruskin had specifically referred. It was then the property of Mr Graham, the collector. It was later bought by the National Art Collections Fund for two thousand guineas and hung in the National Gallery where it is familiar to all. The dim silhouette of Battersea Bridge, exquisitely placed, on the soft blue of the river sky, the faint outline of a barge, appeal now to the critic who recognizes the judgement and perception with which tone and outline are assembled. It appeals more generally as conveying the atmosphere of that vaporous reach of the Thames in the soft night with a remarkable faithfulness. Many people must have seen in actuality just that moment and that effect. Many people then in the court must have seen with their own eyes – even if they did not take it in – such a moment. Yet they had not taken it in. The unfortunate jury certainly had not. Honest fellows, they were puzzled thoroughly. As the Nocturnes were passed round for their inspection their bewilderment grew. One of them was handed across the court for Whistler to verify and on its way an old gentleman with a bald head got a sharp tap from the frame, from which the picture seemed in danger of falling. 'Is that your work, Mr Whistler?' said Sergeant Parry. Up came the eyeglass. 'Well, it was, but if it goes on much longer like that I don't think it will be.'

And when Mr Ruskin's Titian was handed round at the end so that the jury might see the difference between the work of a charlatan and the work of a real master, no difference whatever was perceived. 'We've had enough of these Whistlers,' one said, quite unaware that he was looking at a Titian.

*Battersea Bridge* produced rather more questions than the *Falling Rocket*. 'Is this part of the picture at the top, old Battersea Bridge?' asked Baron Huddleston. 'Are those figures on the top intended for people?' These interrogations produced more laughter, which was rebuked.

'They are just what you like,' said Whistler coolly.

'That is a barge beneath?' 'Yes,' agreed the artist and with faint sarcasm, 'I am very much flattered at your seeing that. The picture,' he added, 'is simply a representation of moonlight.'

It further appeared that *Blue and Silver* had taken one day to paint – after it had been arranged in the artist's mind.

After this, judge, counsel, and jury all trooped round to the Westminster Palace Hotel to look at more pictures, without, it seems, being very much wiser as a result.

Whistler was then further cross-examined by the Attorney-General as to the *Black and Gold*; and again the Attorney-General found that he had met his match in the verbal fence. 'Do you think you could make *me* see beauty in that picture?' asked the Attorney-General.

It was a prime opportunity for the monocle; for the expressive pause; for a survey of the Attorney-General who expected perhaps to ensnare the artist into some confused explanation of the nature of beauty. A long pause, during which a concentrated mockery and contempt could be flashed across the court-room.

'It would be impossible for me to explain to you, I am afraid.' This remark, by Whistler's own reporting, appears in *The Gentle Art of Making Enemies* as 'No! Do you know I fear it would be as impossible as for the musician to pour his notes into the ear of a deaf man.' He credited himself with (Laughter).

On the whole the advantage was, as he stepped down, decidedly towards Whistler. He had, in face of a court inclined to facetiousness, a jury irritated by the incomprehensible, scored. The 'Islanders', as it became Whistler's habit to refer to the British people, were by no means having it all their own way.

The Attorney-General rose in all his majesty at the second sitting of the court. He was, as Whistler might have said, magnificent. He spoke in the authentic accents of Mr Sergeant Buzfuz; and if the latter had had Mr Ruskin as client instead of Mrs Bardell, he could have been no funnier. 'Let them,' said the Attorney-General, 'examine the *Nocturne in Blue and Silver*, said to represent Battersea Bridge. What was that structure in the middle? Was it a telescope or a fire-escape? Was it like Battersea Bridge? What were the figures on the top of the bridge? And if they were horses and carts, how in the name of fortune were they to get off? ...' 'The pictures were strange fantastical conceits not to be called works of art, and Mr Ruskin retracted no syllable of what he had written ...' In reporting this speech Whistler could not restrain himself from as it were dancing on the page round this adversary, from pricking and stinging in marginal notes somewhat disfiguring to his neatly spaced page.

Then the witnesses for Ruskin were called. They were Edward Burne-Jones, William Powell Frith and Tom Taylor.

Thin, fair-bearded, with a look of horrified misery in his blue eyes, Burne-Jones was now subjected to the ordeal of examination. It was dreadful to him thus to be dragged from the beauty of another world, the world of legends of King Arthur, from the Knights who loitered palely in the woods of enchantment and the damsels ritualistic and sad.

There came the brutal, the inescapable question: 'Do you see any art quality in that nocturne, Mr Jones?'

'Yes ... I must speak the truth, you know.' To this remark the alert author of *The Gentle Art* with ever ready sarcasm adds (Emotion).

Guided by Mr Bowen's cross-examination the Pre-Raphaelite granted to the nocturne fine colour and atmosphere. But to the question whether he considered detail and composition essential to a work of art he could not but answer he did. To the following question, whether he found such detail and composition in the nocturne he could only answer that he did not. Asked if he thought two hundred guineas a large price for the picture he said it was, 'when,' he qualified, 'you think of the earnest work done for a smaller sum'. It was, of course, necessary to make a qualification. Two hundred pounds was not very much for a Victorian artist to get. Holman Hunt had had £2,500 for a picture.

'Does it show finish?' went on Mr Bowen encouragingly.

Nervously, Burne-Jones answered at length. The picture

was only a sketch. It was only one of a thousand failures to paint night. At this point Ruskin's Titian was proposed as a sample of finish.

Mr Sergeant Parry objected.

There is a certain sly pointedness in the Judge's comment. 'You will have to prove it is a Titian.' How, he seemed to imply, could one prove anything in this extraordinarily vague and elusive business, about this phantom of art on whose non-existent behalf men struggled so fiercely.

Baron Huddleston recalled the fact, not, he hastened to say, to raise a laugh, that a Titian had been rubbed down and a full-length portrait of George III found underneath.

Burne-Jones, however, expressed confidence that no Hanoverian monarch lurked behind this particular portrait of Doge Andrea Gritti; and that it was a sample of the 'highest finish of ancient Art'.

It may seem odd to the student of art that Titian should have been chosen as the exemplar of finish, his pictures showing progressively a tendency to discard precisely this quality. Indeed, in a letter at the time, Albert Moore wrote in protest. He observed, that the Titian was an early work – that it was distinguished from the later and more valuable work of the master by the very fact that it was more finished, and therefore, being put forward as typical, it was calculated to produce an erroneous impression in the minds of the jurymen. It may be so. It may be doubted, however, whether those honest jurymen would have found the difference between one Titian and another very great. They were unable to see any great difference between the work of the Venetian master and that of the American. On both sides the witnesses were a scratch lot. Burne-Jones was followed by Frith. William Powell Frith, R.A., was then sixty (he lived to be ninety). The celebrity of his *Derby Day* was already twenty years old. He was hugely popular and his academy paintings had more often been fenced in to protect them from the throng of admiring visitors than those of any other academician. He was wonderfully skilful. Even Whistler had remarked that the background of one of his pictures was as good as a

Manet. He had paid several visits to continental Galleries with Millais and made comments on the old masters which were uniformly inept. In spite of his astounding ability he never knew when to stop. He was not even content with telling one story in a picture, he tried to tell a hundred. He was manifestly more interested in these stories, in the pitiful lot of a strolling acrobat at the races, or the delinquencies of an absconding clerk arrested at Paddington station than in the beauty of pictorial art. In his *Reminiscences* he said it was just a toss-up whether he became an Artist or an Auctioneer. 'He must have tossed-up', reflected Whistler. His pictures were of an improving kind, solid in virtue, conscientious in detail, from a Victorian point of view eminently good value. If their fault could have been compressed into a word, it would be – vulgarity, a thing abhorred by Ruskin himself. That Frith should have been chosen to stand on Ruskin's behalf is not one of the least curious features of the case. *Derby Day*, for instance, in subject and treatment was quite outside the range of Ruskin's sympathies. The critic could if he had set his mind to the task have damned it even more heartily than he did a Nocturne. It is possible, however, that Ruskin wanted someone who could not be supposed to be biased in his favour.

In his view, said Frith, Whistler's pictures were not serious works of art. He could not see either in the *Black and Gold* or the *Battersea Bridge* any truth of representation. There was pretty colour, nothing more. There was certainly not two hundred guineas worth.

And finally Tom Taylor gave evidence. 'Poor Law Commissioner, Editor of *Punch,* and so forth and so forth,' described Whistler airily. Tom Taylor was another unlikely ally for Ruskin. A Cambridge man and a barrister, he had been secretary to the Board of Health, and then turned to journalism and playwriting. As art critic of *The Times* he had been one of the scourges of Pre-Raphaelitism. He knew little of pictures, but had built up a formidable reputation through the emphasis and severity with which he stated his opinions. Tom Taylor, a man of sixty, stepped into the box, referred to his long association with *The Times* as his critical diploma, averred that Whistler was not a serious artist; that his work was unfinished and in the nature of sketching.

It was another opportunity for Whistler's retrospective sarcasm. 'To perceive in Ruskin's army Tom Taylor his champion – whose opinion he prizes – Mr Frith his ideal – was gratifying. But to sit and look at Mr Burne-Jones in common cause with Tom Taylor – whom he esteems and Mr Frith whom he respects – conscientiously appraising the work of a *confrère* – was a privilege!'

There was a deadly, an icy implacability about the restraint of his comment on Burne-Jones which must have made the latter's blood run cold. He did in fact go home, miserable, mourning and lamenting the whole wretched business and wishing it had never happened.

The Judge summed up. He made it quite clear that Mr Ruskin had used certain words which, beyond a doubt, amounted to libel. The critic should stick to criticism and not make it a veil for personal censure. The question for the jury was: Did Mr Whistler's ideas of art justify the language used? Did the insult offered – if insult there had been – call for substantial damages? Was it a case for merely contemptuous damages to the extent of a farthing or something of that sort, indicating that it was a case which should never have been brought into court and in which no pecuniary damage had been sustained, or did it call for damages in some small sum as indicating that the offender had gone beyond the strict letter of the law?

In this way Baron Huddleston intimated fairly clearly that he thought Ruskin had overstepped the mark: but that there could be no question of heavy damages – they should be either derisory or small.

The jury deliberated for an hour. It would be interesting to know the exact nature of their deliberations, of the remarks then made; as to these, however, we can only speculate. The time went on. Whistler, it was thought, looked somewhat anxious during the period of waiting. The court darkened in the short winter's day. Candles were brought in.

Preparations were made for the hearing of another case, something about rope, coils of which lay on the solicitors' table. Finally the jury came back and a hush fell on the court. The verdict was for Whistler; but, clearly indicating that a British court had thought it a lot of fuss about nothing and that a purely technical offence had been committed, the damages were – one farthing. Whistler is said to have declared his intention of wearing the farthing on his watch chain. In *The Gentle Art of Making Enemies* he devoted a page to a drawing of the farthing with his emblem, the Butterfly resting upon it, obscuring the head of Britannia and with its barbed tail curling at her feet.

# 3
## Age of Spite

THE first battle of the trial opened a whole campaign and ushered in what may well be called the Age of Spite.

The immediate effect of the trial was damaging both to plaintiff and defendant. It broke the power of Ruskin. He had not appeared in person. It was not possible that he should appear in his mental condition; but the fact remained that the telling words which had been spoken had all been spoken by Whistler. These were the words which stuck in people's minds and were repeated; which have, in the course of time, become classic. The Slade Professor was silenced. He said no more on the matter in print. He threw up the professorship, declaring that he must do so if he could not say what he thought in freedom. He withdrew to the quietude of Brantwood, to muse over pretty water-colour drawings by Kate Greenaway and Mrs Allingham, and punctiliously, when the servant called, 'the sunset, Mr Ruskin,' as if announcing a distinguished guest, to go out into the open and gaze at the streaks of Turnerian crimson in the sky over Coniston Water. In 1883 he made a short reappearance at Oxford but once more illness followed and the remaining years of his life (he died of influenza in 1900) were spent in a state of clouded peace.

It was a victory for the foreigner. There was now no strong champion of an art for the people, serving a moral and social end, save William Morris, and Morris was too much obsessed with the menace of capitalism to waste powder and shot on one mere painter. Painting to him was an idle business, so much so that he was prepared to admit that Whistler was a good painter and to dismiss him contemptuously in the same breath as an insignificant artist. It is true that he perceived and remarked on the grave general issue, but personal hostilities were not in his line. So Whistler, though surrounded by small hatreds and prejudices, was, vocally, triumphant.

At the same time he was ruined financially. With the reverence due to the resources of a wealthy man, one hundred and twenty of Ruskin's friends and admirers clubbed together and raised the amount of his costs, £384 12s. 4d. But no one raised anything for Whistler, beyond the State's farthing. 'The Law allows it, the Court awards it.' Baron Huddleston in the *Punch* cartoon of December 7th, 1878, by Linley Sambourne, is represented uttering these words as he handed the coin to the painter who was depicted with the legs of a penny whistle. Ruskin was symbolized as 'an old pelican in the art wilderness'. On the ground two serpents with wigged heads and forked tongues reared threatening heads in either direction. 'It satisfied,' said Whistler, 'even my taste for curious combinations' – though this was not very much satisfaction.

He had mortally offended his patron Leyland. 'What,' Mrs Leyland heard the high-pitched nasal voice say one day at Princes Gate, 'can you expect from a parvenu?' This remark about the self-made shipowner, uttered in his own house by one whom he had helped, was hardly calculated to keep his support. It illustrates incidentally the mean, the snobbish aspect of Whistler's pride in his artistic caste. Moreover, and more annoying still, he had made impudently free with the house in its owner's absence. He had 'ruined' the dining-room, the famous Peacock Room (now in the Freer Collection at the Washington Museum), by painting over the old Spanish leather on the walls with a peacock design of his own in blue and gold. He invited a throng to see it as if it were a public exhibition hall. Mr Leyland was furious and their relations were at an end.

Howell, of course, was tireless. 'I am most anxious to see Jimmy out of the mess and will do all I can.' If only, he mourned, he had been subpoenaed as a witness at the trial. 'You would have won the case and we should all have been in Newgate,' remarked Whistler. Howell pawned, borrowed, sold. He even bought some of Whistler's pictures himself. He paid ten pounds – and a sealskin coat – for the portrait of Irving. To lend to Whistler he had on one occasion to borrow from Anderson Rose who, in turn, had to borrow from his head clerk. He met a bill (he was so much at home with these paper transactions) given to Mr Nightingale, builder of the White House in which Whistler lived at Chelsea, 'with the money out of my railway verdict, now about to be paid'.

The White House was an incubus. Built by the architect E. W. Godwin in Tite Street, to Whistler's own liking, this attractive three-storied building with its white walls and grey-blue door satisfied his taste and increased his debts, which he could only pay in canvas. Blott, a moneylender into whose hands he had fallen, got the Carlyle portrait as security. The greengrocer, whose bill for fruit out of season was £600, received two Nocturnes in payment.

As a last resort Howell tried to get him a resounding commission – Disraeli. 'If I sit to anyone it will be to you, Mr Whistler,' were the final words of the great politician at their interview. 'And then,' said Whistler, recognizing the art of another sphere, 'he sat to Millais.'

Writs arrived, and bailiffs. The pattern of the old *Vie de Bohème* was revived. The bailiffs were trained to wait at table. 'I had to put them to serve me. Ha! Ha! Excellent fellows, they would not leave me.' One of the bailiffs asked for his money at the end of a week on the plea that he needed it badly. 'Why not have a man in yourself?' suggested his host.

But the legal machinery worked remorselessly on. Whistler was declared bankrupt in May 1879, with liabilities of £4,641 9s. 7d. and assets of £1,824 9s. 4d. Leyland was one of the creditors and committee of examiners. Charles Augustus Howell another. The house was sold to Harry Quilter, art critic of the *Spectator* and *The Times*, collector, amateur painter, and *littérateur*.

Whatever little importance a man may attach to material possessions, even if as an artist he feels he has within him the ability to create more things of value than those he has lost, a moment such as this is bitter, expecially when he has reached the age of forty-five. The greed of strangers, eager for a bargain, the brutal carelessness of those who handle precious objects like so much debris from a ruin, the jocular indifference of auctioneers, the impression that the bankrupt himself has ceased to exist, all this is bound to leave its mark. And as Whistler watched his collection of blue and white knocked down, as he saw the piles of canvases fetching ridiculous sums, and rolls of etchings and drawings thrown out practically as waste paper, one can imagine the hatred that seethed beneath the urbane front, which, plucky as he was, and no one can deny his pluck, he stoutly maintained, the extinction in him of the last grains of sentiment or friendliness to those who had made this outrage possible and had taken part in it.

Hence the peculiar malignance of the painted caricature of Leyland which he left behind – *The Gold Scab or Eruption in Frilthy Lucre* in which his patron was hideously represented as a scaly reptile playing the piano. 'Frilthy' referred to Mr Leyland's frilled shirt as well as to his fortune. But this was only a foretaste of things to come. Whistler determined to wage, as perhaps some of his Southern ancestors waged, a remorseless feud. He would expose these creatures, tear from them every rag of the absurd pretentiousness which they assumed; leave them naked and ridiculous in the eyes of the world. The 'Islanders' had shown him no mercy. He would give no mercy, no quarter in return.

He began to compile an index of folly, the autobiography of a hater, pursuing and hounding in turn each of those whom he considered responsible for his difficulties. Ruskin, first, obviously, because of the trial; Harry Quilter who had the villainy to buy and occupy the White House and belonged to the atrocious breed of art critics; his brother-in-law Seymour Haden and as many more as time went on who happened to get in his way. Thus *The Gentle Art of Making Enemies* came into being.

The style of this work has been described by Max Beerbohm in a description no one could better, as that of a man choking with rage, screaming and pointing a finger with terrible laughter. It recalls a performance by Irving of Mephistopheles, inconceivably malignant. It borrows with a sort of mock acknowledgement some of the tricks of Ruskin's own style, for example the alliteration of the 'pot of paint in the public's face'; and the biblical turn of phrase. It is to be suspected that Whistler consulted a Bible for the express purpose of destroying his enemies. Certainly he did not turn to it for habitual reading or for lessons in Christian humility.

The Parisian style of wit, exact and deadly, the art of concise denigration learnt from Degas was invaluable. Combined with a street urchin's capacity for personal abuse there was here a novel weapon against which seriousness and humour were alike powerless. And the venom of the attack was pictorially symbolized by a Butterfly, originally designed for Whistler by Rossetti as a monogram to sign pictures, adapted now as the badge of war and provided with a barbed tail. *The Gentle Art of Making Enemies*, a patchwork collection of letters to newspapers, occasional epigrams, quotations from his victims with stinging marginal additions, and the text of the author's *Ten o'Clock* lecture, covers Whistler's fighting life from the time of the trial to 1890.

The earliest entry is an assault on P. G. Hamerton, a minor Ruskin, editor of *The Portfolio* and an authority on etching. He, in 1867, had declared that *Symphony in White No. III* was not exactly a *Symphony in White* as it had other colours in it. Thus, alliterated Whistler, did 'profound prattle' find 'its place in print'. 'And does he then in his astounding consequence believe that a symphony in F contains no other note, but shall be a continued repetition of F.F.F.?' (and then the final screech) 'Fool!'

But the serious business begins with the trial, in the account of which Whistler took the opportunity of polishing up and adding to the effect of the remarks he had then made. Scarcely was it over before he had published a pamphlet on Art and Art Critics. Its main purport was to say that the writer as such was not qualified to criticize painting. Ruskin had 'talked for forty years of what he had never done'. The writer out of his depth was next exposed in the person of Tom Taylor, who had made an evidently absurd attack, among other absurdities, on Velasquez. Tom Taylor had frightened the life out of many a painter in his time but he was not used to their answering back or to being made to look silly. He replied with heavy bluster, but Whistler stuck to it that he had killed him 'like a rat, you know, rather cursorily'.

And then the self-appointed Enemy approached, with a gloating, a cannibal pleasure, even with a sort of inverted reverence, the hapless form of Mr Quilter. He created a ludicrous portrait with a characteristic economy of means which makes *The Gentle Art of Making Enemies* more effective in ridicule than such elaborate expositions of hatred as Pope's *Dunciad*. He simply dropped an aspirate, put in an apostrophe and, behold, Harry Quilter, M.A., the notable man of *belles lettres*, the respectable graduate of Trinity College, Cambridge, was turned into a gross, a comic vulgarian. 'Arry Quilter. 'Arry. Viciously, Whistler described him at an exhibition 'an amazing arrangement in strong mustard and cress with a bird's-eye belcher of Reckitt's blue'. No one now, it is to be imagined, would read Quilter's art criticisms but he lives still as 'Arry in the fierce preservative of Whistler's hate.

With the beginning of the eighties, in 1882, a new object of attack appears in *The Gentle Art* – Oscar Wilde.

# 4

## Aestheticism Rampant

IT was natural enough that, sooner or later, the various influences which gave a new and puzzling import to beauty should find a propagandist. They were so strikingly summed up in Oscar O'Flahertie Wills Wilde that it has been carelessly assumed that he was the inventor of 'Aestheticism'. In fact he was merely its vehicle or advertisement. The striking assortment of his plumes, as a young man, was an interesting series of borrowings.

He had approached England, like George Moore before him, as a foreigner, that is to say an Irishman, with the same open and receptive mind, though there the similarity between the two ends: for Wilde came, not from the Homeric country-side, but from the dingy magnificence of Merrion Square in Dublin. There lived his father, burly, amorous Sir William Wilde and Lady Wilde, the poetess Speranza, who maintained a genteel, nationalist salon, which might have been described in a novel by Lever. His education was more regular than Moore's and his talents earlier to show themselves. For though he was idle enough at Portora Royal School, he won an exhibition to Trinity College, Dublin, because of his interest in the classics, and this interest was strengthened at Trinity by the famous professor John Pentland Mahaffy with whom he visited Greece.

Mahaffy was an enthusiast and the nature of his enthusiasm for the ancient world was typical of the Victorian age. Everywhere in the remnants of ancient Greece he saw the evidence of a perfect beauty.

Each age has its own picture of ancient times. To the product of the Elizabethan grammar school (like Shakespeare) Greek culture was legendary and sylvan, a mythology of which the nymph and the satyr were the typical figures. To many an eighteenth-century grandee it represented the perfection of political oratory – conjured up a Demosthenes orating with scroll in hand just as a Pitt or a Burke might speak in the House of Commons. In our own time the effort has been made to stress the half-savage, half-oriental side of Greek art, to dismiss statues, previously accepted as perfect masterpieces, for debased Roman copies, this being in tune with a taste temporarily current for the primitive.

But, to the Victorian idealist, and he may or may not have got his idea from bad copies, or from the great sixth century of Hellas, the triumph of Greece was its creation or representation of a supreme form of human beauty. It was an idea which appealed particularly to schoolmasters because it was the aim of that essentially Victorian institution the public school, to create a human type – to turn a middle-class British youth into a strong and handsome aristocrat. Hence came an artificial emphasis on masculine perfection.

His attention already directed to beauty in this definition, and Mahaffy having done his best to 'make an honest pagan out of him', Wilde went up to Magdalen College, Oxford, in 1874, and in Oxford he had something of that excitement of discovery that Moore had experienced in Paris. Here there were people of an eloquent power greater than Mahaffy's to whom beauty was all important.

The tall, floridly handsome young Irishman went to Ruskin's lectures and took part in the making of the Hinksey road. He haunted the rooms of Pater, met Simeon Solomon there, fell into the spirit of that mystical devotion to art for its own sake in which there was some exciting but unnamed undercurrent.

Pater influenced him more than Ruskin, though from the Professor he may have acquired (if it was not from Gautier) some of that curious interest in gems and precious stones which later was to colour his writings. But as young Wilde knew nothing about art he was all the more prone to accept Pater's dictum that it was a mystery, and, as a mystery, the only interesting thing in modern life. He began therefore to be mysterious. He copied and unconsciously caricatured the languor, the devotional contemplation of the master. He burnt incense in his rooms, not from any personal interest in the High Church but because Pater loved the scented swelling fume in which the magic of dim, past ritual seemed to coil. And he began to collect the 'blue' for which the vogue had been started by Rossetti and Whistler.

All this was very irritating to the average hearty young man. Wilde was not interested in games, an offence in itself, and he was posing, which was a still greater offence. Consequently he became the object of undergraduate violence, which he met with an unexpected mixture of courage and good humour. The leader of a party which set out to wreck his rooms was hurled downstairs by the 'blue china cove' with convincing force; and when another punitive expedition carried him bound and helpless, and dumped him on a hill outside the city, he showed none of the anger which would have completed their triumph but suavely said, 'Yes, the view is very charming.'

At the same time he showed conventional brilliance. He won the Newdigate Prize with a poem on Ravenna and in 1878 took first class honours in the Final Schools. A career of promise was evidently opening out.

But in what capacity? Sir William Wilde had died in 1876 and it was necessary to do something profitable. The example of Speranza, the whole Merrion Square culture, inclined him to be a poet, but one did not make money as a poet nor indeed was he a very good one. 'Why do you not write prose?' inquired Pater. 'Prose is so much more difficult than poetry!'

The first thing to do, evidently, was to make a début in London society, to get to know famous people. He approached the task with the same easy Hibernian assurance as Moore had approached the society of the Parisian cafés. He made acquaintance, among others, as a young and devoted admirer of art, with Whistler who was never averse to a disciple.

It was at one of Whistler's social and celebrated breakfasts, in the year of the Ruskin trial. Watts-Dunton was there. He and Whistler were very friendly at this time. They were both contributing to a new weekly called *Piccadilly*. Du Maurier had designed the cover and Whistler was doing some lithographs. 'Pic' consequently was the nickname bestowed by Whistler on Watts.

The shrewd lawyer glance of 'Pic' took note of the tall young Irishman with the peculiar almond-shaped eyes, the long heavy jaw, and an attractive ease of manner. The more so because Whistler looked very surprised to see him, though the surprise of the host did not in the least disturb the self-assurance of the guest who proceeded to make himself extremely agreeable.

'Who's the smock-faced Irishman, Jimmy?' queried Watts-Dunton.

It appeared that Jimmy had no idea. 'Pic' therefore re-constructed the case in legal fashion. 'You have met him at some dinner where the etchings were being bought, and he jumped down your throat. You gave him a general invitation to come to your breakfast and he has at once taken you at your word.'

'Amazing!' said Whistler. 'Yes, you're quite right. Look how he is jumping down Lady —'s throat over there.'

'And,' continued lawyer 'Pic' worldly-wise, 'by the end of the next season, where you know one person in society the Irishman will know ten.' Wilde equally admired Swinburne; and on a later occasion Watts-Dunton again had a watching brief. All three were present at a gathering at the house of Lord Houghton. The moment Wilde saw the poet he was greatly excited and asked Watts to introduce them. In this, Watts felt, and explained to Swinburne, a certain embarrassment, an embarrassment due to his belief that Wilde was stealing Swinburne's poetic thunder, though he admitted that the young man's deportment was genial, not to say charming.

'Very well,' said Swinburne, 'introduce us. But I will not say a dozen words to him.'

The exchange of courtesies consequently lasted only a few minutes. It was the first and last occasion; but Wilde went to many more of Whistler's Sunday breakfasts and Whistler was quite captivated by him.

Here to Wilde was a fresh revelation. At Oxford he had

been entranced by those who wrote about art, in profound and metaphysical words. But here, in the person of Whistler was the creator himself, not an aesthete, one who had indeed a great contempt for aesthetes, but better still a 'master'. He learnt, or thought he learnt, many more, if not all of art's essential secrets. He heard more pointedly from Whistler than from Ruskin or Pater of the misdemeanours of the bourgeois. Some of the new lessons contradicted his earlier tuition. Ruskin, for example, had rhapsodized on 'Truth to Nature'. Whistler, on the other hand, explained that the artist was superior to nature. But these discrepancies scarcely seemed to matter. In the various remarks of these great men there was at least this common ground that art was a very important thing indeed. At last the path was clear. He, Wilde, would be the defender of art; and as an attitude had been so successful in gaining attention from undergraduates he would intensify this attitude in order to win the attention of the great world. Thus it was the young Magdalen man appeared before the astonished gaze of the capital as a 'Professor of Aesthetics'.

It was a very synthetic 'professorship'. He had the earnestness of Ruskin and Morris; but he had also the flute-like intonation and the dreamy vagueness of Pater; and these things were combined with a little irrepressible humour that hailed from the emerald isle, sharpened up by the Whistlerian wit. His passion for the lily and the sunflower which he held in rapt contemplation may be traced back to the symbolism of flowers typical of the Pre-Raphaelite creed of Truth to Nature. The lily was that of Rossetti's *Beata Beatrix* though it found contemporary appropriateness as a mark of homage to the beautiful Mrs Langtry, the Jersey Lily, who was then the admiration of London. To the general public the most outrageous thing about the professor of aesthetics was his dress. What did it mean, this extraordinary rig, the loose collar and flowing tie, the black braided velvet jacket, the velveteen knickerbockers and silk stockings? It aroused horror. Queer certainly is the figure which appears in a photograph of the time, awkwardly posed against a photographer's backcloth, with one hand pressed on the hip, long hair parted in the middle (in the High Church fashion) and the soulful gaze which du Maurier rendered so well. But even Wilde's dress was not original. Du Maurier in his *Punch* drawings had already invented something like it. It was moreover an aspect of decaying Pre-Raphaelitism, of the protest against Victorian ugliness and the desire to live in the décor of another period. It was almost as if Wilde had borrowed the trappings of an historical picture by Millais.

Yet he was a success, much to the disgust of Swinburne and Rossetti among others. They saw themselves distorted by his sincere flattery. Rossetti, in dark mood, took Burne-Jones to task for 'taking up with the man posing as the leader of the new aesthetic movement'. But Burne-Jones, fascinated by his brilliance, defended Wilde, and two things made Wilde's success conclusive. First, the publicity given to him in *Punch*. Here at last, in flesh and blood, a better and more topical butt than Rossetti or Swinburne, was all that du Maurier had meant to convey by his laughable creations, Maudle the painter and Jellaby Postlethwaite the poet. He fell to work with renewed zest and in *Punch*'s attacks on 'culchah' from 1880 onwards the likeness of Oscar, large, flabby, loose-lipped and soulful, began unmistakably to appear.

Second, was the coincidence of a lecture tour in America and the appearance of the comic opera, *Patience*.

The partnership of William Schwenck Gilbert, the dramatist, and Arthur Sullivan, composer, was already ten years old. D'Oyly Carte, the manager of the Soho Theatre had seen in them the making of an English Comic Opera Company with a theatre of its own after the style of the *Bouffes Parisiens* which Offenbach had opened in Paris. The combination of words and music, lively and satirical like those of the French composer, had already proved immensely popular. *Patience*, produced in 1881, launched D'Oyly Carte's new home of comic opera, the Savoy Theatre.

The parody of rival aesthetes in *Patience* intensely magnified the notoriety of aestheticism and of Wilde himself, a chance result because it was not originally designed on these lines.

Gilbert's idea was to satirize rival curates, as he had done in his *Bab Ballads*. But it had occurred to him that a satire on the cloth might be resented by a great many people and so the curates were replaced by poets. Whose likeness should appear on the stage was also a toss-up to begin with. Swinburne, Pater, and even Whistler were considered possibilities. At length it became obvious that Bunthorne must be Wilde. In *Patience* Philistia made its answer to aestheticism and set its retort to music. The adjective Ruskin was so fond of, 'consummately', became a comic catchword. The attitudes of adoration were stylized. The taste for early Italian art was mocked ('How Botticellian, how Fra Angelican') and the profoundly satisfying conclusion was arrived at that these things 'are very much too deep for me'.

On both sides of the Atlantic the opera caught on. America, eager for culture, even in humorous guise, and for novelty in whatever form it might take, loved it and was prepared in advance to greet the arch-aesthete with enthusiasm. The national weakness for a craze, for exaggeration, attended Wilde's visit with unusual notoriety. His refusal to declare anything at the customs 'except my genius', his disappointment in the Atlantic and the outline of Niagara (in which of course he adopted Whistler's expressed contempt for nature) were repeated with shocked delight. His progress from New York to Boston, to Chicago, to Texas was a triumph. Everywhere *Patience* was being played. The negroes took it up and coal-black Bunthornes postured ecstatically before nigger damozels. At Dallas, the miners' doxies lined the railway platform with nodding sunflowers in their hands to greet the lecturer. In the roaring camps with their wild high spirits and ready guns, in saloons displaying the classic notice 'Don't shoot the pianist, he is doing his best', the velvet clad youth expounded the refinements of the far-off old world.

One can imagine the lynching of an aesthete; but Wilde's personality carried him through. He exerted a strange fascination on all sorts of people. He showed himself quite equal to rough audiences and hard conditions. The manliness of his behaviour was in contrast with the effeminacy with which he was already credited, and even the pioneers and the 'bad men', whether they understood what he said or not, gave him a respectful hearing and applauded the way he stood up to them, pronouncing him a 'bully boy with no glass eye'. From America, Wilde came home with a cowboy hat and a full purse, flushed with success and ready to spread the gospel further.

It was, it must be admitted, a pretty thin gospel. The lectures are not very exciting. Their subjects were 'The English Renaissance' (by which he meant the aesthetic movement), 'The Value and Character of Handicrafts' and 'House Decoration'. He tilted amiably at the 'strange ornaments to be seen in the houses of very charming people ... wax flowers, horrible things perpetrated in berlin wool, endless antimacassars ... which seem to reduce life to the level of an eternal washing day'. Ruskin had said that marble paper was extremely immoral and he himself considered that mirrors were 'one of the unpublished crimes of the nineteenth century'. He became a little shaky on the abstruse question of what he described as the 'stencillings of Japan designed by the first Japanese artists' but came on to firm ground in quoting Morris's exhortation 'not to have anything in the house but what one knows to be useful and thinks to be beautiful' and in an earnest plea that 'handicrafts should be part of the education of every child'.

As far as improvements in recent times were concerned he was optimistic but somewhat vague. 'The wax peach no longer ripens in the glass shade.' Few could be greatly outraged by this mild dilution of the doctrines of William Morris, nor was he outrageous even upon the subject of dress. Vivid colours he said were dangerous, and large checks should not be worn. He was against corset and crinoline and considered the top hat to be wicked and monstrous. Beauty consisted in perfect adaptability to the needs of the wearer. His 'exposition of the application of the principles of true artistic decoration to the interior and exterior of the homes of the people' was so little fearsome as to be widely applauded and many a provincial newspaper spoke with approval of the lecturer's sound judgement and good taste. 'The vast throng,' said a journal somewhat ominously entitled *The Broad Arrow*, 'went away one and all perfectly charmed with the quiet and unassuming manner of the lecturer.'

Whistler, however, was not in the least charmed. He did not share the favourable opinion of a world-wide provincialism, of the *Baltimore American* and the *Dundee Courier*. There was now, in his attitude to the young man who had sat at his feet and listened with awe to his talk, a mixture of personal jealousy and serious disapproval. Here was he, Whistler, a mature man approaching the age of fifty, a man of achievement, who knew what was what, and what he was talking about, and having the devil of a time on those very scores. And now came along this young university fop, still in his twenties, making money and reputation by the monstrous assumption that art was his subject, picking up the good things a genuine artist had said and passing them off as his own. 'I wish I had said that.' There was grimness as well as wit in Whistler's reply to this admiring wish. 'You will, Oscar, you will.'

And when Wilde did not repeat the master he talked rubbish. Who the hell, thought Whistler, cared about the homes of the people? What did wax peaches matter? It was time to warn the interloper to leave the subject of art alone. 'We are of the opinion that with the exception of your epigrams you talk like "Sidney Colvin"' (the new Slade Professor) '"in the provinces", and that with the exception of your knee breeches you dress like 'Arry Quilter.' Here began a brisk exchange of repartee duly recorded in *The Gentle Art of Making Enemies*.

It was a new technique in controversy. It consisted in an apparent friendliness. You administered the blow while you smiled; and your opponent, however effective the blow, smiled back and with apparent good humour countered in as damaging a way as he could. A more subtle form of combat than the straight slanging match which Swinburne had enjoyed, its insulting familiarities might even mislead the casual observer into mistaking them for an amicable joke between intimate companions. Thus Whistler and Wilde, with their free and easy use of each other's Christian name seemed on much better terms than they really were.

The invention of the telegraph also provided a new stimulus to wit or at least a very suitable medium for it. Brevity was the soul of the telegram and Whistler excelled at making the most of its necessarily few words. When Theodore Watts, the friend of Swinburne, hyphenated his name to Watts-Dunton to distinguish himself from the other Watts, there quickly followed Whistler's wire 'Theodore, What's Dunton?' The telegram had also the advantage of being rather more insulting than a letter. A letter implied sitting down, writing with a pen and personally addressing an envelope – but a telegram was a random thought, an epigram put on record in a post office. Thus in the *World* for 1883, as the result of a supposititious conversation in *Punch*, there was published the following telegraphic exchange. From Oscar Wilde Exeter to J. McNeill Whistler Tite Street: 'Punch too ridiculous – when you and I are together we never talk about anything except ourselves.' From Whistler Tite Street to Oscar Wilde Chelsea, came swiftly the riposte: 'No, no, Oscar you forget – when you and I are together we never talk about anything except me.'

A phrase however scarcely seemed sufficient to keep the intruder 'out of the radius' – that is to say, off the artist's preserve – nor did it conclusively explain to the general public the sacrosanct limits of that domain and at last Whistler felt himself compelled to take up the alien instrument in earnest and make a conclusive pronouncement in words. If Ruskin and Oscar could lecture, so could he; and if Oscar could make a success out of a lot of meaningless verbiage, perhaps he could successfully deal in home truths and plain speaking. So it was that in February 1885 at the Prince's Hall in London, the little figure with daintily gesticulating hands and punctuative eyebrows appeared before an audience – to 'preach'. He referred neatly to the amount of current talk about art. Art was, he said, 'upon the town' – 'to be enticed within the gates of the householder' – 'to be coaxed into company as a proof of culture and refinement'.

He then proceeded to explain what art really was. The lessons he had learnt in Paris formed the gist of his exposition. It was the true, the original gospel of art for art's sake.

Art, he said, was selfishly occupied with her own perfection – having no desire to teach, seeking and finding the beautiful in all conditions and at all times. The artist was not a reformer. Tintoretto, Veronese, and Velasquez were not desirous of reforming and improving. Their productions alone were their occupation.

With entire confidence he affirmed that there never was an artistic period or an art-loving nation. The people had no say in the matter of what the artist did. Whistler supported this statement with a fancy sketch of evolution supplied from his ignorance of history. Art had been an unconscious growth – until – the taste of the tradesman supplanted the science of the artist. To say to the painter that nature is to be taken as she is was to say to the player that he may sit on the piano. Nature could not produce a picture though (and here Whistler became almost tenderly lyrical in evidently thinking of one of his own nocturnes) 'when the evening mist clothes the riverside with poetry as a veil and the poor buildings lose themselves in the dim sky and the tall buildings become *campanili* and the warehouses are palaces in the night . . .' then 'Nature who for once has sung in tune sings her exquisite song to the artist alone' (that is Whistler himself).

He then enumerated the parasites of art – the middleman for whom a picture is merely the symbol of a story – the experts 'sombre of mien and wise with the wisdom of books who frequent museums and burrow in crypts', the 'Preacher appointed' (Ruskin of course), the sage of the universities – exhorting, denouncing, directing. The 'dilettante'. This was clearly Oscar. 'The voice of the aesthete is heard in the land and catastrophe is upon us.'

And apart from these disseminators of parody and pomposity, in lonely eminence, was the Master. He was, said the lecturer, 'in no relation to the moment at which he occurs'. (He was again clearly thinking of himself.)

Thus did Whistler loose his bolt on the British people as a whole. He stated in the English language, and it was the first time that it had been done, the attitude of the continental painter; and, as all who adopt the mantle of preacher are prone to do, he took it for granted that this attitude represented a universal truth. The artist was the last aristocrat. The bourgeois was his enemy. His art was superior to nature and unconnected with a nation's life; and if it told a story or became in any way 'literary' it lost caste and merit.

Many objections might have been raised to his argument. It did not occur to him that he had established the smallness of the artist rather than his greatness. The possibility that art might not simply be the result of technique and taste, but a much more vital combination of a great many things was left out of account. He was flagrantly unhistorical and frivolously superficial. Nevertheless he made a deep impression.

The critics had no effective answer. Ruskin in his prime might have answered but Ruskin was out of the fight and none was left who could match Whistler either in wit or vituperation.

Whistler, in fact, almost destroyed a free and unspecialized criticism. Since the time of the *Ten o'Clock* Lecture, few critics have ventured to state roundly that a picture was good or bad, or to attempt to see in it anything beyond the qualities the painter himself intended. As the painter became a law unto himself the critic became a law to nobody.

Incidentally Whistler destroyed the popular confidence in contemporaneous art. It is from this time that a gradual but continuous dwindling of the prices of modern pictures set in. A graph would show a rise until the eighties and a fall which has gone on to our own time. Many separate factors have contributed to this – but the impetus was first given by the clean cut which Whistler tried to make between art and life. If, as it seemed, it was impossible to rely on a great critic; if art was so very specialized a form of labour that none but the artist could know about it, why, then, was it after all such a good investment as it had previously appeared to be, had it not better be left within the mysterious circle of specialists? The withdrawal of public interest was not abrupt – but the truly golden age had come to an end.

Oscar Wilde was among the brilliant audience which listened to Whistler, and Oscar, it is true, raised his voice. 'I differ

5. *The Little White Girl* from the painting by James McNeill Whistler

6. *Nocturne: Old Battersea Bridge* from the painting by
James McNeill Whistler

7. *La Tamise à Londres* from a painting by Claude Monet

8. *George Moore in Paris* from a drawing by Édouard Manet

9. *Oscar Wilde on his arrival in America, 1882*, from a photograph by Sarony

10. *Salomé: L'Apparition* from a painting by Gustave Moreau

11. *Paul Verlaine* from a drawing by Max Beerbohm

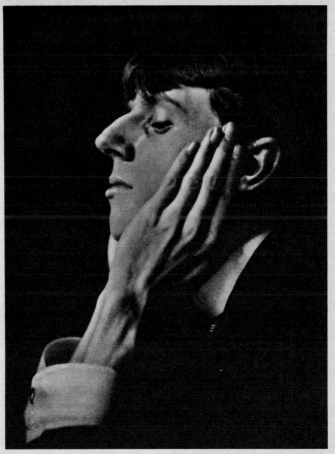

12. *Aubrey Beardsley* from a photograph by Frederick H. Evans

13. *The Eyes of Herod* from one of the illustrations by
Aubrey Beardsley to *Salomé*

entirely from Mr Whistler. An artist is not an isolated fact.'
Nor did Oscar look with favour on the turning of the tables
which made painters out to be more important than writers.
'The lords of life,' he said, 'were Edgar Allan Poe and Baudelaire, not Benjamin West and Paul Delaroche.' With sarcasm
Whistler pointed out the naïveté of the poet in his choice of
painters. He had discovered not beauty in ugliness but ugliness
in beauty. Wilde replied good-humouredly that he had found
'with the aid of a biographical dictionary' that Benjamin West
and Paul Delaroche had lectured on art. 'As of their work
nothing at all remains I can only conclude that they explained
themselves away. – Be warned in time, James.' This was
impudence which must have castigation, and preceded the
elaborate diatribe of 1888 in which Whistler malevolently spat
the question, 'What has Oscar in common with Art? except
that he dines at our tables and picks from our platters the
plums for the puddings he peddles in the provinces. Oscar, the
amiable, irresponsible esurient Oscar with no more sense of a
picture than of the fit of a coat has the courage of the opinions
... of others'.

In this way Whistler vented hatred on all and sundry, and as
the solitary champion of an unpopular cause, ran amok among
the British until no man was left on his legs, darting with an
astonishing turn of speed among adversaries who seemed
hopelessly slow and lethargic by comparison. His hate was
comprehensive. He hated the middle classes. He hated critics.
He hated writers. He hated academicians, in fact he hated the
whole of the nation among whom his abode was fixed. He
found, as other brilliant foreigners have found, an attitude at
once indulgent but at bottom unyielding – and in the long run
perhaps it was he who suffered most. His darts stuck – but at
cost to himself. His quarrels grew smaller and pettier, his selfishness more unpleasant. Worst of all his art began to deteri-
orate. The etchings of Venice with which he sought to
recoup his fortunes are scarcely to be compared with the
earlier etchings of the Thames. 'It must be very tiring to keep
up the role of butterfly,' remarked Degas. 'Better to be an old
bull like me.'

The attack on Britain was renewed in 1887 from another quarter. It was then that there appeared George Moore's *Confessions of a Young Man*.

Moore had come back to London from Paris at the beginning of the eighties. The Irish finances, always so liable to disturbance, had at last broken down. It was necessary for him to work. His vocation he had decided was not painting, but writing, and writing could best be pursued in London.

A change was coming over the capital. The long period of feverish activity which had brought wealth brought increasingly the desire for luxury and extravagance. Everything, it seemed, was well with the nation, except for such minor puzzles as Irish Home Rule and Socialist agitation. Queen Victoria was Empress of India, the head of a glamorous empire. Mr Gladstone and Lord Salisbury alternatively upheld the national dignity. A sunny upland of progress stretched endlessly ahead. The old restraints were loosening. The country was getting gay, inclined to frolic, albeit awkwardly. The growth of London both in area and population had made some other public place of refreshment than the old chop house essential and the growing habit of dining in a restaurant was in itself a social revolution. As entertainment ceased to be entirely domestic both men and women lived the life of the town. The restaurant and the theatre and music hall prospered together. Thus the success of the Savoy operas caused the Savoy Hotel and Restaurant to come into being. The Lyceum under the princely domination of Henry Irving was the rage. The night houses of the sixties were turning into supper clubs and the music halls were becoming a folk institution where the events and characters of the day found a prompt celebration in song.

It was all this that made London tolerable to Moore. The great experience of his life, his acquaintance with the great artists of France in the cafés of Paris, was behind him – indeed the remainder of his life was to be spent in recollection of the dear, dead delights of those days. As he walked out of 'grubby Cecil Street' in the Strand a vision of the Nouvelle Athènes rose up before him. As he discoursed in the Gaiety Bar, his hands waving like the fins of a dolphin, he could not help thinking that his companions were a poor provincial substitute for Manet, Degas, Renoir, Villiers de l'Isle Adam and Catulle Mendès. He drowned his sorrow in such expensive amusement as the fashionable houses of Curzon Street could afford – in the supper parties and champagne with the young lords, in the heavy bohemianism of the 'toffs' who swirled through the West End on a mysterious sea of sovereigns.

Perhaps, after all, London was not so bad. All this was pleasure if not refinement and pleasure in any form was interesting and desirable. Adaptable creature as he was, George Moore began to like it. Even the shabby and sordid aspects of London had their points, especially when you remembered that Zola had written of such squalor in the noble name of naturalism. Looking at Cecil Street through French (or Frenchified) eyes it was positively a worthy subject for a prospective novelist. The landlady, the slavey, and the young actress, parted from her husband, who lived upstairs, the ugly and not very clean rooms, the sordid public house at the corner, the gallery at the 'all, with the gals and the mashers, giggling and shouting, made up a new world not at all to be despised by the writer of prose. He saw himself as the student of ballrooms, bar rooms, streets, and alcoves who would, as the French had done, make these things immaculate and immortal by means of art.

He began to write. He worked on a novel. He wrote articles. He went the round of the Royal Academy on Press View Day, in company with a top-hatted, frock-coated group of critics, thinking mournfully the while of the Impressionists. And he wrote *The Confessions of a Young Man*.

Two books inspired the latter, one French, one English. The French book was the *A Rebours* of Joris Karl Huysmans, a Parisian of Dutch origin. It came out in 1884. It represented a new peak in the search for sensation, though it was in the direct line of descent from Baudelaire's translation of Edgar Allan Poe. Its hero, Des Esseintes, was an exquisite who lived an artificial life. Des Esseintes had a counterpart in real life – the celebrated character Robert de Montesquiou who took a

gilt tortoise about with him everywhere. He had also a counterpart in literature – the Roderick Usher of Poe's *House of Usher*.
He had brought like the demon-driven character of Poe's tale
the cultivation of the senses to the uttermost limits of perver-
sity. He devised for instance a whole orchestration of scents
and perfumes. No vice or curiosity was alien to him and his
overheated imagination grew, in his rooms from which all
outer air and influence was excluded, tropical and monstrous.
He could imagine anything – a visit to England, say, replete
with the bustle of the packet, the fog and the phantom brutal
forms on arrival, the steak pudding and rich, thick Guinness
of the eating house. It only remained to unpack the bags which
were ready for his departure and not go there at all.

In fact he avoided all natural and external experience and
cherished the solitary and unnatural because what was not
nature was art and art was the only worthy condition of
existence.

George Moore saw himself in this light – as one who lived
an exciting inward life, pulsating with adventure and ecstasy,
of a purely mental kind. The other book which inspired him
was Walter Pater's *Marius the Epicurean*.

The same principle was here too, though the emphasis was
not on physical sensation, except in so far as incense and ritual
provided a sensuous background, but on the phases and tran-
sitions of the mind. The scene was laid in the Rome of the
Emperor Marcus Aurelius – a world in transition. And the
soul of Marius was a soul in transition. He lived on the out-
skirts of religion, drawn this way and that, almost persuaded
by a creed and fascinated by the beauty of a philosophy, but
never quite resolved into whole-hearted faith and even gaining
a pleasurable sensation from the doubt which enabled him to
discern so much in Platonism and Christianity alike. The
personality of Marius was partly inspired by a younger Oxford
friend of Pater's, Richard C. Jackson, an authority on Dante
and Greek art, a sort of monkish philosopher. In stilted and
elaborate phrase Pater acknowledged this inspiration. He
addressed Mr Jackson thus : 'Even as the hyacinth sprang
from the blood of Hyacinthus so shall all that I have gleaned

from *thee* swell *thy* fame to kiss posterity therewith.' At the same time there was much in Marius of Pater himself. Marius derived an aesthetic pleasure from the religious that came within his experience; and so did Pater. A wealthy High Church clergyman of his acquaintance, the Rev. George Nugée, had founded a chapel in a poor quarter of London, dedicated to St Austin. Several houses near by, in the New Kent Road, were transformed into a 'Monkery' – it was a 'hot-bed of so-called Romanism'. The riches of the father of the Priory and the brethren were applied equally to the lavish decoration of the buildings and the promotion of a working men's club. Week-day services were held to 'awaken a religious spirit' in the people of the district, services 'which were dight with gem and gold and sacred song'. There were processions with banners, and St Austin's became famous – to the discomfort of its founder who did not want sightseers but simply to make sincere Christians.

Frequent were the absences of Pater from Oxford, when he slipped off to St Austin's Priory at Walworth. There was a special pleasure in the luxury so discrepant with the shabby surroundings. It was detached, and its detachment was pleasing to him. It was possible to carry off the priory in the mind and place it down mentally, in some long-distant age, whose life had no present meaning, to lose all sense of significance as one snuffed gratefully at the incense fume, like the cloud from some magician's vial in which there took shape visions of beauty. It was in this way that Pater conceived the recurrent exaltation of spirit in his Marius. It was a form of pleasure that he himself felt. He was prepared to admit that 'religion enlarges a man's perspective', but he would go no further; and he admitted, to the distress of Mr Nugée, that the only thing that inclined him towards the Church of England rather than to Nonconformity (whose leaders' merits he fully appreciated) or to Rome (which demanded too great a submission) was that ritual which satisfied the aesthetic emotions. Thus *Marius the Epicurean* was a 'confession' – the confession of one who placed art before faith.

But George Moore was attracted not only by the argument

but by the language. For the first time he had come upon an English writer to whom the form was important as well as subject matter – who took as much care as did Flaubert to compose a sentence, to find exactly the right word, to enclose a thought in an appropriate and often complex rhythm. It was possible then, in the English language as well as in French. He would try it himself.

The *Confessions of a Young Man*, completed when he was thirty-four, was pervaded by the spirit of Moore's two models, though it lacked the intensity and tautness of either. It had not the macabre note of *A Rebours* nor the restraint of Marius. He took aestheticism cheerfully, with, as Pater remarked, an 'Aristophanic joy', and he created a character himself – the gay, impudent, inquiring, impressionable Moore – with a remarkable literary art.

In his light and apparently casual and even rambling paragraphs there was presented also a fragmentary history of 'art for art's sake'. Moore recalled how, on reading *Mademoiselle de Maupin*, he 'stood as if enchanted before the noble nakedness of the elder gods', had been enthralled by the 'great exaltation of the visible over the invisible'. He spoke of Baudelaire, of Verlaine, Rimbaud, Mallarmé, of living French writers as if they were the only writers who counted for anything, of living French painters as if they alone were important.

And this salutary corrective to island self-esteem was interspersed by a genial onslaught on the nineteenth-century conscience. 'Education' – that should be confined to clerks; 'Democratic Art' – art was the antithesis of democracy; 'Pity' – pity was the most vile of all vile virtues; 'Christianity' – he hated 'the pale socialist of Galilee'. Respectability, the villa, the lending library whose censorshp had kept the country apparently moral for forty years, were held up to ridicule.

'Oh!' exclaimed George Moore, 'for excess, for Crime!' This was the 'questionable shape' in which he spread the continental gospel and battered once again at the now scarred edifice of Victorianism.

Meanwhile Oscar Wilde went to Paris and entered on the second of the quite distinct phases which mark his career.

Fresh from the success and financial profit of his American tour he found himself in a world to him as new as the one he had just left and in a literary atmosphere which previously he had only known at secondhand.

As he had sought out celebrities in London, so now he sought them out in Paris. He met the solemn and exquisite de Goncourt who carefully recorded the wild exaggerations with which Wilde merrily enlivened the account of his travels. 'Extraordinary,' murmured the scholarly diarist as he noted down the fact that in Texas a theatre was turned into a law court at the conclusion of a performance and that the audience shot at the bodies of criminals as they swung on the stage.

He met the popular writer Daudet and the symbolist Mallarmé, whose word-music, suggestive and obscure, was already arousing esteem; and as in London he had worshipped Lily Langtry, the Jersey Lily, so now he paid homage to Sarah Bernhardt, who ranked almost with Queen Victoria in his admiration.

Wilde discovered, with some surprise, that Whistler's views were not so individual and original as he had thought. There was for example that oft repeated Whistlerism that a sunset was vulgar, that the best nature could do was to imitate art. It seemed that Gautier and Baudelaire had anticipated this remarkable inversion. Baudelaire had said that nature has no imagination and Gautier had praised Baudelaire's *Fleurs du Mal* as a creation of art from which nature was entirely absent. Huysmans, in this wonderful new book *A Rebours* that everyone was talking about, said the same thing – Nature was a *banal agence* – crude and commonplace material of which the artist condescended to make use but to which he could never become subservient.

This effectively disposed of any remaining attachment that Wilde might have had to his whilom Professor's 'Truth to Nature'. Always theatrical, he was quite prepared to adopt a new pose. So now he dropped completely the pose of his aesthetic period. Gone were the velvet breeches, the silk stockings, and the page-like mop of hair, the medieval soulfulness, the Pre-Raphaelite yearning. Instead there appeared the *flâneur* of the boulevards, a gay cosmopolitan, sipping absinthe, smoking scented cigarettes, and dressing the part of the dandy, the continentalized dandy on the model described by Baudelaire. In fact after Bunthorne came Beau Brummel. Whereas before he had carried a lily he now had an ivory-topped cane in imitation of, as a mark of respect for, Honoré de Balzac, and the only remnant of his enthusiasm for flowers was the buttonhole of the man about town.

Paris had on him almost exactly the same effect as it had on George Moore, except that he had little contact with the painters. His interest in the visual arts had never been more than superficial and he had loudly proclaimed the supremacy of literature, but the French example caused him to pay a new attention to form and style. Flaubert, Huysmans, affected him profoundly and the strangeness of the beauty they sought, not the commonplace healthy beauty of nature but a *beauté maudite*, accursed and infernal. Huysmans himself had envisaged this beauty through the mystical paintings of Gustave Moreau. In the *Apparition* of Moreau, Salomé loaded with a barbaric profusion of jewellery danced lasciviously before the King while there appeared, blazing and forbidding, the ghostly head of John the Baptist. Huysmans had devoted some remarkable passages to praise this mystical art, more moving and impressive than their source. From him and from the *Herodias* of Flaubert Wilde evolved the passionate prose poem of his own *Salomé*; which he wrote at a sitting in a café on the Boulevard des Capucines, while the orchestra at his request played wild Tzigane music. And from *A Rebours* he conceived the first notion of *The Picture of Dorian Gray*, 'the strangest book (Dorian Gray) had ever read. It seemed to him that in exquisite raiment and to the delicate sound of flutes, the sins of the world were passing before him ... It was a poisonous book ... ' In this way Wilde translated the French decadence into terms of English decadence.

Decadence in the eighties was an accepted literary term in France. Like many such general terms it had acquired several shades of meaning. It had been used disapprovingly by critics and in two senses – as a decline from what was natural, healthy, and vigorous in life, and as a literary style. Thus Baudelaire and Huysmans were popularly considered decadent in the principles they expressed. To those who did not distinguish between writing about vice and practising it, their works were depraved and corrupt. The court which condemned the *Fleurs du Mal* could have little doubt that the work was decadent in this sense, without appreciating either its tormented conscience or the beauty of language. On the other hand, the word decadent was applied in a particular sense to indicate a mannerism and a suggestive power of words, a departure from classic principles, just as medieval writers in Latin might be said to be decadent. But however much the purist might insist on this meaning, it was not commonly used with such strictness. The term of disapproval was adopted out of bravado by the writers to whom it was applied, and with all its flavour of wickedness. Only a poet could do justice to all it suggested. 'I love,' said Verlaine, 'this word decadence, all shimmering in purple and gold. It suggests the subtle thoughts of ultimate civilization, a high literary culture, a soul capable of intense pleasures. It throws off bursts of fire and the sparkle of precious stones. It is redolent of the rouge of courtesans, the games of the circus, the panting of the gladiator, the spring of wild beasts, the consuming in flames of races exhausted by their capacity for sensation, as the trump of an invading enemy sounds.' The maker of dictionaries might jib at such a definition but it was in this exciting shape that it made its appeal to artists. It made romance out of exhaustion and excess.

Certainly Decadence appeared in these colours to Wilde. The alluring thing about *A Rebours* was that it was 'poisonous'. He added to his repertoire of opinions the approval of excess in which great French writers had been and were so wholehearted. With the necessity of having enemies and objecting to nature on which Whistler insisted, it made up a new attitude, 'shocking' in a fresh manner, and expandable almost to the size of a philosophy, by the variations of paradox. His habit of paradox was growing. If the proverbial wisdom and accepted maxims of the mass of mankind were natural, then to convert wisdom into art it was only necessary to turn it upside down or inside out. Consequently he was able, by a slight exertion of his singular cleverness, to produce the effect of a refreshing truth, hitherto undiscovered, brought to light by a seeming profundity of thought. 'If one tells the truth one is sure sooner or later to be found out.' 'One should be careful to choose one's enemies well.' 'Nothing succeeds like excess.' However simple the recipe the result was none the less effective and as truth is many-sided it sometimes looked as if in reversing the accepted he had made an important discovery.

Such was the Oscar Wilde who after his period of wandering settled down in London in the eighties. He was much changed. The earnest pleader for child craftsmanship, the advocate of refined schemes of interior decoration, had become an ultra-sophisticated man of letters, reoriented, if not re-educated, by his sojourn across the Channel.

Society and the Press were somewhat disappointed at finding him so far departed from the aesthetic pattern. A Bunthorne was unique but Beau Brummels were by no means unusual and were not such good fun. A man of thirty, respectably married, with a charming house in Chelsea, dressed (even if somewhat loudly) according to the prevailing fashion, he seemed to have no eccentricity left and except for the marked brilliance of his conversation to advance no claim to attention.

Aestheticism was no longer front-page news. Labour was murmuring and muttering, ready even to make a half-hearted attempt at revolt. Home Rule for Ireland was a question absorbing to politicians and populace. Wilde was out of the limelight for the time being especially as he adopted the unspectacular role of working journalist. The receipts from the lectures were not everlasting. He could not live otherwise than extravagantly and he had a home to keep up. To make money by his pen was an obvious step and in at least one respect his aesthetic background proved of use – in the matter of dress and decoration. His occasional articles on these subjects, deploring the bustle and other contemporary modes, were well received – and in 1887 he became the editor of *The Woman's World*.

Pleasure and Hatred were now established as the dominant

motives of the talented men who, however static the rest of the population might be, led the way in change. The balance had shifted from the Victorian attachment to Hard Work and Christian Socialism.

The pattern of hatred was intricate. It was not only a distaste among artists for the mob, the *canaille*. They had a distaste for each other. They were lone wolves who bayed at the public and snapped at each others' flanks.

It was partly a question of nationality. The Francophile American Whistler found English ways disagreeable because he could not understand them. George Moore and Oscar Wilde, though they were more good humoured than Whistler, were Irishmen, and as little bound as Whistler by the conventions from which Englishmen departed so seldom. Each wished to have the exclusive privilege of beating Britannia as a man might beat his wife, resenting similarly the attempt of anyone else to beat her.

The Pre-Raphaelite spirit of mutual help was dead or dying. The conviction that everyone was naturally an artist was replaced by the conviction that no one was an artist (none other at least than he who held the belief) until he should have pursued a long, lonely path of his own and run the full gauntlet of sneers and abuse. The comprehensive nature of Whistler's hatred has been described, but a small true anecdote illustrates a typical lack of sympathy.

He was standing one day in the Arts Club when an acquaintance approached. 'There is a young man here, Mr Whistler, who admires your work tremendously and would so very much like to meet you. He wants to be an artist.' One can imagine the youth, standing apart, but hearing the conversation very well, anxious to express his admiration, eager for a crumb of encouragement. Abruptly came the comment, 'Poor devil.'

And the 'Master', already thinking of something else, turned brusquely round and made off.

So was presumptuousness chastised. Let him get on with it, this young mister whoever-he-was, who probably never would be an artist anyway. Rossetti would not have behaved in this fashion. He would have encouraged the young man. It was in some such manner that he had first met Burne-Jones and launched him on his career. But now so far were things changed that masters had no encouragement to spare and thought only of themselves.

Wilde laughed at Moore; and though his laughter was not so merciless as that of Whistler, it was shrewdly directed against Moore's literary pretensions.

'He conducts his education in public.' Moore, according to Wilde, had discovered the sentence and flushed with triumph had gone on to the discovery of the paragraph. When someone asked him if he had read one of Moore's novels he remarked, 'I hear it has to be played on the piano.' There is less than his usual good humour in the answer he gave to someone else who inquired:

'Do you know George Moore?'

'Know him, I know him so well that I haven't spoken to him in ten years.'

These were 'good things' and the good things had to be seasoned with malice. Walter Pater, the original aesthete (and fifth columnist, as he might be termed, of the aesthetic invasion), had his own quiet society. The pretensions of Wilde were distasteful to him. It seemed to him that Wilde had parodied his ideas and caused the discordant blare of publicity's trumpets to drown that small, exquisite sound of flutes. In the eighties he had settled in Earl's Terrace, Kensington (with a motion of repugnance against Oxford people and Oxford ways), and he saw quite often the self-appointed disciple. There was something of comedy in their meetings – Pater, hunched, thin, and old, though only fifty or so, and Wilde, flashy, tall, with a half-guinea buttonhole and an opulent fur-trimmed overcoat. But when Wilde hired a cab to take them to a place of amusement a hundred yards away on the other side of the street Pater, who never paid a bus fare if he could possibly help it, was quite indignant; and when Wilde inscribed books to him with the words 'Homage to the great master' the recipient was almost furtively embarrassed and uneasy. A delicate and restrained distaste peeped out on the occasion when he had been lecturing at the Literary Institute in Albemarle Street, in the almost inaudible murmur usual with him. As they were going out he said, 'I hope you heard me, Mr Wilde.'

'We overheard you,' replied Oscar genially.

'Really, Mr Wilde, you have a phrase for everything.'

'A phrase for everything.' It was a rebuke, censuring, with as much emphasis as Pater thought decent, the inevitable, the ready-made remark; to emerge more definitely in his comment 'the strange vulgarity which Mr Wilde mistakes for cleverness'. Even vulgarity, to Pater, could be strange.

Moore also professed to idolize Pater, and in a literary way was no doubt quite sincere, though he described him with candid malice as 'a very ugly man, an uncouth figure like a figure moulded out of lead', 'a vicarage Verlaine'. He expected brilliant conversation but was disappointed. 'Now and again the conversation flickered up, a little light appeared in the vicar's mind and one remembered what Pater said, not because he said anything remarkable but because it was Pater who said it ...'

Eventually it penetrated even through Moore's self-complacency that Pater was bored with him. 'The evasive eyes' were perhaps looking round for a means of escape. The 'abnormal fear both of himself and of his listener' was perhaps an abnormal fear of Hibernian candour and talkativeness. 'I began to doubt whether he wished to see me and kept away ...'

Pater did write a charming and quite cordial letter about *The Confessions of a Young Man*. Once more Moore's hope of a personal friendship revived. Once more they were dashed. 'When I went to London I met the same formal man, as kind and polite as ever; but seemingly a little more distant.' They met at dinner 'in the dullest houses in London – houses where I seldom went ...' Moore tried art, literature, sport, and women – surely, he thought, the last subject must produce some conversation. But no, Pater would not talk – and Moore at length retired baffled.

There might be degrees or qualifications of the prevailing

hatred – it varied from savage insult, more or less good-natured jest, to a studied inaccessibility; but the main fact was, as Wilde said, 'Friends don't much matter but enemies are important.' The artificiality of letters had invaded human relations or, in the phrase so constantly reiterated, 'nature was creeping up to art' again. The tone was at once more intimate and less human – and in their remarks the men of the day stylized themselves and were as undeviating from their chosen part as the *dramatis personae* of the older English comedies who were named according to their characters. They played a comedy of manners, against the gilded and luxurious background of the West End of London.

After the long years of Victorian seriousness it was a refreshing change. It is not necessary to suppose an entire lack of sincerity or earnestness, but certainly these qualities were something you kept to yourself and for which, in conversation at least, you subsituted a cynical front.

You were earnest only about such matters as a candid parasite could be – and you favoured both luxury and squalor, not caring, as an earlier breed of reformers had cared, whether these things were right or wrong, but cherishing them as the substance on which you lived.

It is surprising to remember that while the *bons mots* were flying, and sparkling trivialities passed to and fro, there still lived an artist with an aim in life, William Morris, ready even to destroy his own art, in what he believed to be a cause for the advantage of all men and women. Or, was he then and for that reason, no artist? The thought, the question, lights up the problems that 'art for art's sake' had brought with it, the gulf that it had made between man and man.

# 5

## Pleasures, Serious and Otherwise

PLEASURE with its corollary of vice or self-indulgence was a more profound business than Hatred which so often took the shallow form of malice and spitefulness rather than a deep and principled enmity. Pleasure soared and wallowed. It was ecstasy and disgust. It devoured and nourished. Enticing and terrible; it led to torture, to wisdom, to the unknown.

So, at least, it seemed to the nineteenth-century rebel. 'No, I do not seek happiness,' said Oscar Wilde in one of those disturbingly prophetic utterances which traced beforehand the pattern of his life, 'but Pleasure, which is much more tragic.'

The conquest of pleasure is one of the triumphs of the twentieth century. Its exacting machines require the steady touch of a hand and mind free from all intoxicants even those purely of the imagination. Excess is a matter of diagnosis and prescription. Pleasure has become serious and utilitarian.

Then, it was a land unexplored still and the writer was the pioneer of mental experience. It may be that his was the first step in the curious and in some respect dismal process of conquest. Poems which seemed at the time of their publication to attack all morality were the necessary preliminary to the revision of a code. The poet was a 'seer' – prophet or soothsayer, like the ancient *vates*; who anticipated, even while he seemed to flout, the lawyer and the doctor. Baudelaire may have laid the foundations of psycho-analysis.

Such statements are speculative. Nevertheless the fact of a persistent revolt against the principles and inhibitions of the middle class cannot be questioned. The poet renouncing the well-worn ways was determined to know personally the tragic, the dangerous, the miserable tracts of the land from whose nearer and more agreeable parts he had not previously attempted to wander.

Such a man was Paul Verlaine whose name in the seventies and eighties began to be heard with esteem on both sides of the Channel, coupled with that of Arthur Rimbaud. Together they carried a step farther the research which Baudelaire had begun. They spurred each other on as Gautier and Baudelaire had done. They presented an even more formidable combination.

Verlaine! squinting and villainously ugly, his suppurating limbs wrapped in vile rags, the consumer of a prodigious amount of alcohol, supported by the earnings of street-walkers and the charitable replies to begging letters; the would-be assassin and self-confessed homosexual; the connoisseur of prisons and the habitué of hospitals. Debauched and snivelling he resembles the old Karamazov of Dostoevsky's novel, in his capacity for an endless degradation lit by flashes of insight and even humour; his fits of mawkish repentance alternating with fits of maudlin ferocity. He was, if not the greatest, one of the greatest French poets of his time. From a Victorian point of view it was incredible that he could be so. What would Tennyson have thought of him, if (as Verlaine threatened he would, given the necessary cash) he had sought out the Poet Laureate and invited him to translate his works? How Quaker Elizabeth Robins shrank in terror and repugnance from the satyr-like face so unpleasantly close at a London dinner-table. How upset Mr Murdoch of the school at Lymington, Hants, would have been if he had known the full story of the frog who taught French to his young and innocent pupils.

Rimbaud has left an even stronger impression. With talents altogether unusual, he was in many respects a typical adolescent whose characteristics were enlarged as if under a magnifying glass. At the age of sixteen, tall, raw-boned, dirty-minded, arrogant, boorish, with a head full of words and magnificently defiant ideas and with a precocious pipe between his teeth, he might have been a clever, oversize schoolboy. But he was more than that. He had a genius, not so easy to explain. It expressed itself in his behaviour by a ferocious hostility to everything that was respectable, including not only the bourgeoisie but literature itself: in poetry which set old forms at contempt and adventured into the unconscious.

The period during which he and Verlaine consorted together as if demented, went through a series of violent and
scabrous episodes, was a pantomime of decadence. They ran
the gamut of sensation. Rimbaud attacked Verlaine with a
knife. Verlaine shot at and wounded Rimbaud with a gun.
They were arrested in Brussels on a charge of unnatural vice.

The policeman at the corner of Old Compton Street, Soho,
would have looked much harder at the two foreigners (when
they came to London) if he had known their full history.
'Mme Smith', at the lodgings they took in Great College
Street, Camden Town, might have thought twice before
taking in these peculiar boarders.

The partnership did not last long. By the end of the seventies Rimbaud with a savagely erratic change of course had
become a gun runner to Abyssinia, wrote no more poetry,
came to an early and miserable end in 1891.

Verlaine remained, settling down to a steady rhythm of
squalor, translating it into poetic symbols which echoed and
yet purified it. Nothing was more remarkable about him
towards the end of his life than the serenity and self-satisfac-
tion of his demeanour. Wicked to the last, though with a mel-
lowed wickedness that seemed so much a part of his gifts as to
deserve admiration rather than censure, he was now a kind of
saint who died, amid the murmurs of regretful esteem of
literary followers, in the mingled odours of absinthe and
sanctity.

What strange compulsion was it that caused a clerk of
twenty-seven and a youth of sixteen to join together in a series
of frantic escapades which caused the elder to wallow in the
gutter, and to continue throughout his life to hold a balance of
poetry and debauch? Was it simply an accident of personality?

Against that there is some circumstantial evidence. There
were too many like cases happening within the same period to
be put down to accident. The mood first signalized by Baudelaire, with his deliberate cultivation of vice, was following its
appointed course.

To be successful in such a highly experimental career
required force both of character and of ability. Especially was

this combination needed in England. Up to a point the antics of Swinburne and Simeon Solomon resemble those of Verlaine and Rimbaud. There is the same protest, the same impish satisfaction in being outrageous, the same desire to explore forbidden ground; but in the puritanical island the consequences were heavier to bear, the weight of society's reproof pressed harder on the individual, than in France.

So it was with the unfortunate Solomon. From being the centre of attraction in fashionable coteries, and a celebrity in art, he became a pariah. His imprisonment sentenced him to social death. Pre-Raphaelites, whose honoured associate he had been, looked askance, expunged his name from the diaries meant to be read by those who should come after. And his friend Swinburne, himself tottering on the brink, looked upon his fall with a horror which in due time turned into indignation. The fact that the wretched little man had been an acquaintance was actually a menace – and the first expressions of Swinburne's distress were altered by 1879 to the opinion that he was 'a thing, unmentionable alike by men and women as equally abhorrent to either – nay to the very beasts – raising money by the sale of my letters to him in past years, which must doubtless contain much foolish burlesque.'

There seems no doubt but that Simeon did sell the letters. He was capable of anything – except the ability or the wish to go seriously forward with his art or to extricate himself from the position in which he had landed himself. He was entirely passive. Transferred to an asylum, on the sympathetic ground that he was not responsible for his actions, he was one day sent out to post a letter. It was assumed that he would take the opportunity of escaping, but he came back and would have stayed indefinitely, until at last he had to be turned out. Evicted, he sank without effort to the lowest possible level.

There was in this a lurking anger – he felt a grievance against society and he showed it by that kind of obstructive helplessness which causes people to lie down in the street in front of moving vehicles. Friends and relations did what they could. He took what they gave him, drank, sank back. It was impossible to help him. A frame-maker in Kensington used for a time to supply him with chalks and paints and gave him the freedom of his workroom; but the other workmen objected so much to his extreme dirtiness and to his bad language that the agreement came to an end. He found refuge in a pleasant house in a remote part of Devonshire and the family found him most courteous and attractive – that is, until he found means of getting drunk, which terminated this episode. The dealers tried to make him paint. He took their money and produced no pictures.

He became a character of the underworld. He sold matches in the Mile End Road, lived in doss-houses, begged from passers-by, associated with thieves and blackmailers, was constantly and hopelessly intoxicated.

He boasted (like Verlaine) of his prisons, and like him also showed a sort of mischievousness which almost made his life appear a prank played upon the social system.

There is some doubt as to whether he really did burgle Burne-Jones's house or whether it was one of his inventions; but in either case it is in keeping with this mischievous turn. As the story goes he and a burglar friend broke into The Grange, where Simeon, being strongly fortified for the occasion, dropped pieces of silver with a clatter, argued with his mate and finally brought down the eminent owner of the house – who let them go with a caution.

It may have been this same distorted sense of a joke that led him to send pictures to the Royal Academy representing spiritual but physically complete beings, wearing aureoles round parts of their persons not usually submitted to public inspection. None of these were accepted.

Much changed from the handsome little pagan of yore, bald, bearded, bent, Simeon Solomon, while the drama of the eighties and nineties was being played out, shuffled along in the gutters of the capital, a hopeless outcast, a warning to any others who might take aestheticism too seriously or translate into reality the poetical figment of sin.

An odd thing, however, was noticed when he died in the workhouse dining-hall. Those who gathered round were amazed by the perfect serenity of his features, as if he were content to have traversed the barren ground and in it had found what he wanted.

2

Nor was Simeon Solomon alone in his melancholy adventures. There were others equally gutter-crazy – possessed by that malady for which it was necessary to invent a term, *'nostalgie de la boue'* – the craving for abjection. They were, like him, refined and sensitive persons of talent, but whether through incapacity to take their part in a middle-class world, through some congenital defect or through that fretful call for excess, the romanticization of 'sin' which had become the literary theme, they each sought, and even with eagerness, a sordid destiny. There was a whole crop of island Verlaines, who flourished, if that is the word, in the feverish atmosphere of London in the nineties.

The capital was frivolous, equipped to spend the wealth accumulated in black and dreary toil. There was, too, a feeling of climax as the end of the century approached, as if the date was also a spiritual terminus, and before the millennium of the twentieth century should be reached the nation must have its fling. Quicker poured that spate of sovereigns through the West End of London. The globes of the gas lamps receding in long lines were an incitement to adventure. The huge gin palaces, built in the seventies and eighties, offered a wonderland of cut and stained glass, a profusion of coloured and barbaric ornament, a rich choice of inexpensive alcohol, sparkling in the bottles contained in massive wooden shrines, like Renaissance tombs. 'Mirth and the lamplighter' hurried westward on the romantic evenings, full of fog and noisy with hansom cabs, to the velvet-cushioned restaurant of Agostino and Stefano Gatti in the Strand, to M. Nicol's café in Glasshouse Street, to the theatre, to the Tivoli, the Alhambra or the Empire music halls – perhaps to hear Charles Coborn sing 'The Man who Broke the Bank at Monte Carlo', to laugh at the cockney genius of young Matilda Alice Victoria Wood (the great 'Marie Lloyd') or slim Vesta Tilley's impersonations of 'the Piccadilly Johnny with the little Glass Eye'.

Through this bubble-world of Cockaigne wended the outcasts. As early as 1874 the pessimistic outlook of the artist, unable to live anywhere except in the great city yet finding in it neither hope nor subsistence, was expressed in 'The City of Dreadful Night' by James Thomson who found 'all alike crushed under the iron yoke of Fate'. Believing this, thinking himself 'much better dead than alive' he sank into a broken condition to which despair, alcohol, and narcotics contributed equally. He alternated between excess and collapse which destroyed his chances of livelihood and produced gnawing agonies of self-abasement. 'In one fit of frenzy I have not only lost more than I yet know and half murdered myself (were it not for my debts I sincerely wish it had been wholly) but justly alienated my best and firmest friends.'

The end of this life-in-death was grim. Thomson was thrown out of his small room in a Bloomsbury lodging house which the landlord declared he had tried to burn down. He slept in the street and the doss-house, and his best night's rest was at the police station. In actual kindliness he was sentenced to fourteen days' imprisonment which he spent in hospital.

In June 1882 he crept like a wounded animal to the rooms of Philip Bourke Marston, the blind poet. He asked to lie down on the bed. Concerned, groping in his perpetual darkness Marston touched the face of his visitor – felt, blood. William Sharp, Marston's friend, who had arrived, saw with horror that Thomson was dead of a dreadful haemorrhage. He was forty-eight. So finished a poetic genius in this prosperous land.

Sometimes Simeon Solomon, prowling the streets, met a worn, wild, neglected looking man with a straggling beard, wearing an old brown cape and looking like a pedlar in an old Dutch etching. His name was Francis Thompson. He was a failure of the provinces. Already an opium addict, he had come to the capital from Manchester, where his father was a doctor, 'without hope and with the gloomiest forebodings, in the desperate spirit of an *enfant perdu*'. Naturally absent of mind, dazed by opium, consumptive, he lived in a dream on a shilling a day. He accepted the situation apathetically, though he learnt how to spend the shilling to the best advantage. For example, a penny was allotted, not to the purchase of a cup of tea but of tea itself. Water could be boiled in the common kettle of the lodging house and thus several cups were provided. He learnt the slang of thieves, discussed life gently with a murderer, shuddered at the foulness of his fellow outcasts' talk, was befriended, like De Quincey, by a girl of the streets.

Sometimes he slept on an oblong box without a lid, containing a mattress and provided with a leather coverlet or apron, in a 'Refuge'. Sometimes it was the Embankment or under the arches of the Adelphi. And he saw

> the places infamous to tell
> Where God wipes not the tear from any eyes.

Two people befriended him: a bootmaker in Panton Street and Churchwarden of St Martin-in-the-Fields, John McMasters, who employed him for a while; and Wilfrid Meynell, editor of *Merry England*, a magazine with many distinguished contributors. Meynell saw merit in a manuscript that one day reached him from an unknown author. A postscript to the letter enclosed with it requested, with the hopelessness typical of its writer, 'Kindly address your rejection to the Charing Cross Post Office'.

That no answer came to the editor's acceptance was also typical. Thompson had drifted off into the wilderness of pavements. It was as if some strange fish had been fetched up from the deep, or some timid creature of the jungle had been brought into an explorer's camp when at last he was coaxed into appearing in Mr Meynell's office, with a thin shirt barely covering his wasted chest, a ragged coat, and gaping shoes through which his bare feet protruded. That he now was, to some extent, rehabilitated was due to the kindness and sympathy of Meynell. He was sent to a private hospital to be cured of his opium addiction and the nineties saw the appearance of his poetry whose qualities secured recognition: 'Why can't I write poetry like that?' said Oscar Wilde. 'It is what I have wanted to do all my life.'

Nevertheless he was little changed by the measure of praise and the possession of a competence. A humble pensioner of existence, he seemed to feel himself not entitled to anything other than the bleak life he had known and his favourite haunt in his later years was the gloomy waste of Kilburn's bricks and mortar. Dying slowly of consumption, he would sit, holding out tremulous hands to the fire in the Skiddaw public house at the corner of Elgin Avenue and the Chippenham Road. 'Oppressed with fatality' he breathed his last in the Hospital of St John and St Elizabeth in 1907. 'Once step aside,' he had said shortly before, 'from the ways of comfortable men and you cannot regain them. You will live and die under the law of the intolerable thing called romance.'

Yet however hardly the city might treat these men, however much they might hate it, it had a fascination for them. They endured its hardships with a deliberate self-sacrifice, a loving-loathing; they were self-impelled to martyrdom. This was also the case with George Robert Gissing, the novelist.

Gissing left England under a cloud as a young man and spent some years in America. Returning, he became a needy recluse, an observer of and a participant in the struggle for survival in its shabbiest and dreariest forms. Austerely, he recorded the blighting effects of poverty as he had experienced them, remaining, until towards the end of his life, determinedly in a state of threadbare misery.

Disease and their own incapacity to earn a living inclined James Thomson and Francis Thompson to self-indulgence and self-destruction. A sense of social injustice moved Gissing to write of Clerkenwell. More influenced than these by the French cult of 'art for art's sake', though the two similarly-named poets conformed closely to its type, were Ernest Dowson and Charles Conder. They display a period likeness not concealed by the fact that one was a painter and the other a writer. The dreamy Conder, a Londoner who had spent a long time in Australia, had turned cosmopolitan, gravitated to France and was more at home in the Rat Mort in the place Pigalle than in his native city. In him and Dowson are to be seen the familiar symptoms, the lurking consumption, the savage need for squalor or excess, the self-abasement, linked with a delicate art. France was their favoured country and Dowson's appreciation of the French realists became a genuine passion for the equivalent of what they described in England. In Paris he haunted the market quarter of Les Halles and in London the district round the docks, where he discovered anew the bitter savour of the conditions in which lived the proletarian poor. He came into possession there of a mouldering wharf on the river front, decaying and rat-haunted, where he lived for a time in romantic isolation. He made some effort, without success, to find a substitute in London for the friendly Bohemian and artistic circles of Paris where ideas were conceived and movements born, but the cafés of Soho did not provide the right atmosphere – and the Rhymers Club, which met in an upper room of the Cheshire Cheese in Fleet Street, whose poet members smoked church-warden pipes and drank beer out of pewter tankards, lacked the verve which it ought to have possessed and perished in the uncongenial air. Finding polite society unbearable Dowson took his pleasure indiscriminately in the taverns round the Strand, and his favourite eating houses were the cabmen's shelters in which he was well known. He invented for himself a hopeless romance which led him to spend many hours gazing in speechless adoration at a foreign girl in a Soho restaurant, after which 'desolate and sick of an old passion' – to quote his most famous poem – he 'cried for madder music and for stronger wine' and becoming extremely drunk, astonished those who knew his ordinarily gentle manner by his angry violence and furious language. As consumption advanced he hid in his lodgings, refused to see a doctor, let himself starve; until a friend who found him one day, practically penniless in a 'Bodega' and scarcely able to walk, took him off to a cottage at Catford where Dowson died in 1910 at the age of thirty-three.

Such was the purgatory of the gay nineties, the intolerable

romance to which so many artists who lived for the sake of their art were doomed. The prevailing gloom of the picture throws into stronger relief the metropolitan glitter of which it was so much a part – there was one place, even, where the artist's hell might be temporarily confused and merged with a mere bohemianism. This was the Café Royal in whose interior the décor of the Second Empire was successfully transported to London.

Its red plush and marble tops appealed to the nostalgia of those who had been delighted with Paris, the derisive mock pomp of its gilt ornaments and endless mirrors was enlivening to the powers of conversation, and far out beneath the surface of Regent Street stretched cellars containing the rarest and choicest wines that France could afford.

There wit sparkled, enmity smiled, the poor were entranced by splendour and the rich by talent. Sometimes Dowson came here, surfeited with the streets, finding it neutral ground between the society he disliked and the nether-world to which he was so irresistibly drawn, discovering there the typical balance of the time between pleasure and ruin.

There was in France a parallel between painting and literature. Thus the painter was fascinated more by the spectacle of pleasure than by the religious and historical themes which had formerly been his preoccupation. Manet could make a masterpiece out of a bar at the Folies Bergère. The shimmer of glass, the reflexions of amusement seekers in crowded perspective, the waitress emerging as strangely amid the foam of champagne as an aphrodite from an iridescent sea, were sufficient for him; made it unnecessary to seek 'noble' subjects.

There was that kind of almost religious exaltation in Toulouse-Lautrec's scrutiny of the music-hall and of the haunts of vice which appears in the poems of Baudelaire. How like the two men are! in their fastidiousness, their physical suffering, their feverish interest in excess governed by an austere and uncompromising artistic principle. A descendant of the Counts of Toulouse who terrorized the Albigensians, a dwarf in size, Lautrec separated himself disdainfully and perhaps even with a sense of hurt, due to his stunted physique, from the sporting life of the provinces and the attractions of metropolitan high life to become the historian of the night world of Montmartre. To the study of ageing women of pleasure, with sagging chins and shapeless bodies, in whose eyes there is an immense vacancy and about whose tightened lips an obscure anger, the little man brought as much reverence as one painting the most ideal type of madonna. In the dolorous nocturnal haunts of those mentally warped as he was physically, he found realistically that alternative to the everyday world which Poe and Huysmans had imagined in words. It was by an appropriate chance, an inevitable accident, that when on a visit to London, where an exhibition of his works passed unnoticed except for some expressions of disfavour, he should paint Oscar Wilde, in the days immediately before his trial and conviction, the pasty mask of a beau, the picture of Dorian Gray at the instant of dissolution.

Through the medium of a different temperament, that of Degas, the same interest in pleasure appears, though with a greater detachment and more cynicism. But even when he was least cynical, he was still a universe apart from the insular view of the ideal painter; and this was shown most conclusively when the famous painting known as *L'Absinthe* was exhibited in London in 1893.

The real title was not *L'Absinthe* but *Au Café*. It depicted a man and woman sitting at a café table with glasses before them, a scene not at all unusual in the French capital nor necessarily lacking in decorum. In fact the man was a skilled and respectable engraver, M. Desboutin, relaxing quietly and pipe between teeth, contemplating the agreeable spectacle of the street. The drink in the tumbler before him was, actually, nothing more harmful than black coffee. The woman with him was a well-known model. Nevertheless the invented title was condemnation in itself, Absinthe. The baneful liquor that drives men mad. What, thought those to whom the idea of a picture without a purpose was unbelievable, could this mean save that here was an emblem of the sorry results of self-indulgence. To Walter Crane, designer and disciple of William Morris's socialism, it was 'a study of degradation, male and female'. 'Arry Quilter, not silenced even yet by Whistler's mockery, was loud in denunciation in the *Pall Mall Gazette*. 'An expression in painting of the deplorable side of modern life', said W. B. Richmond.

Even George Moore tripped up. In an otherwise laudatory review he allowed his pen to wander in a description of the model. 'Heavens! what a slut! A life of idleness and low vice is upon her face: we read there her whole life. The tale is not a pleasant one but it is a lesson.' But when the battle was really joined, he quickly recanted. He confessed his error in his own naïve fashion. He should not have written 'that abominable phrase "it is a lesson".' Only D. S. MacColl, the militant critic of the *Spectator*, spoke consistently and emphatically in support of Degas and against the incurable affliction of the Philistine who would never know what painting was.

To see this controversy in the light in which it appeared at the time it is instructive to consider who then or thenabouts were popular in Britain. The academicians were still at work on classical and historical subjects. Sir William B. Richmond, R.A., who was so severe on Degas, had finished not long before what he considered to be his best work, *Venus and Anchises*. 'Probably,' he admitted, 'few who see it will remember that Venus is supposed to have visited Anchises, whose handsomeness was celebrated far and wide, on Mount Ida.' And the distance between Mount Ida and Montmartre was to him impassable. 'I am a thinker,' declared G. F. Watts, 'who happens to use a brush instead of a pen.' Thus in his picture *Love and Life* the aim was to show that love, 'by which, of course, I mean not physical passion, but altruism, tenderness' leads man to the highest life. Evidently there would not have existed much mutual understanding between him and Toulouse-Lautrec.

Frederick Goodall, R.A., had received two thousand guineas for an Egyptian composition – *The Ploughman and Shepherdess*. To make himself familiar with Egyptian sheep ('different from our European breeds') he had imported a whole flock which he kept on a farm at Harrow Weald. Sir Laurence Alma-Tadema, R.A., was meditating an elaborate reconstruction, both architectural and human, of the Baths of Caracalla. Marcus Stone, R.A., had recently painted *A Sailor's Sweetheart* in which a pensive young woman in bonnet and early nineteenth-century dress leaned on the wall of a seaside garden and gazed sadly over the water, thinking – well, one scarcely needs to see the picture or describe it farther to imagine the rest.

To reflect on the dreamy and sentimental world of fancy which enabled these good simple men to ply their trade enables one to understand better the shock which the sharp realism and even cynicism of French art inflicted, which led Holman Hunt to 'warn the world that the threat to modern art, meaning nothing less than its extinction, is "Impressionism"'.

And yet the foreign influence, the 'seed blown oversea from a ruined garden', as George Moore described it, had caught root. As early as 1886 a group of painters who had worked in the schools of Paris had met together to make their plans. It was suggested that they should call themselves 'The Society of Anglo-French Painters'. They eventually formed The New English Art Club.

It was one of several movements of reform towards the end of the century. Whistler himself had attempted to convert the Royal Society of British Artists into an art centre but the conservative elements were too much for him. There was a mutiny. 'The "artists" came out and the "British" remained – and peace and sweet obscurity are restored to Suffolk Street – Eh! What? Ha! Ha!' The early days of the New English Art were similarly marked by dispute and secession. The 'Glasgow' School withdrew in a body. Others, the open air landscape painters, formed a school of their own at Newlyn. Leighton, president of the Royal Academy, predicted that 'the second year would try, and the third probably disband them.' The president was wrong. Through the nineties the New English Art Club continued to hold its ground and by the time King Edward came to the throne, it was an accepted institution filling that place which the Pre-Raphaelite movement had occupied a generation earlier.

But the French accent of painting in Britain gives only a faint flavour to the nineties. It was a young draughtsman, not a painter but an artist in black and white, who gave the period a peculiar stamp. His name was Aubrey Beardsley.

He arrived on the scene at a moment when the wit, dandyism, preciousness, and artificiality which had been active for thirty years, fused and flared up.

The wit of Whistler had enlivened the town all through the eighties, but *The Gentle Art of Making Enemies* was not published until 1890 when its author was aged fifty-four; and thus the mordant jester seemed newly born.

Oscar Wilde had been celebrated for his brilliance, his attitudinizing since 1880. But it was not until the nineties that he came into his own – in 1891 with his story *The Picture of Dorian Gray* and then with the series of sparkling comedies which took London by storm. It was the third of his incarnations and the most natural to him. Where should such a capacity for talk as he possessed show itself to advantage except in the theatre. The comedy of manners which he had played hitherto in life needed only a slight adaptation to be transferred to the stage and his epigrams acquired a new savour when put into the mouths of a mythical English aristocracy. Bulky, brimming over with high spirits, he basked in triumph, in the new era, expanding with genial egotism. When Herbert Beerbohm Tree, the actor, found him writing on the script of *A Woman of No Importance* and said, 'What are you doing?' he answered, 'I am making some slight changes in the text,' and then, 'but, after all, who am I to tamper with a masterpiece?'

In 1890 Aubrey Beardsley was eighteen – a clerk in the Guardian Insurance Office, seemingly one of those insignificant youths of whom Gissing wrote, pale, tuberculous, resigned to a dismal office routine from which there could be no escape. Struggling with the disease which already racked his thin bony frame he had almost given up certain splendid ambitions he had conceived during his schooldays at Brighton. He had then begun to draw. The piano duets which he played with his sister Mabel had given them some local fame as musical prodigies. But such accomplishments were not unusual. He was outwardly just a clerk – though if one had been able to look into his mind, there would have been seen a strange medley of learning and aspiration, an imagination haunted by *Madame Bovary* and *Mademoiselle de Maupin*, a secret intention to be great among the great.

In 1891 he secured an introduction to Burne-Jones. Always mindful of that wonderful year in which he himself had timidly approached Rossetti as a youth, had received from him precious counsel and encouragement, Sir Edward received him kindly. Perhaps in the portfolio-clutching boy before him he saw reflected his earlier self. Warmed by Burne-Jones' sympathy Beardsley began to imitate his style, and to draw sad figures in medieval garments, like a convinced Pre-Raphaelite.

At the same time Beardsley admired Whistler. He read *The Gentle Art* when it came out and made up his mind to be a wit on this model – to speak with a cutting and elegant turn of phrase, to scorn the middle class from which he came. It was in 1891 that he visited the Butterfly's famed Peacock Room. There was another stimulus. The patterns in blue and gold-leaf with which Whistler had ruined Mr Leyland's Spanish leather put fresh ideas into his head. The 'Japanese' patterns impressed him. He began to look out for and copy Japanese prints, and just as the earlier aesthetic movement had casually mixed Botticelli and 'blue and white', so now he began to combine Burne-Jones and the Japanese Utamaro in his drawings.

Aymer Vallance, associate of William Morris, now introduced him to that great man. The interview was a disappointment. Morris perhaps suspected in the curious visitor, his immature work, some vein of thought or feeling hostile to his own. At all events he was discouraging and therefore Beardsley tried elsewhere.

By chance these efforts led to a sort of emulation of Morris.

The publisher Joseph M. Dent had in mind the production of editions of the classics, comparable with Morris's Kelmscott Books but less costly. He determined to begin with the *Morte d'Arthur* itself, so long the quarry and inspiration of the Pre-Raphaelite artists. He talked over the question of an illustrator with Frederick Evans of that 'university of city clerks', Jones and Evans' bookshop in Cheapside. Mr Evans bethought him of Beardsley, a regular visitor to the shop, whose drawings he had so often been shown. Strange to say the recommendation was accepted and Beardsley fell to work, wild with delight.

The aesthetic movement abounds in hybrids; and in the drawings in which Aubrey Beardsley suddenly began to display an astounding talent there was something so hybrid as to be monstrous. To William Morris it was as if a subtle corruption had invaded a pure ideal, as if beauty had lost its soul and, retaining outward fairness, seemed yet the more fiendish. It was a copy of his work, 'an act of usurpation'. It was also a parody. He was very angry when he saw Beardsley's Lady of the Lake telling Arthur of the sword Excalibur and he was with difficulty dissuaded by Burne-Jones from writing to Mr Dent in remonstrance.

But by the end of 1892 Aubrey Beardsley had lost interest in the *Morte d'Arthur* and done most of the drawings for it he was to do, though not all that had been commissioned. A series of events now directed him into a more congenial path. Aymer Vallance introduced him to the art critic C. Lewis Hind, who was looking for material for a new art magazine. In the first number of this magazine, *The Studio*, edited by Gleeson White, there appeared as a result an article on Beardsley by Joseph Pennell.

Joseph Pennell was a Philadelphia Quaker, whose great passion in life was Whistler. It was an admiration shared with his wife, earnest Elizabeth Robins Pennell, who had first heard of the Butterfly from the lips of Oscar Wilde on his American lecture tour. They had come to England in the eighties to write up Old Chelsea for the *Century Magazine* and found it so congenially disagreeable that they had been there ever since. They treasured every remark made by Whistler, who in their view could do no wrong. In praising Beardsley however Pennell ventured for once to run counter to his hero, who chose to regard the young man as just one more wretched amateur, for whom indeed he showed some personal dislike. 'Why do you go with him?' he asked, 'he has hairs on his hands, hairs on his fingers' ends, hairs on his toes, hairs all over him.' Nevertheless the article was written, and a drawing of Salomé reproduced with it was seen with interest by the publisher John Lane.

John Lane, in 1889, had set up a bookshop with Elkin Mathews, had also begun to publish books at the Bodley Head in Vigo Street. He was seeking new talent. Here evidently was the artist to illustrate the English translation of Wilde's play-poem which had first appeared in a French version. The drawings by the young man of twenty-one positively overpowered the writing and made the book his. John Lane was encouraged to appoint him art editor of a new quarterly, called, with a suggestion of the 'yellow-back' French novel, *The Yellow Book*. In 1894 with the publication of *Salomé* and *The Yellow Book*, Beardsley became famous. It was more than fame. He had positively created or expressed the essence of the age. He seemed the very spirit of 'decadence'. In him were all the various qualities summed up in that word.

These strange drawings were highly artificial. The uncompromising opposition of black and white set nature at defiance. The decorative lines were decadent in that they formed an elaborate and sterile system, as if of symbols whose meaning and purpose had ceased to exist or were profoundly hidden. They were decadent in another sense: that is they were full of troublous suggestions of the sub-world of vice, of exhaustion, and of excess. It was an inner existence that Beardsley had put down on paper, of sexual images and fantastic literary reveries. He had a sort of innocent familiarity with evil, he communed with the leering dwarfs, the bloated, epicene figures that peopled the depraved landscapes and grotesque interiors designed by his pen, as a child might

14. *The Abbé* from one of the illustrations by
Aubrey Beardsley to *Under the Hill*

15. *Oscar Wilde* from a portrait by Henri de Toulouse-Lautrec

16. *Katie Lawrence at Gatti's* from a painting by Walter Richard Sickert

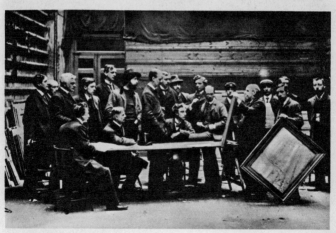

17. *The Last Jury of the New English Art Club at the Dudley Gallery, 1904.*
Back row, from left to right: Walter Russell, David Muirhead, Alfred Rich,
Ambrose McEvoy, Henry Tonks, Augustus John, D. S. MacColl, P. Wilson
Steer, Muirhead Bone, Francis Bate. Front row, seated: Fred Winter, Fred
Brown, Roger Fry, William Rothenstein

18. *Danseuse sur la Scène* from a pastel by Edgar Degas

talk with fairies. He invented a mythology which could only be explained by that other mythology of modern times – psycho-analysis.

His daily occupation with the Guardian Insurance Office had caused him to execute his first drawings at night; and this became a settled habit. Like Huysmans' hero he cultivated seclusion. The room had to be darkened before he could start work, the candles lit in two tall ormolu Empire candlesticks.

Deliberately he made himself a figure of mystery.

*The Yellow Book* and Beardsley's art were a new phase of aestheticism, increased the breach between aesthete and Philistine. *The Times* called the new quarterly 'a mixture of English rowdyism and French lubricity', mourned that if this was the new art we were much better off with the old. *Punch* had its fun about 'Mr Danby Weirdsley'. Even Oscar Wilde (who had not figured in the *Yellow Book*), buying it for a railway journey, threw it out of the carriage window in impatience.

But of Beardsley's success there was no doubt. It created or helped to create a feeling of tension in the atmosphere as if the country were touched by madness or its character had changed overnight into something new and strange.

And in fact crisis was at hand. The strange movement of defiance and abasement which had affected so many clever people in so many different ways was now to be joined by the gayest and most dazzlingly brilliant man of the time – Wilde.

# IV
# DÉBÂCLE

## I

'STOP to let this man get out! I invited him for a drive but he is not a gentleman.'

The cabman pulled up without surprise. Cabmen are never surprised – too many queer things happen in the course of their rovings for that. Two toffs having a quarrel. That was all.

A young man flushed and worried-looking got out. A portly man remaining inside angrily motioned the cab onwards. The little drama took place on a rainy London afternoon in the year 1895.

The speaker was Oscar Wilde. It was his friend, Clyde Fitch, the American dramatist, who left him, at whom the unpleasant words were spoken. It seemed a pity for their relationship had previously been cordial. Wilde had encouraged the younger man to write, and the latter had dedicated his first book to Wilde. So friendly were they that Wilde would send him a telegram now and then, useless, but as a mark of affection, simply to say 'What a charming day it has been!' And this had to happen.

The fact was that Oscar Wilde was being talked about – and in a way that was not at all favourable to him. The repressed, scandal-eager society of the time gave to the stifled rumours and hints it interchanged a growing ugliness and portentousness. 'Best steer clear of him,' they were saying, 'he has a bad reputation.' 'He is making the country too hot to hold him.' 'It's notorious that he ...' and then the heads drew closer together and voices sank to a shocked undertone.

Was it true? That was what Clyde Fitch had wanted to know, what people were saying, that his esteemed and brilliant friend was one of those with a perverted fondness for their own sex which led to practices rendering them liable to criminal prosecution. At least he should be informed so that he could deny and scotch these rumours. But Wilde had made no vigorous denial. He had passed the matter off lightly with one of his typical remarks, 'To the pure all things are impure,' something of that kind. But Fitch persisted. He wanted a plain answer. Wilde obstinately refused to discuss the matter and with the slamming of the door of the cab their relationship ended.

The rumours, together with Oscar's behaviour, were making more than one of his friends uneasy. Frank Harris, for instance. Frank Harris was no plaster saint. He had knocked about the world and seen life. He had arrived in London in 1882 by way of Galway, Liverpool, New York, Chicago, Kansas, Heidelberg, and Paris. He had been a bartender and a lawyer at the Kansas bar, a cowboy, and a schoolmaster. Educated in 'go-getting', he had forced his way on to the *Fortnightly Review* and the *Spectator*, had become one of the persons of the nineties as editor of the *Saturday Review*.

As an editor he was ambitious and adventurous. He wanted the most able contributors and the most original articles he could get. Among others he had picked for dramatic criticism a thin, sardonic, red-bearded Irishman, nearing his fortieth year and clad in an odd woollen suit, with a passionate belief in the theatre, whose first play had been written and heartily hissed. This was George Bernard Shaw. Wilde, naturally, was one of the friends of this active and genius-seeking editor who championed his plays, and yet, there was that in Wilde which made him uneasy. It was not comfortable to see him in the Café Royal with some frightful smirking lads who looked like newspaper sellers or stable-boys, discoursing to them with that elegance and beauty of language which had become second nature, on the glories of ancient Greece and the noble nudities of the Olympic games and thereby producing the most offensive sniggerings from his regrettable audience. Decidedly this was not right conduct for a man of Wilde's culture and eminence. Frank Harris, voluptuary and man of the world, was shocked.

If Wilde's friends were shocked his enemies gained a new malignance. His success as it was professedly intended to do had made enmity. His affectation offended the clubman, irritated the dull-witted. Even newspapermen were inclined to dislike by his contempt for their craft. He made enemies among those he had never met. Thus a young author, Robert Hichens, having made acquaintance in Egypt with some of Wilde's circle, was moved to write a novel *The Green Carnation* in which Wilde was held up to ridicule and innuendo. One of these enemies was formidable indeed. It was the eighth Marquess of Queensberry, distinguished as the inventor of the Queensberry rules of the boxing ring.

The Marquess disapproved of the literary friendship of his son and Wilde. The sporting world to which he belonged was precisely that most suspicious of artistic pretensions and attitudes, whose contempt was ever ready to turn into truculence, explosive violence. He disliked Wilde, to begin with on general grounds, and instinctively, as so many did, for his cleverness, his easy wit, the implied superiority of his attitude, perhaps for his appearance of being superbly happy. Mistrustfully he met him on one occasion with his son Lord Alfred Douglas at the Café Royal; though even he was not proof against the man's charm. They spent hours in the discussion of – atheism. The mistrust of the Marquess was allayed. Wilde was after all a most agreeable and amusing person. He was ready to endorse the enthusiasm which Lord Alfred shared with so many others for Wilde's ability as an artist and conversationalist – until finally the mounting tide of rumour left no doubt that he was not a desirable companion and the Marquess felt it incumbent upon him at all costs to pull the man down and expose him.

This was the background for the second of the great aesthetic trials of the century.

What produced, in Oscar Wilde, his infatuation, can be discussed now scientifically. 'I have always maintained,' wrote Bernard Shaw, 'that Oscar was a giant in the pathological sense of the word and it is this which largely explains his weaknesses.' This may be so. There is nothing at least to disprove it. If Speranza had not wished to have a girl instead of a boy, it might have been that Oscar would have had a more normal constitution. It is reasonable to assume that if medical or biological science could supply the explanation, it should also have been charged with supplying the remedy.

Other factors may also be considered. Perhaps if he had not gone to Greece with Mahaffy, had not so thoroughly acquired that admiration of male beauty which was to be found in the books and sculpture of ancient times, the danger would have been avoided or at least remained latent. And the same applies to his reading and knowledge of the French 'decadents'. If he had not, for example, so greatly admired the perverse nobleman of Huysmans' *A Rebours*, so much so that he copied from that book his own *Dorian Gray*, he might have pursued a safer course. But if Poe and Baudelaire had not influenced Huysmans, *A Rebours* might not have been written. There are many links in the chain. There seems to be something inevitable, a fatality in what happened. It is said, George Moore among others said it, that books do not influence conduct, though a very strong case can be put up against this opinion. Books are a product of life. It may be asserted that the whole aesthetic and decadent movement was a protest against the repressions of the century and that Wilde happened to be the individual destined to stand in the forefront when the great clash came.

The effects of repression, that is to say of the secrecy and terror with which the subject of sex was invested by the most prudish century in history, were not limited to the writer. The impression which was skilfully created at the time that Wilde was a unique monster, an impression that has been perpetuated, was of course untrue. As one proof of this there exists the undeniable evidence of a whole system.

Unnatural vice was commercialized and organized. Its profits were largely made from blackmail to which the prevailing strictness of morality gave an extraordinary power. Oscar Wilde, different from the rest only in talent, was one of a number of poor flies who buzzed into this most sinister of webs. At the centre of one web was a man called Taylor. His lair was at the upper part of a house at No. 13 Little College Street. A 'gentleman of good birth', who had been educated at Marlborough School, he had been into and come out of the Militia, had inherited £45,000 and getting through that had been declared bankrupt. His occupation, subsequently, was vague; but at those heavily curtained rooms in Little College Street, musky with burning incense, there were 'tea-parties' at which gentlemen were introduced to a choice collection of grooms, hotel doorkeepers, sacked valets, unemployed waiters and other hobgoblins who would do anything for money. And at some later stage of their acquaintance these soft-minded gentlemen would find that they were, in the objectionable language of their protégés, 'rented', that is to say, blackmailed. 'We all got money by blackmailing. All those I have spoken of got money in that way. I never knew them do anything else.' Such was the confession of one of them. They were, said Wilde, 'wonderful in their infamous war against life. To entertain them was an astounding adventure'.

In his strange hallucination which permitted him to see an Antinous in an Alf Parker, Wilde went to these mysterious tea-parties, and behind him trod, not specifically on his trail but certainly on that of Taylor's, the heavy silent foot of the law.

That heavy silent foot followed Mr Taylor one Sunday in 1894 to a house in Fitzroy Street. In a midnight raid, eighteen men were taken into custody and charged at Marlborough Street police station. Among them was one 'dressed in a fantastic female garb of black and gold'. It was difficult however to make a precise charge. The circumstances somewhat resembled those of that case of the Queen *v.* Boulton in which Swinburne and Simeon Solomon had been interested many years earlier. 'They are most of them known, your worship', said Superintendent Sheppard, who implied in these words a certainty of some discreditable knowledge, but no evidence was put forward and Taylor and the rest were let go.

Wilde was incapable of being warned by this ominous business. Madly he danced onwards, scattering sovereigns, warm epistles in pouting, purring prose, inscribed gold cigarette cases, lavishing conversation and champagne on guttersnipes in the restaurants of Soho and the Strand.

And here it was that the terms of art and life became so strangely mixed. It was an undercurrent in Wilde's life of which many of his friends were unaware. It was the dark reverse side of his lavish admiration of an ideal beauty, an ideal companionship in the pursuit of art. It was distinct from his admiration of the talent and spirit of a young poet like Lord Alfred Douglas. That was on another plane. And yet to the Marquess of Queensberry it seemed that the suspicion of that dark, reverse side however far removed from friendships in the world of culture should withdraw from Wilde's writings all esteem, should withhold all personal communication.

In a scene which had a strong accent of melodrama he visited Wilde at Tite Street, with another man to act as witness. He accused him of having been turned out of the Savoy, threatened to thrash him in public. With dignity Wilde surveyed 'the screaming, scarlet Marquis', rang the bell, told the servant, 'You see this man, he is the Marquess of Queensberry, the most infamous brute in London, and he is never to be allowed to enter this house again.'

Queensberry, however, was set on trouble. He arrived at the first night of *The Importance of Being Earnest* with a load of vegetables with which he proposed to pelt the author. His next move was that message left with the porter at the Albemarle Club which read 'To Oscar Wilde posing as a somdomite' – a mixture of legalistic caution, bad spelling, and malignance.

What was Wilde to do? He could ignore the Marquess, in

which case undoubtedly the persecution would go on. Or he could take legal action and attempt to silence his noble adversary in that way. To the dismay of his friends and of others who by no means welcomed the ventilating of this particular issue, he went to law.

2

'SENT TO THE STOCKS, BY BELTED BRITON, THAT HE MAY THERE BE PELTED WITH
UNCLEAN EGG BY THE PHILISTINE OF THE MARKET, IN HIS UPRIGHT WRATH ...'

These words almost suggest the conflict of Wilde and Queensberry. They are, in fact, part of the 'Argument' of the stinging butterfly, Whistler, in the account of his case against Sir William Eden. This dispute was contemporaneous with that other and more serious affair. Both were incidental to the trail of litigation which accompanied the age of Spite and Frivolity and the haughty aesthetic régime.

'One really can't live in London,' said Whistler, 'without a lawyer.' He had or thought he had more than one cause of offence.

Firstly, du Maurier was bringing out *Trilby* in *Harper's Magazine*. Nearly forty years had elapsed since he and Whistler and Poynter and the rest had lived a Bohemian life in Paris and yet here it was, in minute detail just as if it had happened the other day, their rooms, their friends, their quarrels and loves, preserved all that time in du Maurier's retentive memory. It was also a success. It was tender and sentimental. There was no harsh realism and the fate of Trilby herself was a tragedy of irreproachable charm. But it was most unpleasant to Whistler – for there was a description of himself, unmistakable in the author's delineation, though the name was Jos. Sibley; and a very unflattering description it was.

Whistler promptly consulted the indispensable lawyer. He also declared his intention (as du Maurier wrote in some distress, to Armstrong) of using physical violence.

... J.W. seems to me to have gone quite crazy – however, there's nothing I can do now – and I really don't see what he's aiming at – unless it's notoriety – an endeavour to keep his memory green in England ... Nor can I, after all this virulence on his part, attempt anything in the shape of an apology – if I were to delete 'Joe Sibley' in the coming volume (which I would do were he to write me a decent letter) he would say I was in a funk – So I can't even do that. What *does* he want? I can't very well go and call him out – fancy the roars of laughter over there! Nor can we very well have it out with fisticuffs! *à notre âge, et dans notre position!!!* I suppose he *does* mean to come and 'hit me in the eye' as he always called it – so I must look out ...

But extreme measures were not required and the reference to Whistler was altered by its author out of all recognition.

He had a less cause for offence and a more formidable antagonist in Sir William Eden, Bart.

The baronet was in the great tradition of eccentric English gentlemen, that is to say he combined the manly, forthright appearance and some of the routine of the squire with unpredictable tastes. He was six feet in height and well built in proportion, with red cheeks, light blue eyes, a moustache and beard of reddish brown, and tufted and imperious eyebrows. He wore a cap and suit of small brown check – The 'Eden Tartan', but he hated dogs, children, pipes, and whisky. A sportsman, he could not tolerate sporting pictures. England's green and pleasant land did not appeal to him, but he had a great aversion to red in the flower beds and visited any gardener who offended in this way with his ire. He painted in water-colours, travelled restlessly and took a delight in French painting. His 'immaculate Degas' was one of the great comforts of his life.

It was in 1894 that the dispute arose. The baronet negotiated through George Moore for a portrait sketch of his wife to be made by Whistler. There was some vagueness about the fee but a minimum was established of one hundred guineas and as the portrait was 'about the size of a sheet of note-paper' this minimum was paid. Whistler took offence at the amount, painted over the sketch and kept the money.

It would seem that he could scarcely defend this procedure legally and Sir William was determined to bring him to book. He instituted an action in the French courts as the transaction had taken place in Whistler's Paris studio. The Civil Tribunal of the Seine gave judgement against Whistler, ruled that he should refund the price, hand over the picture and pay damages. Whistler appealed, full of republican rage against the aristocracy and of contempt for Moore, 'the expert (*sic*)' who 'had made himself a spurious reputation as advanced connoisseur and cultured critic.' The suit, which dragged into the Court of Appeal and was not concluded until 1897, confirmed the previous judgement up to a point, demanding of Whistler the hundred guineas and costs though allowing him to keep the picture. He affected to consider this a triumph though it was but a poor one; and of course it in no way appeased enmity. The baronet bluntly declared that than Whistler 'there never was a more vulgar and indomitable cad or a more vain and vicious beast. The man thinks no one dare collar him'; and the latter, implacable as always, could not even endure that his friends should know Sir William; and to one whom he saw walking with the baronet in the street he alluded thereafter as Judas Iscariot.

The affair of 'the Baronet and the Butterfly' is not of great importance though it is interesting in the light it throws on two contrasting, self-willed individuals. But it raised no major issues as the Ruskin trial had done. The artist was behaving pettily. That amount of right he had had on his side against the powerful critic was no longer his. The witty sallies he included in a new booklet were no longer backed by a just indignation but were spiteful merely. From the rue du Bac he made an ironical gesture 'to those Confrères across the Channel who, refraining from intrusive demonstrations with a pluck and delicacy all their own, "sat tight" during the struggle' – though there appears little reason why they should have done otherwise. It was now with an almost puerile conceit, a wilful disregard of right and wrong that Whistler insisted on the privilege of the artist caste.

*

It is possible that as Wilde meditated the means of subduing
the Marquess the example of his litigious friend (or 'enemy')
was in his mind. Adept in imitation, he may have seen
himself like Whistler, an epigrammatic witness, skilfully
reducing counsel to impotent silence: asserting, as Whistler
had done in defiance of Ruskin, that the artist was a lord
among men, whose ways were not to be called in question,
whose genius overruled all bourgeois limitations. If that
were so he sadly underestimated many things: the superior
combative qualities of Whistler, the great difference between
two cases in only one of which lurked the suggestion of
criminality; the power of an opposing barrister to put an
unexpected and dubious interpretation on even the most
innocent occurrences; and, most of all, the shaky foundations
of his own position.

There is also the possibility that he foresaw the whole
wretched case in prospect – that some kind of inverted
heroism made him go forward – had he not said that one
must always go forward – to face obloquy and martyrdom.
That conception of sacrifice, of renunciation, was never far
from the minds of the investigators of sensation, Baudelaire
and Verlaine. If the inquisitors of the middle-class world
were to crucify him would that not be a noble death, con-
demning them and causing him to live for ever? Not so
much a Christian death as like that of the belated Apollo of
Pater's tale – Denys L'Auxerrois in his *Imaginary Portraits* –
when 'the pretended hunting of the unholy creature became
a real one, which brought out, in rapid increase, men's evil
passions' and the body was borne along in front of the
crowd, 'torn at last limb from limb'. There was also the
thought, whose appalling horror had its own fascination,
that the death might be an ignoble one, whose ignominy
should be more intense than nobility and constitute a
martyrdom of a new kind whose sordidness was without
mitigation.

What he later declared to have been the most ignominious
and unpardonable action of his life was to have appealed to
society for help. And society said in effect, 'You have defied

my laws all this time and now you seek their support. The law you have invoked shall be rigorously applied to you.' No man, he remarked, ever fell so ignobly or through such ignoble instruments. But the die being cast, he went on without hesitation and, on 2nd March, 1895, John Sholto Douglas, eighth Marquess of Queensberry, was charged with publishing a certain libel concerning Mr Oscar Fingall O'Flahertie Wills Wilde. The second hearing took place a week later. The trial began at the Old Bailey before Mr Justice Henn Collins on 3rd April, 1895. Sir Edward Clarke was leading counsel for Wilde, Mr E. H. Carson, Q.C., M.P., Oxford acquaintance of Wilde, appeared for the defence. The crowded court, though the crowd was exclusively of men, testified to intense public interest.

This, the first act of the celebrated and frightful drama, lasted for three days. Some of the sordid tangle beneath the surface began to reveal itself on this day; but equally in prominence was the issue whether Wilde's own writings were or were not 'immoral and obscene'. The writings particularly cited were *The Picture of Dorian Gray* and the series of epigrams, 'Phrases and Philosophies for the Use of the Young', which had come out in a publication called *The Chameleon*.

Lantern-jawed, bleak, harsh, Edward Carson, when the preliminaries were over, rose to cross-examine. Near by sat the Marquess of Queensberry wearing a Cambridge blue hunting stock, mumbling beneath his breath and casting furious glances at his enemy who was dressed most correctly in a dark tight-fitting frock coat with a white collar and tie of decorous black.

It was not the sort of case Carson much cared about. He had, after all, been a fellow student of Wilde though he had not liked the man. He had respect if not for his personality and his writings at least for the classical scholarship which had so much excelled his own. He had, moreover, a bad cold on this day. He began his questioning in subdued tones as one wearily performing a distasteful duty; but shortly the off-hand demeanour of the witness called forth his energies and the trained legal faculty began to probe with deadly effect.

*The Chameleon*, it had already been stated by the prosecution, was not a creditable publication nor one with which Wilde would have associated himself if he had known its character in advance. It was a piece of amateur 'decadence' and its trend was homosexual. Unmistakably so was the story it contained, 'The Priest and the Acolyte'. But if the defence could show or suggest that Wilde approved of 'immoral literature' so much was gained to them. Now he could not by the nature of his aesthetic position admit the existence of any such thing; and to that extent the position was parallel with that of Whistler in his libel suit against Ruskin: Wilde could only maintain that the story was to be adjudged good or bad as a work of art.

'You have no doubt whatever that that was an improper story?' asked Carson.

'From the literary point of view,' answered Wilde, 'it was highly improper. It is impossible for a man of literature to judge it otherwise; by literature, meaning treatment, selection of subject, and the like. I thought the treatment rotten and the subject rotten.'

He would not admit that a writer should be limited in his freedom to say anything, to write of any subject. He admitted only the right to criticize its style.

Carson persisted: 'You are of opinion that there is no such thing as an immoral book?' – 'Yes.'

The expected affirmative paved the way to an ingenious trap: 'May I take it that you think "The Priest and the Acolyte" was not immoral?'

Lightly, Wilde evaded it. 'It was worse, it was badly written.'

'Do you think the story blasphemous?' – 'I think it violated every canon of artistic beauty.'

'That is not an answer.' – 'It is the only answer I can give.'

Counsel sought to exasperate the witness. 'I want to see the position you pose in' – and twice more the question was asked, 'Did you or did you not consider the story blasphemous?' Finally Wilde was compelled to answer that he did not consider the story blasphemous, though he did think it disgusting.

Having extorted this answer Carson proceeded to show that 'The Priest and the Acolyte' was very blasphemous. He reminded the witness that when the priest in the story administered poison to the boy he used the words of the sacrament of the Church of England. 'That,' said Wilde, 'I entirely forgot.'

And once more came the maddening question: 'Do you consider that blasphemous?' It was not perhaps the right moment to say that the artist has no religion except his art. Wilde compromised. 'I think it is horrible. "Blasphemous" is not a word of mine.'

And then came what all this was leading up to. 'I think you will admit that anyone who would approve of such an article would pose as guilty of improper practices?' Wilde was a little incoherent in reply but made clear that he objected to the story and fell back on the generalization, 'I do not believe that any book or work of art ever had any effect whatever on morality.'

'Am I right in saying that you do not consider the effect in creating morality or immorality?' – 'Certainly, I do not.'

'So far as your works are concerned, you pose as not being concerned about morality or immorality?' – 'I do not know whether you use the word pose in any particular sense.'

'It is a favourite word of your own.' – 'Is it? I have no pose in this matter. In writing a play or a book I am concerned entirely with literature – that is, with art. I aim not at doing good or evil, but at trying to make a thing that will have quality of beauty.'

Carson then proceeded to Wilde's own writings. He dealt in heavy-handed fashion with the light froth of the 'Phrases and Philosophies'. The harsh, cold-laden voice gave a grotesque emphasis to their frivolity.

'There is something tragic about the enormous number of young men there are in England at the present moment who start life with perfect profiles and end by adopting some useful profession?'

'I should think,' remarked the author, 'that the young have enough sense of humour.'

And from these epigrams they passed to the more serious matter of *Dorian Gray*, on which temper rose higher, for Wilde valued it and Carson disliked it more.

It was Carson's intention first to show that it had been necessary to expurgate the original text which had appeared in *Lippincott's Magazine* five years before. Wilde denied that the text had been modified. He had made additions. There was one instance in which Mr Walter Pater, 'the only critic of the century whose opinion I set high', had pointed out a passage liable to misconstruction and this he had altered.

Pater (who died of rheumatic fever in 1894, the year before the trial) seems to have thought highly of *Dorian Gray*. In 1891 when other critics were running the book down he had given it appreciation in *The Bookman*. 'His genial, laughter-loving sense of life and its enjoyable intercourse goes far to obviate any crudity there may be in the paradox . . .' 'Clever always, this book, however, seems intended to set forth anything but a homely philosophy of life for the middle class – a kind of dainty Epicurean theory, rather . . .'

Walter Pater had considerably altered his earlier views of life. He had in contradistinction to his pupil come more and more to prize asceticism and self-discipline.

If Oscar Wilde had been a prudent man he would have reflected long on the later life of his teacher. 'A vicarage Verlaine', Moore had called Pater. In the ambiguous nature of some of his utterances, there were those who had discerned an encouragement to licence. In his younger days he had created the impression of being a mild case of satanism. The message of the Renaissance had been 'Enjoy yourself'; and yet as time went on he adopted subtle, cautious yet none the less important, emendations to it. You became an artist by extracting sensation from life; by giving your own impression of the world; by saying what you had to say in the most direct and exact manner possible. But good art was not precisely the same as great art. Greatness came 'if it be devoted further to the increase of men's happiness, to the redemption of the oppressed ... or immediately as with Dante, to the glory of God.'

Less inclined than his pupil to be influenced by catchwords and fashions, Pater came back continually to the profound thought of Plato – to his conception of an invisible world of absolute beauty. The approach to this celestial condition must surely be through spiritual means; and thus Pater found an oblique justification of virtue – as an approach to this cleansed and final form of beauty. As the merit of a high church service was aesthetic – so there was aesthetic merit in a life whose restraints were in themselves a form of artistic expression. The strenuous task-work, the laborious, endless education of the ancient Spartan was pursued to the end that he himself might be a perfect work of art 'issuing thus into the eyes of all Greece'. You could be an ascetic as well as a rake for the sake of art. The only reason for being good was if you thought it was beautiful.

Wilde's Epicureanism was unsatisfactory to Pater. At the same time he emphasized the fact which others overlooked that *Dorian Gray* had 'a very plain moral, pushed home, to the effect that vice and crime make people coarse and ugly' – an aesthetic moral, but still a moral. There is indeed little, if anything, for the moralist to complain of in Dorian Gray. His sins are the merest abstraction. 'He who finds them has brought them,' said Wilde.

Carson was determined to see in them the author's own.

'This is in your introduction to *Dorian Gray*. "There is no such thing as a moral or immoral book? Books are well-written or badly-written." That expresses your view?' – 'My view on art, yes.'

'Then I take it, that no matter how immoral a book may be if it is well written, it is in your opinion a good book?' Wilde somewhat incautiously said 'Yes'. He might have objected that a good book could not be an immoral book, on the grounds that art for art's sake was superior to both morality and immorality. Instead of that he said 'Yes, if it were well written so as to produce a sense of beauty, which is the highest sense of which a human being can be capable.

If it were badly written it would produce a sense of disgust.'

It was a very difficult matter to explain in court. The delicacy and even the sharpness of distinction was lost. For example how was one to say that it all depended on the attitude of mind that the writer brought to the work, that the scrupulous observation of the novelist made it necessary for him to record without gloss or comment the nature of humanity in all its forms; that his morality consisted in being true to his imagination, in being bold enough to state what it prompted and apt enough to give it its most perfect form?

Still less was it possible to explain that official morality was hypocritical and cant-ridden, in its own temple to which one had come to seek redress.

'Then a well-written book putting forward perverted moral views might be a good book?' – 'No work of art ever puts forward views. Views belong to people who are not artists.'

'A perverted novel might be a good book?' Carson pressed. – 'I don't know what you mean by a "perverted" novel.'

'Then I will suggest *Dorian Gray* as open to the interpretation of being such a novel.'

Wilde was now really angry. He sprang to the defence of his creation. 'That could only be to brutes and illiterates. The views of Philistines on art are incalculably stupid.'

Personal antagonism was growing. The eminent barrister was stigmatized as a brute and an illiterate. Well, they would see. The next move was to show that Wilde was alone in this attitude: that the 'brutes and illiterates' represented society as a whole, a conclusion calculated to arouse indignation in those typical representatives of society, the twelve good men and true.

'An illiterate person reading *Dorian Gray* might consider it such a novel?' Again, with spirit came the answer, 'The views of illiterates on art are unaccountable. I am concerned only with my view of art. I don't care twopence what other people think of it.'

'The majority of persons would come under your definition of Philistines and illiterates?' – 'I have found wonderful exceptions.'

'Do you think that the majority of people live up to the position you are giving us?' – 'I am afraid they are not cultivated enough.'

'Not cultivated enough to draw the distinction between a good book and a bad book?' – 'Certainly not.'

The 'ordinary individual', that tender and virginal plant, was introduced into the examination at this point.

'The affection and love of the artist of *Dorian Gray* might lead an ordinary individual to believe that it might have a certain tendency?' asked Carson, using the ambiguous word 'certain' with sinister implication.

'I have no knowledge,' was the answer, 'of the views of ordinary individuals.'

So far Wilde had held his own. The enemy had tried various openings but made no serious inroad on his position. Nor did the following interchange in which Carson suggested that certain passages of *Dorian Gray*, which he read, were improper, have serious effect.

'I have adored you extravagantly,' quoted Carson.

'Do you mean financially?' mocked Wilde.

'Oh, yes, financially. Do you think we are talking about finance?' burst out the angry barrister.

'I don't know what you are talking about,' shrugged the witness.

Once more Wilde asserted that he was not concerned with the ignorance of those who might see something wrong in *Dorian Gray*. He admitted that he had been influenced by a French book called *A Rebours*, though he declined to be cross-examined upon the work of another artist. That, he said (with the respect for a *confrère* that Whistler had insisted on) would be 'an impertinence and a vulgarity'. Nor was the satanic masterpiece of Huysmans further called into question. Sir Edward Clarke succeeded, on an appeal to the judge, in stopping further reference to it.

But now there came a new phase of literary inquiry – a

letter which Wilde had written to Lord Alfred Douglas, a paraphrase of which had appeared in the form of a sonnet by the French poet Pierre Louÿs in another mushroom publication, *The Spirit Lamp,* 'an Aesthetic, Literary, and Critical Magazine'. It was, said Wilde, a 'prose-poem'. The prose-poem was much cultivated in France. Baudelaire had devoted great pains to its lapidary perfection. Huysmans' hero, Des Esseintes, considered it the supreme form of literary art. No doubt Wilde had had his French models in mind when writing this letter in a somewhat extravagant and artificial form. 'Your slim gilt soul walks between passion and poetry', etc., etc.

The 'prose-poem' did not represent Wilde's literary style at its best. Like most letters read in court it had a tawdry, even a ludicrous sound. Read by a forbidding-looking barrister with a bad cold and a Dublin brogue the effect was none the more poetical.

'I can suggest for the sake of your reputation that there is nothing very wonderful in this "red-rose-leaf lips of yours"?' – 'A great deal,' said Wilde, 'depends on the way it is read.'

'Your slim gilt soul walks between passion and poetry,' snuffled Carson. 'Is that a beautiful phrase?' – 'Not as you read it, Mr Carson. You read it very badly.'

Anger flared out. 'I do not profess to be an artist and when I hear you give evidence I am glad I am not.'

The case was now leaving aesthetic ground. It was shortly to be diverted from the level of prose poems, to take leave of that sphere in which it seemed the main questions were debatable points of taste in literature, to sink to a quicksand underworld in which the scene and the personalities except for the entangled figure of Wilde himself were entirely changed. Questions were asked about a person 'of no occupation' but 'seeking a post as a clerk' and also a passage to America, who it was implied had attempted to blackmail Wilde; about the associates of his blackmailer. It appeared that the acquaintanceship of Wilde with young men outside his own social sphere was really in question, a publisher's 'office boy', a newspaper seller at Worthing.

The defence had not been inactive. The heavy, legal foot of ex-Inspector Littlechild had plodded persistently on the trail. Many facts had been stored up to be sprung in due time as a series of bombshells. There was a definite new trend in the affair – a hum of surprise and attention in court, but Wilde's answers were still in a light vein.

'He sold newspapers at the kiosque on the pier?' – 'It is the first I have heard of his connexion with literature.'

'What was he?' – 'He led a happy idle life.'

'Was his conversation literary?' – 'On the contrary quite simple and easily understood. He had been to school, where naturally he had not learned much.'

Wilde had given this seaside Ganymede an inscribed cigarette-case, a copy of *The Wreck of the Grosvenor*, a silver-mounted crook-handled grape-vine stick, had fitted him out with a suit of blue serge and a straw hat with a band of red and blue ('That I think was his unfortunate selection'); had taken him to the Albion Hotel in Brighton.

It was on this note and with the prospect of further revelations to come that the first day of the trial ended.

3

From the beginning the case had not lacked interest. The first day roused interest to excitement. There was a feeling that something important was happening. The excitement was coupled with a rising anger. Had the artist a right to the position beyond that of other men? beyond good or evil? Should books be written and the claim made for them that they were works of art when they were immoral in tone and suggestion? Was the famed aesthetic movement a cover for personal licence – or even an incitation to it? So all the problems implied in the phrase 'art for art's sake' came forward in a manner that could not be denied attention; and the instinctive answer to the first two questions was No; the instinctive feeling that the aesthetic movement was self-condemned.

There were those who looked forward with an unpleasant

delight to scabrous detail. There were those who took a sporting view of the 'duel of wits', who followed and applauded the verbal thrust and parry – but in sum the phenomenon of public attention was much more terrible than either – the 'periodical fit of morality' was rising to a frenzy.

An analysis of this frenzy would reveal many different motives – the horror of the Victorian paterfamilias, bull of a jealously protected herd, whose purple cheeks puffed apoplectically as he sensed an additional threat to the many threats which surrounded the sanctity of home life; the alarm of sinners who felt that they themselves might be dragged into an unwelcome prominence; the agony of snobs, anxious to disown the acquaintance they had courted; the economic jealousy of demi-mondaines and street walkers; the hypocritical concern of those who thought it all so sad and thereby made it doubly sordid, the triumph of those who hated art and could not forgive genius; the mean cruelty of those who could not bear others' success and rejoiced to see its abasement. These certainly were elements in the now rapidly growing enmity to Wilde. And more frightful still was the apparent stirring of a primeval human lust for sacrifice. Apart from and more important than the pathological details of Wilde's case was the century's own problem of repression. The primitive instinct was to solve it, as other general problems of humanity have been solved, by a martyrdom and on Wilde devolved the role of martyr. The tabu had been broken and the superstitious rites which ensued were unrelenting.

On the second day, Thursday, 4th April, 1895, it became clear that, in fact, though not yet in formality, Oscar Wilde and not the Marquess of Queensberry was on trial. The aesthetic issue also had disappeared. It was no longer possible to answer epigrammatically on matters of Culture. The cross-examination was on a different, a lower plane. The miserable reality of those delusive visions of joyous classical youth, of carefree beauty became evident in a further citation of the writer's young friends. They appear before the mind as a series of Phil May drawings, with pale sharp features and small crafty eyes, old in the knowledge of the city's under-world, the inevitable product of the city's slums. It was a damning point to that class-conscious period apart from any other circumstances that a man like Wilde should have so far ignored the barriers of caste.

'Did you know that Parker' (one of the two brothers introduced to Wilde by Taylor) 'was a gentleman's valet and the other a groom?' asked Carson. – 'I did not know it but if I had I should not have cared. I didn't care twopence what they were. I liked them. I have a passion to civilize the community.'

'Was there plenty of champagne?' (referring to a dinner at Kettner's) – 'Well, I did not press wine upon them.'

'You did not stint them?' – 'What gentleman would stint his guests?'

'What gentleman', came the sneer, 'would stint the valet and the groom?'

It was a dreary business, this monotonous series of questions about names and places. Wilde seemed depressed and bored. He muttered some of his answers with an impatient exclamation. It was the mood for which counsel waits, ready to spring on the unguarded admission which loss of patience might produce. Carson was alert.

He asked Wilde if he had ever shown affection for a servant in Oxford.

Impatiently and with his characteristic desire for effect, Wilde answered: 'Oh dear no. He was a peculiarly plain boy. He was, unfortunately, extremely ugly.'

Carson pounced. It was precisely the admission he had wanted. Why did Wilde mention his ugliness?

'I do not know why I mentioned that he was ugly, except that I was stung by the insolent question you put to me and the way you have insulted me throughout this hearing.'

But still the sharp, staccato question was repeated time and time again.

In the further course of the trial, it became obvious to all that the case was lost. Carson's speech for the defence, begun on Thursday and continued on Friday, the last day of the trial, deadly in itself, was alarming to all in its proposal 'to bring before the jury the young men one after the other, who had been in the hands of Mr Wilde, to tell their unhappy tales.' It was, he said, 'even for an advocate, a very distasteful task'. He was warming to the work, nevertheless, when Sir Edward Clarke threw up the sponge. The withdrawal of the prosecution not only absolved Lord Queensberry but, as it involved the proof of justification, left open the way to further proceedings against Wilde. The Marquess's thoroughness ensured that everything possible was done to set these in motion. The Director of Public Prosecutions at once received from Queensberry's solicitor a copy of all the papers in the case. Two detectives, employed by the Marquess, lounged in Sloane Street opposite the Cadogan Hotel, whither Wilde drove off and where he conferred with Lord Alfred Douglas and his brother. On the information laid before the Home Secretary, Mr H. H. Asquith gave instructions for Wilde's arrest.

If the trial be considered, apart from all personal matters, as an aesthetic issue, it would seem that he had failed miserably. As a result of it the public was convinced that Wilde's books were immoral; that if he was a genius he was an evil genius. They were confirmed in their belief that a book should inculcate moral sentiments and that the best authors were the most respectable.

It could have been pointed out that his books were entirely free from obscenity; that no word he used was indecent in itself; and that whatever innuendo might be found in his writings could only be apparent to those whom it was beyond their power to harm. It could have been emphasized as Pater had quietly said that *Dorian Gray*, apart from the beauty of its style, was a most moral production – that it might, if one wished, be construed as a warning against indulgence rather than an encouragement to it. It could have been said that to take a few laughing phrases and heavily appraise them in a court of law, as if they had been intended for anything beyond a play of words, was to show a deplorable absence of humour.

But this emphasis was not given. Nor would it have

conveyed the true inwardness of the case if it had been. To say that Wilde's art conformed, in spite of suggestions to the contrary, to the standard of propriety demanded by the middle class would have been to give away all the principles he had upheld. As well might Baudelaire have maintained the improving nature of the *Fleurs du Mal*. Wilde claimed, implicitly, moreover, not only the artist's right to say what he liked, but also his right to go his own way in living. Not only had he transgressed, in fact, against the moral regulations laid down, but he did not believe in those regulations. If he had really spoken out in court it would no doubt have been to this effect; but, as he had claimed the protection of the law, he realized only too acutely that he could not say he disowned its standards; and thus he was only half-hearted in defence and in a position that was false from any standpoint.

The second act of the drama was now about to begin – the trial of Wilde himself – though it was taken for granted that he was 'damned and done for'. The populace booed. The prostitutes danced in wild delight outside the Old Bailey. The sale of the books, the vogue of the plays was at an end. The Press, then much more malicious and personal than it is at the present day – reflecting accurately the period of spitefulness – was without mercy. 'He appears to have illustrated in his life the beauty and truthfulness of his teachings ... The best thing for everybody now is to forget about Oscar Wilde, his perpetual posings, his aesthetical teachings, and his theatrical productions. If not tried himself, let him go into silence and be heard of no more.' Thus, *The Echo*, the London evening paper, in a leading article on the day of Wilde's arrest.

It was assumed, and for various reasons hoped, that he would go into silence. The way was open. In a few hours he could have been across the Channel. It was not until the last boat train of the day had left the London terminus and at about half-past six in the evening that Detective Inspector Richards and Detective Sergeant Allan came to the Cadogan Hotel with a warrant for his arrest.

Why he did not go, why he remained in the hotel drinking hock and seltzer, smoking endless cigarettes, turning over and casting aside newspapers full of reviling is a question of considerable interest.

Was it a display of that courage, even though of a passive kind, in which he had never been lacking, a determination to see the thing out? Or was it that paralysis of the powers of will and action, which after a great shock renders the victim incapable of movement and decision? It seemed as if there was an undeclared necessity in it – as if it was inevitable that, willingly or not, he should complete the symbolic ritual of an outlawry – final and more appalling than any of those previous outlawries which had so far marked the progress of the aesthetic movement.

With a sort of relief he put on his overcoat, took up his hat and gloves and went off, with the officers, in a four-wheeled cab to Scotland Yard.

The record of the subsequent proceedings; of the first trial at which the jury disagreed; of Wilde's release on bail; of the second trial, at which, together with Taylor, he was found guilty and sentenced, covers a period of nearly two months. The details are dismal. The sparkle of epigram would now have been woefully out of place, nor was there any such sparkle. The reiteration of evidence, the accumulation of petty and squalid backstairs detail, was tedious. Being so, it made each day appear interminable and thereby extracted from it a refinement of torture. There was none of that breathless interest which attached to Carson's brutal master-piece of cross-examination – which made the observer feel as if he were watching some clumsy but savagely powerful hunting dog bounding on the trail of a hare, nimbly twisting and turning but ever losing ground. The effect of Carson's effort was still potent: but his successors in the prosecution were not of the same calibre. Sir Edward Clarke had gener-ously continued to act for Wilde, in spite of his knowing full well that he could derive no personal advantage from it of any kind, and his humane defence is one of the few attractive features of the case; but he was unable to dispel the grimy and depressing cloud which overhung it.

It is in the fact of being an aesthetic martyrdom that the proceedings concern this narrative and some salient features require to be noticed. First, is the insistence of the law on the unpardonable iniquity of Wilde. 'With regard to the gravity of the case, I think there is no worse crime than that with which the prisoners are charged.' This is the statement made by Sir John Bridge, at Bow Street, when committing Wilde and Taylor for trial. As a superlative, it demands a test.

No doubt then, as the worst of crimes, it had always been punishable by a vigorous sentence. But in fact it had not. Wilde's offence had only figured in the statute book since the Criminal Law Amendment Act of 1885, when on the motion of Mr Labouchere an amendment had been inserted, making it punishable by one year's imprisonment with or without hard labour. A further amendment, to extend the period of imprisonment to two years, raised no objection and was added to the Bill. It might reasonably be said therefore that the 'worst of crimes' was only recognized as an afterthought in a comparatively recent piece of legislation.

But the same emphatic language was used by Mr Justice Wills in the final trial. Sir Edward Wills, who was at some pains, though with little relevancy, to explain to the jury that he had not had a university education, said that the case was a most difficult one. He would rather try the most shocking murder case that it had ever fallen to his lot to try than be engaged in a case of this description. This statement is also interesting enough to require analysis. Was it the fact that then a good clean murder was on the whole preferable, because it was less harrowing to legal emotions? Was a utilitarian crime preferable because its motions were more intelligible? Was it less reprehensible to have poisoned one's aunt for her money than to have entertained a Fred Atkins at the Savoy? In that case it would seem that the sentences should be reversed – that the judge should condemn the paederast to death and the poisoner to two years in gaol (with or without hard labour). Perhaps that was Mr Justice

Wills's view. 'It is the worst case I have ever tried.' The severest sentence that the law allows 'in my judgement ... is totally inadequate for such a case as this.' Allowing for the repulsion that the normal person feels towards unnatural behaviour, there is a strain of superstitious hysteria in this pronouncement. There was also an ambiguousness in the judge's statement that Wilde had 'been the centre of a circle of extensive corruption of the most hideous kind among young men'. Wilde might with some truth have claimed to have been the victim of young men, already corrupted after a different fashion by a hideous commercial organization against which the law provided no sanction. The only count in the indictment by which the corruption of youth could have been maintained was that concerning the somewhat weak-minded publisher's assistant; and on this count the jury declared him Not Guilty.

The unique importance given to Wilde's misdemeanour by judicial horror was further emphasized by carefully excluding any suggestion that there might be others who had offended likewise. Names were written down on pieces of paper. Witnesses about to blurt out a name were sharply headed off. References to 'the Birmingham gentleman', the 'two American gentlemen', the 'elderly man in the city', the 'foreign nobleman', all of whom had been lured by their regrettable whims into the thieves' kitchen of vice, remained vague. The total effect was that Wilde appeared to stand alone, as a Nero, and to those who did not distinguish overmuch in the evidence even as a species of Fagin.

The interval between the two trials when Wilde was released on bail saw torture intensified. Stirred by the unrestrained abuse of the Press, the tide of morality had taken on an ugly violence. Every door was closed to him. No hotel would receive him. Gangs of roughs pursued him. With a face flaccid and grey, panting and dishevelled, he came at last to his brother's rooms with a despairing request for shelter.

That even now there was the possibility of getting away; that melodramatically Frank Harris urged him to go; that a swift conveyance was waiting, a yacht with steam up lay ready at Erith; all this is on record. Let him lie low for a while and it would all blow over. The possibility of escape was a dreadful agony in itself – the hope it stimulated, so painful that he could not or would not face it. He went back to hear himself condemned – and to leave the dock as a convict.

Once more the street women danced their wild carmagnole, the roughs jeered. 'Down with the aristocrats' was the cry. Moral indignation became dreadfully like an orgy. No circumstance was lacking to make punishment comprehensive. Wilde's income had been derived from the profits of his books and plays and now these were at an end and he was destitute. His books were withdrawn from circulation. The comedies which had been having long runs were taken off. *An Ideal Husband* at the Haymarket quickly succumbed. *The Importance of Being Earnest* at the St James's Theatre dragged on into May, although the name of the author was removed from the bills and programmes. Then that too was withdrawn. Handcuffed, between two policemen, Wilde was conveyed from one place of misery – the prison, to another – the Bankruptcy Court.

The house in Tite Street was plundered. In this respect though with greater indignity the result was like that of the Ruskin-Whistler trial. The artist, who had been rash enough to try conclusions with society was sold up. An inquisitive, careless rabble tramped through the rooms, and there was scarcely an appearance of order about the sale. Yet again, a collection of 'blue and white' was dispersed. Whistlers went for a pound or two. Letters and manuscripts disappeared without trace. In this way the Philistines took a disgraceful advantage of their enemy's fall. Like the medieval townsfolk of Pater's story they would have plucked this Dionysus of the vine and the reed limb from limb, if they had been able. Once more, and this time in a quite macabre fashion, nature crept up to art. Dionysus himself was incarcerated at Reading Gaol. It was almost the same as if he were already dead.

## V

# THE AFTERMATH

I

## The End of the End of the Century

THE *Yellow Book* too was dead (or dying). The whole period was dead and those who had most represented it were required as scapegoats before the moral balance of society could be restored. Aubrey Beardsley was one of them – a fact which he bitterly resented. It was taken for granted in this little café-world of the nineties, where Christian names were so freely bandied, where everyone seemed to be on such familiar terms, that Beardsley and Wilde were the closest intimates and that Beardsley therefore also must be boycotted. It was an ironical assumption. Their relation was no more than that friendly hatred so typical of the time. Beardsley had not liked Wilde. He thought him condescending: Wilde seemed to take it for granted that *Salomé* had created its illustrator, whereas his illustrator considered the reverse to be true. 'Dear Aubrey, he knows France so well – he has been to Dieppe, once.' This was wounding to the vanity of a young man, especially one who considered himself at least as well versed in French literature as the author of the remark. Nor was Beardsley in any sympathy with Wilde's weaknesses, with which despite the erotic cynicism of his own drawings he hated to be linked. Whether it was the poet William Watson or the novelist Mrs Humphry Ward who urged on the boycott the fact remains that Beardsley contributed to the *Yellow Book* no more.

The period however was not to die without a struggle. Beardsley, aged twenty-three, grappling with a severe return of his disease, in difficulties now that his main source of income was removed, found a new lease of life in the proposal to start another magazine. The proposal came from a remarkable man, Leonard Smithers.

He was a pale-faced, fair-haired man with a thick-set elegance and, according to a journal of the time, 'singularly clear-cut aristocratic features'. In his personality there appears a compound of the homely and the fantastic. He had been a solicitor in the West Riding of Yorkshire. He had set up in London as a second-hand bookseller and had added to this the function of publisher. A true creature of the decadence, he loved luxury and revelled in the unexpurgated. He handled no useful or edifying books, but only those of a dubious or imaginative kind and from the little shop he swiftly rose to palatial offices, a house in town and country.

His emissary was Arthur Symons. Symons was one of the young leaders of the aesthetic movement. A Cornishman, born in Wales, he prided himself on not being Anglo-Saxon. From Pater, at Brasenose, he had first learned of beauty; and long periods spent in France had made the French outlook habitual to him. He revered Verlaine and Mallarmé and was chief among the group which induced Verlaine to leave his hospital for a while and lecture in Oxford and London. He experienced an anxious triumph in the presence of the monster of genius in his rooms in Fountain Court, where Verlaine consumed a great deal of gin and poured out 'the confessions of a lifetime'.

Symons found Beardsley 'horribly white'. He wondered if he had come too late; but the message was tonic in itself. A name for the new magazine came instantly. *The Savoy*. At once Beardsley began a new series of drawings – and his best drawings. They reflected, as in the illustrations to Pope's *Rape of the Lock*, his deep attachment to the artificial eighteenth century, to that book which was the inspiration of so much 'decadence', *Mademoiselle de Maupin*.

Yet his was now a life in death, an emotional history, terrible but without sentimentality or pathos. Beardsley was now triply excluded from his world: by the devouring progress of consumption; by the deliberate forgetfulness of the public, which erased him from mind along with Oscar Wilde; and by the intense egoism with which he shut himself off from interest in the life around him and in dreams borrowed from art.

The erotic romance he now wrote (for it was his ambition to excel in writing also) called *Under the Hill* shows how little, in spite of his repugnance for Wilde, he had lost that strange intimacy with and appreciation of vice fantastically projected and personified in his drawings. In its monstrous conceits of attire, 'fans of big living moths', 'masks of coloured glass', 'wigs of black and scarlet wools'; its description of exquisite lechers and unearthly fops, its stilted and precious language, *Under the Hill* echoes the drawn designs.

This erotic purgatory stood in some undefined relation to religion. It was now that Beardsley came much under the influence of the poet-priest John Gray who gradually influenced him in the direction of Roman Catholicism. Having invented a hell it was necessary that he should seek for a heaven. The spirit in revolt, questing after a tortured fashion for new and transcendent pleasures, and discovering at last with inexorable certainty that they were impossible to find or did not exist, was the more inclined to obey at last. It was said of Huysmans that after writing such a book as *A Rebours*, having explored every sensation, and dared every ban, the author could choose only between a revolver bullet or the feet of the cross. Huysmans chose the latter alternative. Oscar Wilde was impelled irresistibly along the same path. So, too, in terror, yet driven nevertheless to run to the end of the gamut of sensation was Beardsley.

He lived with a continuous intensity. The story goes that he produced one day from that black satchel which gave him, it was said, the look of 'a man from the Prudential', the elegant and masterly designs with which he had illustrated *The Rape of the Lock* for the inspection of Whistler. Scornfully, the Butterfly began to look, then with increasing attention. He said at last 'Aubrey, I have made a mistake. You are a great artist,' whereupon Beardsley to Whistler's discomfort, for sentiment was alien to his genius, burst into tears.

What to make of these tears one scarcely knows. They indicated perhaps a gratified vanity, out of nervous control, and an acute realization of the doom hanging over his head, a movement of pity for those other drawings he would not live to carry out.

Tuberculosis was gaining on him and although he asserted that he could not work except in London, the hope that attaches to a change of climate took him to the Continent, to Dieppe first and eventually to the South of France. The short and functional letters he wrote home to Smithers were concerned mainly, apart from money matters, with the description of his bouts of illness.

Smithers kept him going. The seeming prosperity of the town and country house, the palatial offices did not give an accurate impression of his means. He was often in straits himself; but he showed himself dependable. To the end he continued without demur to give the support he had pledged. It was to him that that famous final letter of Beardsley, the letter of the erring repentant, was addressed.

Menton.

Jesus is our Lord and Judge
I implore you to destroy all copies of Lysistrata and bad drawings . . .
By all that is holy all obscene drawings

AUBREY BEARDSLEY
– In my death agony.

It was 1898 and he was then twenty-five.

## The Difficulty of Being Earnest

In what way could the artist, after the awful interlude of two years oakum picking in a 'model' prison, resume his life and his work? And if he did resume his work, what form was that to take?

That was the difficult question which confronted Oscar Wilde when in May 1897 the gates of Reading Gaol opened and thrust him back into the freedom of an unfriendly world.

A Verlaine would not have found it so difficult. Impervious to anything that society could do he would have restored his niche, cunningly played the cynical child and the misunderstood saint, as it suited him, have continued to write poetry and collect disciples on whom he would impose in some remarkable way a veneration equally for his stoic behaviour and his matchless rhythms. It was remarkable, indeed, that Verlaine himself had contrived to control his prestige, to give as it were his own valuation of the various untoward events that had happened to him in the course of his life so that people spoke laughingly and almost affectionately of his outrageous escapades, condoned his prisons and found in his hideous aspect and physical decay the venerable outward signs of one detached and wise beyond the wisdom of ordinary men. His vices had become not glamorous but abstract, the legendary foundations of a philosophic attitude which caused him to be compared, as a figure, with Socrates. But Wilde, for several reasons, was unable to achieve a status of this kind. He was not able to take a philosophical view of his own past or to set it in any tolerable relation with his whole existence. His capacity for defiance was much smaller than that of Verlaine. The bleak reality of the trial and the brick fortress into which he had been flung remained a bleak reality and towered uglier and more monstrous after his release than they did before. His art, reviving, might have dispelled that cold and withering shadow, lessened it gradually as a new succession of brilliant works came forth. Instead, it pined and the shadow grew larger and more withering.

He was a man of society – that is to say of a frivolous and wealthy circle. He required its praise. Cut away from it, he lacked the very substance of his inspiration. He was not adapted to a shabby and penurious life – only to luxury and success. He was, unlike Verlaine, haunted by respectable feelings which in themselves exaggerated his misery. Almost he adopted the pose of the society that was hostile to him as he had once adopted the pose of Whistler, made an attitude of conscience and condemned himself.

Sebastian Melmoth was the name which he chose to assume. Could any in itself have been more subtly grotesque and appropriately unsuitable? Taken from the novel of one of his own distant ancestors (Charles Robert Maturin) it suggested in some odd way and perpetuated that figure of a gross, dandiacal *roué* which he appeared in the eyes of Britain. Rehabilitation might have been more effectively sought under the guise of Smith or Brown.

A Marxian observer of the nineties would note the narrow boundaries of art for art's sake – the artist's complete absorption in his own sensations, his lack of interest in humanity, his artificially confined subjects, the poverty of matter underlying the parade of gorgeous epithets and exotic images. This also was one of Wilde's new difficulties. The artificiality of his earlier writing seemed inappropriate to his present condition. 'Why don't you write a play?' asked his friend, the French writer André Gide, who had watched his career with interest and concern. Mournfully Wilde answered that he was incapable of it. How could he write a gay comedy about the kind of people who had crushed him?

Yet he could not undertake a literary conversion. He was aware of the new note in European literature outside France, the literature that was not aesthetic but was concerned with views and problems, the plays of the Norwegian Ibsen, the novels of the Russians. He could not write like this. At present, he said, all thought had retreated to Norway and Russia, where the sun never shines. For himself he preferred the sun.

It is true that the idea of redemption was at first strong in him. He admitted in the Russians the great quality of pity; and he criticized in Gustave Flaubert's *Madame Bovary* the absence of that quality. He said of himself that he had gone into prison with a heart of stone, thinking only of pleasure, but afterwards, his heart being broken, pity had entered into it.

In June 1897 he wrote, in thanking Will Rothenstein for words of encouragement and offers to help, an account of what he thought to be the change in him. He was ashamed, he said, not so much of having been in prison as of having led a life unworthy of the artist. 'I know simply that a life of definite and studied materialism and philosophy of cynicism and a cult of sensual and senseless ease are bad things for an artist. They narrow the imagination and dull the more delicate sensibilities.' With isolation for thought and freedom from the hunger for pleasure he imagined he could still write better than ever. But it was less a statement than a speculation. How could he genuinely deny the material world which so definitely existed for him, the gay philosophy which was so indispensable to the exercise of his delightful humour? Penitence itself was disappointing though it was in this mood of tentative sincerity and love for mankind, of theoretical self-discipline that he wrote *The Ballad of Reading Gaol* and *De Profundis*.

The little classic ballad was published by Smithers. No one else would issue the work of the discredited man. Originally it appeared without the name of the author. In the seventh edition the name crept on the title-page in brackets. But it was the last important thing he did. In the three years of life that remained to him after prison, spent at Dieppe, at Naples and finally in Paris, he was increasingly without purpose or direction. Fastidiously he refused to write in the French periodicals which made him tempting offers because of his notoriety. Desperately he tried to behave as the literary master in the manner of Verlaine. His talk was as sparkling as ever and he would often fascinate his audience by some fable or improvised story which he told with almost a pathetic earnestness as if to convince both himself and his hearers that he still deserved the respect due to the lord of language. But always there hovered at hand that withering shadow, disconcerting and silencing him, turning the admiration of his loyal supporters into a pained compassion. There were former friends who cut him dead. These even included Aubrey Beardsley, savage at an association which seemed to entangle him in an aura of viciousness which he strongly resented. 'It was *lâche* of Aubrey – a boy I made,' said Wilde. There were middle-class strangers who rose in public places when he came in and left with expressions of stony disapproval. There were restaurants which refused to entertain him because someone had complained of his presence. A constant awareness of being still watched and persecuted poisoned brief intervals that might have been happy and brought back with all its vividness the agony he had undergone.

Laurence Housman has described such an occasion: how in 1899 he and Robert Ross waited at a café on the boulevard des Italiens, to entertain their friend to lunch, to surprise him with the presence of another friend whom he had not seen for 'three disintegrated years'; how at once they came under the spell of Wilde's conversation, listened, losing sense of time, to one of his stories, told with a strange undercurrent of passion, found, then, that meanwhile the friend they awaited had been in, seen Wilde, and left promptly. The savour had gone from the meeting. Wilde excused himself and left them.

In such circumstances he had not disciples but sympathizers, who as often as they tried to admire the writer found themselves diverted to pity for the outcast. This was a sentence of death from which, with too great a submissiveness and too little rancour, he made no appeal. When he was dying in 1900 ('beyond my means' as he characteristically remarked) he was still capable of a humorous view of his extraordinary predicament. 'If I were to survive into the twentieth century it would be more than the English people can bear.'

And even death could not bring forgiveness or redress the balance between a misdemeanour committed in life and what he had permanently contributed to literature. Hatred followed him beyond the grave, preserved the *éclat* of his disgrace and obscured the memory of his works. Many years had to pass before his plays could be revived. Even now there is a prejudice against him though not quite on the original grounds. In our highly political and strongly sociological period the absence of serious purpose and, still more, the implicit mockery of being serious does not commend itself. To be epigrammatic is an error of taste and wit is out of date.

But Wilde's career remains an extraordinary symbolic martyrdom. He said he had put his genius into his life and only his talent into his writings. This is usually taken to mean, and no doubt he himself so intended it, that his conversation was better than his books. Whether it was, in fact, is questionable. There is the same cleverness in both. Yet he did put his genius into his life by giving it a sacrificial pattern and completing the aesthetic movement with its greatest sensation. By that, something ultimately was gained. The rational and scientific discussion of the 'unmentionable' followed gradually but inevitably after the notorious trial, to the benefit of morality it may be thought rather than otherwise.

## 3

## A Reformed Character

THROUGH the lace curtains draping the windows of a hideous, semi-detached Victorian house in Putney there often peered a big, pale, anxious face with a heavy moustache drooping about the mouth. It remained here until, from the direction of the High Street, there came into view a small figure flitting along with quick bird-like steps. The face looked relieved, disappeared and, shortly after, the small figure, that of an old man though with a curiously childlike air and an appearance of glowing and perfect health, opened the door of the house and went in.

The face belonged to Theodore Watts-Dunton, the critic. The house, No. 2, The Pines, was his. The small figure was that of Algernon Charles Swinburne who lived with Watts-Dunton, and the walk along Putney Hill, across the Heath and back, was a regular part of his strictly controlled and disciplined life.

When Wilde died in 1900, Swinburne, then sixty-three years of age, with nine more years to live, had already spent twenty-one in virtual imprisonment. Since that day in 1879 when Watts, at the appeal of Lady Jane Swinburne, had taken a strong hand and haled off the poet (then far gone under the influence of alcohol) to stay at Putney, he had lived a life entirely at variance with what his poetry implied.

There is a curious parallel between this prolonged and celebrated durance and that of Wilde. Just as surely, though by slower degrees and without the grim panoply of crime and punishment, the vital spark in Swinburne was crushed, the massive power of middle-class society was exerted and the defiant artist was condemned to respectability. 'Watts is a solicitor,' Wilde himself had remarked, 'and the business of a solicitor is to conceal crime. Swinburne's genius has been killed and Watts is doing his best to conceal it.'

Yet Theodore Watts-Dunton was a good, a serious, and

well-meaning man. A solicitor and the son of a solicitor, he had come from a home in St Ives, Huntingdonshire, which was impregnated with the hopeful Victorian theory of evolution. To set things in order, to make people better, to record a continued improvement, this was his conception of life. Literature and Art fitted into this conception but like rich estates which had been allowed to sink into a neglected wilderness, offering scope for a conscientious steward who would clear the undergrowth in the plantations, dismiss the parasitic servants, recall titled owners to a sense of duty, pore over accounts, and present, at the end of each year, a satisfactory and increasing balance on the right side. It was in this spirit that he had become the friend of Rossetti and Swinburne. In both he respected the presence of those two meritorious abstractions Literature and Art. They were heirs to wonderful estates – yet how sadly neglected, how much there was to do for each. His interest grew as he reckoned up the possibilities of canalizing genius, by shutting off those side channels through which it ran to waste, by excluding those unfortunate acquaintanceships which led it astray, and being able to point not only to an increased but to a healthy and systematic output, benefiting mankind by its trim irrigation much more than by its previously undisciplined outpouring.

It was, thus, natural that he should make Swinburne his special care. Rossetti was a problem even to him. He had a circle of friends, too large to be eliminated without great difficulty; and he was not an easy subject for the exercise of control, being masterful even when he was very ill. On the other hand Swinburne was easily influenced. He was like a child, trustful and confiding. He was lonely, except for undesirable boon companions such as Charles Augustus Howell. He was a genius running to waste, drinking brandy in most harmful quantities. A perfect case for reclamation.

It meant that you had to devote your life to this beneficent labour; but Watts-Dunton did not mind that. It was the sort of occupation he wanted. After all he was a writer, too, a critic of poetry, and, although he did not presume to compete with the great ones, a poet. Would he not benefit by constant association with a man destined for immortality and transfer, by its means, some needed element to his own writing?

He set to work methodically. The first thing was to restore Swinburne to physical health. To do that it was necessary to stop him drinking, and to set up a steady routine of rest and exercise. From the sanctuary of The Pines with Swinburne under his own eye Watts-Dunton was confident that he could keep away such bad influences as Howell – in fact this he very effectively did. He proceeded next to cut off alcohol by slow and steady degrees. He spoke slightingly of brandy, praised port as the true poet's drink. They drank port. Then he cooled towards port, and praised burgundy as the drink of Swinburne's beloved France. They drank burgundy. From burgundy they went on by the same process of suggestion to claret and finally to the 'wine of the country'. 'Shakespeare's brown October, our own glorious and incomparable British beer', as Watts-Dunton lyrically described the bottled ale to which at length he reduced his charge.

The little poet began to recover. His recovery was helped by regular walks across the neighbouring heath and common. The walks became a settled habit. He seemed to have lost his craving for excess and though his frailty was constitutional his eyes became clear, his countenance took on the tones of health. The experiment so far had been a success.

Time went by. Almost, in this placid round, it ceased to exist. Yet it was fully occupied. There were books in plenty. There were poems and articles to be written. Occasional, carefully chosen, strictly supervised, visitors lent interest to the periods of relaxation, and in the evenings Swinburne was able to give free rein to his passion for reading aloud. Watts-Dunton found no boredom in these readings; and even had he been bored his pride in maintaining the interest of Swinburne, of keeping him so harmlessly engaged would have prevented him from admitting it.

But in the kindness of Watts-Dunton there was a not precisely sinister, but terrifying element. His affection and care were devouring. No smallest detail that concerned Swinburne escaped his notice. When a guest came he would watch anxiously while Swinburne talked, as if he were constantly taking his mental temperature, and when signs of excitement began to appear he would implore the visitor to say no more but to leave it to him to induce the poet to lie down and sleep. Swinburne was capable of excitement on subjects which to others might appear merely academic and these were black-listed. 'We don't mention Hazlitt here,' Watts-Dunton would whisper. 'Neither I nor Swinburne care to talk about him on account of his abominable treatment of Coleridge.'

Occasionally Swinburne would mutiny against the unremitting tenderness, the implacable care of his guardian, or would display signs at least of finding it oppressive. There were times when the guardian, launched upon his favourite subject of discussion, the gipsies and George Borrow (whom Watts-Dunton had positively seen one day in his youth, swimming in the sea at Yarmouth), would render Swinburne almost lifeless with ennui; when another of many references to the critic's article on 'The Renascence of Wonder' would seem more than he could tolerate; when he objected to being told to go to bed or change his wet things; but never did mutiny become serious. The poet of freedom was in complete subjection. His sentence at The Pines was a life sentence.

Anger and amusement were aroused in the outside world. Those were angry who felt that Swinburne was made ridiculous and that to prevent a poet from living as he pleased, no matter what the conditions, was to tamper with his destiny and thwart his natural fulfilment.

Edmund Gosse, the biographer of Swinburne, was very cold in his references to Watts-Dunton. A. C. Benson, in his essay on The Pines, allowed a certain distaste to penetrate through his essayist's urbanity. Looking on that kindly visage, he found an adjective of repulsion. A 'clotted' moustache. That was how he described the hairy fringe that drooped over Watts-Dunton's lip. It was an offensive word in its suggestion of an unhygienic tangle. It helped to build up the essayist's picture of a domestic ogre. On the other hand Max Beerbohm, inspired to write a small gem of description, found exquisite subtleties of humour in the relation; and if the essence of humour exists in the incongruous then at The Pines there was humour and to spare. The tiny genius and the anxious, mothering presence. The stuffy villa and the world of ideal beauty of which its lodger had dreamed. Liberty and propriety. These were the opposites and irreconcilables which, brought together, formed the substance of one of the great comic legends of English letters.

The patience with which Watts-Dunton restored Swinburne to physical health was applied equally to his opinions. The error of his early life having been pointed out it was necessary to indicate and correct the errors of his early works and by degrees to turn him into a man of principle. Watts-Dunton was careful to explain the harmfulness of ill-advised words, the difficulty of suppressing them when printed. They were like some poisonous growth, he said, which, cut down, root and branch, still lived and even gained a fresh vitality from suppression. The simile made a deep impression. It seemed at length to Swinburne that certain of his earlier poems had been of this kind and he was only restrained from suppressing them by the fear of directing fresh interest towards them. He began to deplore his outbursts against Christianity. The rebel, republican, and internationalist merged into the moral patriot, conservative and insular.

Like the very genius of Respectability, Watts-Dunton presided over this transformation anxiously, putting in every now and then a word, with an almost diabolical skill, that would sink into the poet's mind and infect him with the critic's attitude to life.

There was Whistler for instance whom Watts-Dunton disliked, with whom Swinburne had so long been friendly. 'A bit of a charlatan,' breathed Watts-Dunton. Would not Algernon write something to counterbalance the painter's impertinent intrusion into literature? Algernon was persuaded. He wrote, impetuously and wordily, his attack on art for art's sake, on the art of Japan and the 'fortuitous fripperies of Fusi-Yama'. He protested against the idea he himself had once held that the appreciation of art was limited to the few. The article was friendly to Whistler himself but ironic enough about those things he liked to cause the breach Watts-Dunton desired. Whistler answered, with brief sarcasms, and with a kind of regret which was not entirely due to his sense of dramatic effect. 'Have I shot down the singer in the far off when I thought him safe at my side?' 'Cannot the man who wrote Atalanta ... be content to spend his life with his work which should be his love ... that he should stray about blindly in his brother's flower beds and bruise himself?' Then this mood, in which Whistler metaphorically brushed a manly tear from the eye, passed, hatred reasserted itself. 'I have lost a *confrère* and gained an acquaintance, one Algernon Charles Swinburne, outsider, Putney.'

It was very convincing to hear Watts-Dunton lauding the superiority of England to other countries, and airing the safe, sound views that were tried and tested by time. The airing of these views was so often repeated that insensibly the hearer came to look on them as his own. So Swinburne became more and more patriotic and conservative and without perceiving any inconsistency in himself (how could one notice a change of direction when so isolated from the world?) at length came to hold precisely opposite opinions from those he had previously held. The indignant European liberalism which had made him so fervent in the cause of Italian freedom became a hearty Toryism which led him to oppose Home Rule for Ireland with a frantic vehemence and to denounce Mr Gladstone as the Liberal advocate of the measure. His language, ever unrestrained, poured out in denunciation during the eighties. 'See the man of words' (Mr Gladstone) embrace 'the man of blood' (Charles Stewart Parnell), he said when the defeat of the Home Rule Bill in 1886 and the consequent Unionist majority of Lord Salisbury threw Gladstone and the Irish leader into a close political alliance. Gladstone was the 'hoary henchman' who was responsible for Gordon's death. Parnell was the 'crownless King of holy Liarland'. 'The Ballad of Truthful Charles', which Swinburne wrote for the *St James's Gazette* in 1889, placed in the mouth of Parnell the refrain 'I meant to cheat you when I said it', referred to the Irishman's having told the House of Commons in 1881 that 'secret societies had ceased to exist in Ireland', and his subsequent statement, 'It is possible I was endeavouring to mislead the House of Commons on that occasion'.

How was it that Swinburne who had written an Appeal on behalf of the Fenians condemned for murder in 1867 was now equally hot against the assassinations in Phoenix Park? It required a nice distinction in homicide, which with verbose casuistry Swinburne set forth in a letter to *The Times* in 1887.

One can imagine Theodore Watts-Dunton the while, chuckling softly and rubbing his hands. Algernon was being kept busy, throwing himself into his writing. That was good. Moreover he was recanting, recoiling from early error and showing the most proper spirit. Better still. It remained only for him to speak out as loud and clear as the great Tennyson on other patriotic themes.

And Swinburne did. A truculent patriotism was growing in the country which in itself was a reaction against 'decadence'. After the many years of peace the nation required to remind itself of its power, to reassure itself that it had not grown soft, and enervated by pleasure. It was a popular sentiment, which had first been given expression in the music halls. The 'Great MacDermott' had hurled defiance at Russia from behind the footlights.

> We don't want to fight, but by Jingo if we do,
> We've got the ships, we've got the men,
> And we've got the money too.

Jingoism, thus first defined, had taken a parallel course with that of pleasure-seeking, become flushed and excited as the end of the century, with its suggestion of climax, grew nearer. The romantic imperialism to which Disraeli had given shape was assertive. The series of small but celebrated campaigns against the Dutch farmers of South Africa brought the excitement to a head. Among the patriotic voices then lifted, the voices of W. E. Henley, Rudyard Kipling, Alfred Austin, and Henry Newbolt, none was more emphatic than that of Algernon Charles Swinburne.

The lover of France, he who had considered himself practically a Frenchman, was now converted into a determined enemy of 'the French hounds', who were so scurrilously criticizing the acts of Britain.

> We have not alack an ally to befriend us
> And the season is ripe to extirpate and end us.
> Let the German touch hand with the Gaul
> And the fortress of England will fall.

It seemed clear to Algernon now that he had in his youth greatly over-estimated the importance of Baudelaire and the admirable qualities of his nation. And while Whistler was eagerly studying the papers each day for the news of some fresh reverse for the 'Islanders', Swinburne was describing the Boers as 'fiends' and 'dogs' to be scourged. This was indeed a change of tune. There was even the possibility, when Tennyson died in 1892, that Swinburne would become Poet Laureate: 'I am told,' Queen Victoria is reported to have said, 'that Mr Swinburne is the best poet in my dominions.' If the appointment had been offered and accepted it would have been a masterpiece of irony. In the pre-Putney days Swinburne had never mentioned Tennyson without some strong epithet of abuse. He had regarded Tennyson's King Arthur as 'a wittol and a prig'. The stately movement in harmony with the Victorian system, the praise of its labours and science, the approval of its 'increasing purpose' had aroused in him a passionate dislike, while Tennyson himself had shown an equal animosity to the cause which Swinburne had so long represented. Thus had the Laureate expressed himself:

> Art for Art's Sake! Hail, truest Lord of Hell!
> Hail Genius, Master of the Moral Will!
> The filthiest of paintings painted well
> Is mightier than the purest painted ill!
> Yes, mightier than the purest painted well
> So prone are we toward the broad way to Hell.

And this broad way was so manifestly that which Swinburne had pursued until the narrower path to Putney Common had been pointed out to him. How could he then wear the mantle of one so opposite to himself? It was fortunate, on the whole, that he was not chosen as Laureate. He was set aside however not because he had been anti-Christian and anti-mortal but, by some oddity of official ruling, because he had once said something derogatory about the Czar of Russia.

Softly moved Watts-Dunton to and fro with gentle firmness setting the little poet's ideas in order. One thing he did not set in order was his style. To that distinguished critic, style, indeed anything that might realistically and not romantically be called 'Art', does not seem greatly to have mattered. He cared about Algernon's health and the propriety of his sentiments, but as little about whether his poetry were good or not as any old and ignorant nurse.

He 'got into the way of praising'.

He would say a poem was good whether he thought it was good or simply to humour the writer and keep him happy. In a letter to T. J. Wise Swinburne wrote of a new poem: 'Watts – as I possibly had told you – says (what a man generally likes to hear of his latest work) that it is the best poem I ever wrote.' The editors of the collection of his letters add the note: 'It may be observed that Watts said this on every successive occasion.'

Moreover the indulgent critic was perfectly ready to praise poems he had not read. Thus Coulson Kernahan reports that Watts-Dunton confessed he had not seen a memorial sonnet by Swinburne, appearing in the *Athenaeum*, in spite of the fact that he himself, in an article in the very same number, referred to the sonnet as 'noble'. There was a kindly absence of scruple in this. So long as Swinburne was happy and 'busy' it did not really matter at all.

In that curious architectural shell, which like a marine organism had sucked into and retained within its chambers the most varied collection of matter, bad Italian paintings, an oriental cabinet reminiscent of the days of friendship with Whistler, water-colours by J. W. Inchbold, a Proserpine by Rossetti gazing, mystically sad, at the solid Victorian comfort of chair and sofa, Swinburne worked away industriously, but, as far as the living world was concerned, in an intellectual vacuum. He showed little interest in new men, spoke harshly of Yeats and never of Kipling, did not like Stevenson and thought Hardy should not write poetry. He worked on subjects set by Watts-Dunton and little suited to his genius, like the nature poems of *A Holiday Excursion*; on interminable bombastic tragedies; on prose appreciations, especially of the minor Elizabethans, whose enthusiasm was riotous and unchecked; but never more did he write as he had written before the days of his suburban captivity; and his death in 1909 was that of one who had outlived the adventure of his youth.

# 4

## In the Days of King Edward

THE trial and conviction of Oscar Wilde had seemingly brought the aesthetic movement in Britain to a halt. It had caused a wholesale literary and social fumigation. An exaggerated robustness was one of the consequences. Poets, no longer velvet-collared, absinthe-sipping, were now a hearty and virile race, tweed-clad, pipe-smoking, beer-drinking, Sussex-downs-tramping. They broke into rousing choruses, discarded subtlety for the sake of a cheery lilt, and proclaimed that Philistines could also sing.

The subject of sex was buried beneath fresh layers of discretion, beneath cryptic phrases and obscure turns of speech which might or might not conceal some romantic or extraordinary secret. At least this was so among those who still looked upon literature as the art of concealment and cherished decadence in its decay. '*Fin-de-siècle*' lingered on as a term of respect for wickedness. 'So *fin-de-siècle*' murmured the ladies about some interesting indiscretion, behind their ostrich-plumed fans.

Puritanism itself learnt the art of double-talk, of *double-entendre*, making itself more interesting and concealing the meagreness of its emotions by means of long ambiguous sentences and artfully allusive scraps of French. Thus in the later novels of Henry James, the strict propriety of the author was made indeterminate in outline by the innumerable wrappings in which it was hidden and two of his characters would converse so irrelevantly that the reader if he were to make head or tail of them must ask, not what had been said but what might, conceivably, not have been said. Sometimes the reader would be tempted to wonder finally if this tantalizing 'what had not been said' really contained a meaning proportionate to the number of words suggesting it.

It is indeed with as great a wonder as if surveying some remote historical period, ancient Crete or ancient Egypt, that

the twentieth century now looks back upon its own begin-
nings. The Edwardian age, which lasted from 1901 to 1910,
whose characteristics persisted until 1914 when the first great
stroke of a war without precedent drew its gashing and
cauterizing cut clean through the social body, seems a kind of
void, an interlude in modern development.

This was so even though many new things were stirring.
The typical inventions of our own time were already in train,
but it was too early to perceive their great material possibilities and consequently there seemed to be a pause – between
the age of steam and the age of internal combustion. The
motor-car, making its first effective appearance about 1895,
was still a whim of the wealthy, who swathed in furs, veiled
and goggled for the ride, were figures of popular fun. The
flying machine was experimental and did not fly any distance
before 1908. Wireless telegraphy, proved practicable by Mar-
coni in 1896, was not yet developed. The cinematograph was
in its early days. On all this alarming and miraculous release of
forces, the Edwardian era looked with a characteristic good-
humoured imbecility and lack of understanding.

The new woman was well established. She was pedalling
briskly about the countryside on a bicycle, playing golf,
hockey, and lacrosse, skiing in skirts 'as short as she had the
courage to wear'. The suffragettes had begun their campaign
for the enfranchisement of women. And yet at precisely the
same time 'femininity' was overpowering. Dresses billowed
and foamed, waists were constricted to a point beyond even
Victorian endurance, huge hats riotous in velvet and satin
drooped beneath a monstrous panache of feathers. The
boudoir was heavy with perfume and embanked with flowers
in whose combined odours hung also the acrid scent of husband's or lover's cigar. It was not until war was declared and
woman had gone into factories and put on uniform that her
emancipation really began.

It was, this age of gilt, one of enjoyment, one of those
delusive lulls which occur infrequently in the tempestuous
history of mankind. Living was cheap and prosperity was still
growing. At the same time it was importuned by stern

mentors and critics and uncomfortable phantoms, though of these it took little notice. The Russian soul palpitated before it. The historical research of Karl Marx condemned it. The plays of Ibsen flung back its social problems. George Bernard Shaw and the Fabian Society sought to undermine its institutions. Some day these revolutionary creeds and works would have an effect – but they were powerless to disturb the complacency of this period which had made for itself an old régime of its own.

Our unfortunate century was born middle-aged. It had none of the ardours and ideals of youth. Genial, false, and well provided with the world's goods it ate, drank, and was frivolous after an elderly fashion. Hence there was in many of its productions a queer vacancy, a bonelessness, an absence of aim – manifest, for instance, in the *art nouveau,* the 'new art', in which solid forms disappeared in amazing twists and contortions, ornaments of glass dripped cloudy tears, ashtrays looked like spent dum-dum bullets. This aberration came from Vienna under the inspiration of the English arts and crafts movement and left its traces in every home.

The triviality, the nullity of life became interpreted with some as an amiable philosophy. The small underbred man, undignified and comical, is thus seen in Grossmith's *Diary of a Nobody.* On the other hand there were many among the young who fretted at being born into a time when nothing ever happened, when it seemed as if nothing would ever happen (though in the latter respect their fears were groundless). The pathetic heroes of H. G. Wells' sociological comedies, decent but vulgar, with a thwarted desire for romance, for escape from insignificance, are typically Edwardian. Their creator lamented them, seeing behind them a past which they did not understand and in front of them a future with which they could not cope.

And yet the period had its own splendour. For a long time Royalty had mourned, reclusive. But now the dust-sheets were removed from the furniture of Buckingham Palace and Windsor Castle. The prince, who in 1901, at the age of sixty, ascended the throne, was a good European, the 'Uncle of

Europe', of whom as long ago as 1881 Disraeli had said: 'he has seen everything and known everybody'. A true cosmopolitan, he set himself to dispel finally the legend that England was insular. He restored the circulating magnificence of society, the international routine of pleasure. Hereditary princes of the Empire, and Russian Grand Dukes (and how many of them there were) formed the brilliant accompaniment of his European journeys. The Riviera shimmered with titles. Every month, for the King, had its appointed destination, Biarritz in March, Paris in April, London in May, Ascot in June, Cowes in August, Marienbad in September, the shoot at Balmoral in October. With an incomparable gesture he could even create in a foreign country a resort (like Le Touquet) which had not existed before.

And curiously enough, this reopening of communications matched or marched on parallel lines with the aesthetic movement. That interest in, and even subservience to, the spirit and the aims of French literature and French art which in the face of all opposition had steadily grown since the early days of Whistler and Swinburne, was now given official sanction. It is true that conversations with President Loubet were more effective than readings of Baudelaire in producing this understanding; but there were some who found a political meaning in King Edward's preference for a *Sole Soufflée à la Marigny* at the Café Anglais.

The friendliness of the old tie with Germany was waning. The death of Queen Victoria had, for the German Kaiser, helped in this estrangement. There was in his attitude to his European uncle a mixture of jealousy, respect, and resentment of his commanding position. It was not merely a question of fashion though even the quiet authority with which the English sovereign decreed that the bottom button of the waistcoat should be left unfastened, or established the popularity of the Cronstadt or Homburg hat, was galling. A symptom of the Kaiser's desire to excel was the super-yacht *Meteor II*, with which he hoped to beat the *Britannia*. In this naval race, the Prince (as he then was) did not care to compete. He thought of selling his yacht; 'Castellane is so flush with money that he might be inclined to buy her – and compete with his brother-in-law'. The Marquis de Castellane, who had married the sister of a millionaire, was, however, too busy building a Trianon of pink marble in the avenue du Bois to go in for yachting. But, such minor matters apart, the real naval race was on; in which Britain had no intention of allowing Germany to excel; and behind the Entente, that cordial friendship of France and her island neighbour, was the huge and ominous realignment of contending nations.

But the outline of war was not yet conspicuous. The fierce competitive energy of nations was plainly manifest only in the pavilions of international exhibitions. To the fore was a courtly ritualism, the ceremonious interchange of silver whist markers and gold cigarette cases in the corner of which some accomplished craftsman had wrought an enamelled and jewelled butterfly; the practice of the less strenuous but competitive sports and pastimes, horse racing, pheasant shooting, and bridge at small and (after the Baccarat affair at Tranby Croft) carefully selected house parties; and, not least, the satisfaction of appetite. The upper classes combined large eating and drinking with a discrimination derived from France. The royal menus are such as to startle a strictly rationed age. The glass of milk at seven, the breakfast of boiled eggs, bacon, fish, potted meats, and coffee; the luncheon, including lamb and chicken, the large tea, the dinner, at a quarter past eight, in which *Potage à la Tortue* was followed by *Turbot garni de Merlins, Bouchées à la Reine, Cailles à la Financière, Cimier de Daim rôti, Selle de Mouton, Faisan rôti,* completed by at least three sweets such as peaches and cream, soufflées, and Venetian ices, was barely translatable into our austere language of vitamins. A dinner of this kind, broken in the middle by a *sorbet* to assist digestion, was washed down with Rhine wine, champagne, and liqueur brandy, and finished with a superb Corona or Henry Clay.

The artist, in this epoch of international enjoyment, was of course affected in one way or another by its main characteristics. In some it produced a corresponding routine of travel. There lived in Tite Street, Chelsea, in these years a tall, burly, bearded man with a sanguine complexion and prominent blue eyes, Bostonian by descent, though he had been born in Florence and brought up amid the art treasures of Italy. His name was John Singer Sargent. When King Edward came to the throne Sargent was forty-five, and was painting the daughters Ena and Betty of the celebrated and wealthy Jewish art dealer Asher Wertheimer.

He painted the 'fair Stars and Stripes', the American heiresses, who now came in increasing numbers from the land of marvels across the Atlantic: the native Edwardian beauties; and the Jewish men of wealth who now commended themselves at Court and in Society for their intelligence, international outlook, and skill in finance.

Of them there were many. There was Baron Maurice de Hirsch, who came from Bavaria, had added to the ancestral fortune by financing railways and settled in Paris after the Franco-Prussian war. The King stayed with him at his Austrian estates, though his host was barred from the Court of the Emperor Francis-Joseph by the prevailing anti-Jewish sentiment, and followed with the keenest interest the fortunes of his horse 'Matchbox' in the Paris Grand Prix. There was Sir Ernest Cassel, who came from Cologne, whose financial genius had produced him £5,000 a year a bare two years after he began to work in England as a clerk, who applied himself with success to the supervision of the royal economies. Royal favourites also were Arthur Sassoon with whom the King would walk arm in arm on the front at Brighton, and Baron Ferdinand de Rothschild with whom he shot at Waddesdon.

It was in this world that Sargent moved as to the manner born. His greatest activity in portrait painting coincided (and ended) with the Edwardian age and he was to depict it at once glittering and prosaic. Though a shy man he was, by upbringing, fitted for social life and his skill was of that easy and unerring kind which, while conveying at the time an impression of remorseless truth, rarely failed to please the sitter by its revelations; so that those who went to him because it was the thing to be 'painted by Sargent', dreading the psychological scrutiny, more often than not were relieved to find that they were more interesting than they thought. An internationalist, Sargent lived in London but was not of it. His bag was always packed for sudden departures. His valet Nicola learned not to be surprised by the swiftness of a decision to travel. Between 1884 and 1906 Sargent crossed the Atlantic at least twelve times. This was apart from his European journeys, for Italy remained to him the centre of civilization.

Others, however, partly because of the period interest in France and because it is the natural tendency of art to follow wealth, attached themselves more closely than before to that country and to the round pursued by its rich visitors. Dieppe may be said to have been the cultural bridgehead.

The breezy fishing port was a convenient intermediate point. It was linked with Britain by the Channel packets that moored in its safe, deep harbour, by the chalk cliffs that signalized its short distance from the English chalk, sixty-four miles away. Its castle, captured and destroyed at intervals in past wars between the two nations, remained an additional symbol of their nearness to each other. For artists the church, St Jacques, with its fourteenth-century portal, roughened and crumbling in the strong sea air, its water-front, arcaded, bilingual, held a powerful fascination. The indented coast line with its cliffs and pockets of sandy beach had been a haunt of painters since the early nineteenth century and the days of Delacroix and Bonington. Its moods of sky and sea had lured thither the Impressionists, Monet and Pissarro, Renoir and Degas.

In troublous times Dieppe had been a place of refugees. Louis Philippe had come this way from Paris when his bourgeois monarchy had fallen – this way too had come families sent to safety after the Franco-Prussian war. When Paris fell and the communistic spirit of the Parisian masses showed itself, when barricades were erected, and the rue de Rivoli echoed to the sound of shots, Dieppe was the sanctuary of aristocrats and politicians. In the place des Tribunaux one might meet, at the same time, in the seventies a visiting Lord Salisbury and rusticating M. Thiers.

Conversely here had come Britons who for one reason or

another sought refuge or rest – those who had decided to lie low at the height of some insular scandal, or for some other variety of escape. And at one time it had been full of dying and doomed Englishmen of talent – Aubrey Beardsley struggling with his dreadful cough, Conder and Dowson, pale and languishing in its seaside air, Oscar Wilde writing home with a pathetic gaiety his hopes for regeneration.

It was the haunt of aestheticism still. The French writer Marcel Proust stayed there, nursing his asthma, writing of an inner world of mental and emotional life which made more subtle and intricate than ever the long-continued quest and cult of sensation. The high-life which he depicted was that 'old régime' which touched and joined hands with its more substantial equivalent across the Channel – a world of snobs, not that is to say of aristocrats who maintained a familiar even if superior relation with the 'lower classes', but of those who through fastidiousness or fear refused contact with them altogether; a world of revived, assumed, grotesque, and mysterious titles, the more mysterious for their existence in a republican country; a world, finally, preoccupied, as Poe and Huysmans had been preoccupied, with devising a secretive and subjective entertainment. Combining the illusions of pleasure and the sick-room, it was the sort of phantasm that is dispelled like a mist by the breath of external reality and the briskness of action.

The house of a noted pathologist, M. Blanche, was in Edwardian days a meeting place of Anglo-French culture. The pathologist had married an Englishwoman. The family had moved to Wilton Place in London during the Franco-Prussian war. Jacques Émile, the son, remembered seeing Frenchmen and Germans coming to blows at the Alhambra Theatre in Leicester Square while the war was on. It was in Dieppe that he became familiar with Walter Richard Sickert whose work it was to popularize in Britain the later stages of Impressionist art.

\*

Sickert was a man at the tail-end of a movement. He followed in the steps of Whistler and Degas. He was influenced by his contact with them both.

Like Whistler he had an international background. His family was of Danish origin. His grandfather, Johann Jurgen Sickert, had been a painter and head of a firm of decorators employed in the royal palaces by Christian VIII of Denmark. His father Oswald Adalbert Sickert was born at Altona, had painted, worked for the German paper *Fliegende Blätter* and settled in England in 1868. The conquest of Schleswig in 1864 had made him a German. For a while, peaceably accepting his new nationality he had lived in Munich: but to save his sons from conscription in the German army he had adopted the nationality of his English wife, whom he married at Harrow in 1859. Walter Richard, eldest of six children, was born in Munich in 1860.

His early surroundings reflected some of his later tastes. At Dieppe, where the family stayed for a while on the way to England, the small boy began to learn French and his first view of London was gained from the dingy northern vantage of Islington, for which he retained an affection. After leaving King's College, and being discouraged from painting by his father, he went on the stage, having a natural bent for acting, and played some minor parts in Irving's company; but when in 1881 he became engaged to a young woman of wealth, Miss Ellen Cobden, his father's objection to an artistic career was withdrawn. He worked for a while at the Slade School – and then met Whistler.

The result was that he became a disciple. He followed Whistler into a tobacconist's shop and asked if he might come to his studio. The Master was graciously pleased to accept this adoration. He advised leaving the Slade. 'You've wasted your money, Walter – there's no use wasting your time too.' For several years the young man's devotion was unlimited. He painted at Whistler's side in Tite Street. He wrote articles championing his work. He accepted good-humouredly the irritable despotism. 'Why didn't you pay the interest, or whatever it is called?' snapped master to disciple when it was reported that a gold medal Whistler had won at Amsterdam had been bought in a pawnshop. 'How like you,' drawled the master bad-temperedly when Walter dropped an etching plate. 'How unlike me,' he said a few moments later when he dropped the plate himself.

Gradually Sickert became infected with Whistler's sharp-tongued wit, still more with his veneration for France as the fountain-head of modern painting; and soon he went there himself.

It was in 1883 that Sickert, a young man of twenty-three, sharp-featured, nearly six feet in height, watched anxiously a deal case, darkly outlined against the starry sky over Dieppe as it swung from a crane. He was anxious because the crate contained a masterpiece – the now world-famous portrait of Whistler's mother, on its way to the Paris Salon. Walter had been entrusted with its care. It promised to be an exciting visit. He had letters and copies of a catalogue of his etchings from Whistler to be delivered to Degas and Manet. Moreover he was to be the guest of Oscar Wilde who was staying in Paris at the Hôtel du quai Voltaire.

Oscar Wilde quoted Degas' own version of the visit, which was characteristic. Degas contrived to suggest a brusque and insular egotism, riding roughshod over the desires of the host. He had been awakened at an early hour by a great knocking and ringing. He had attempted to excuse himself from seeing anyone on the plea of bronchitis, to which his visitor had answered, 'I don't want to talk. I have come to see your pictures. I am the pupil of Whistler and I bring you the catalogue of his etchings.' In masterful silence the pupil had examined Degas' pictures and statuettes, pronounced, finally, approval. 'Good, very good. I will fix an appointment for you to-morrow at your studio at ten o'clock.'

Whatever element of malice there was in this anecdote there is no doubt that Sickert got on with Degas, much better indeed than with Whistler. Still another lawsuit severed the connexion of these two. It had to do with the question of whether the term lithograph can be applied to the print taken from a drawing on transfer paper as well as from a stone. It is consequently of small interest to most people and is mainly remarkable for a superb display of judicial ignorance. 'What are Degas?' asked the judge.

It was with a certain pleasure that Sickert was eventually to observe the triumph of the humble boatman Walter Greaves whose pictures, to the annoyance of the Master and the anger of his devoted Joseph Pennell, were hailed as better than Whistler's. 'The meek have triumphed,' said Sickert, 'as they have done so often in the history of the world and will do again.'

The intimacy with Degas, however, lasted until the outbreak of the first world war. In the murky studio in the rue Victor Massé, among the piles of canvases, the mass of easels, the litter of the printing press, the dancing girls in red wax with dust-covered skirts fixed in startling and life-like poses, they formed a mutual liking which was to continue. Although the story, which Sickert himself repeated, was 'piquantly distorting', the frightening wit of the great recluse appeared less frightening to the young man than it had appeared to Whistler himself. Perhaps it was because in Degas Sickert recognized a sense of reality with which he was in sympathy, a massive geniality, a more philosophic and weighty sarcasm than that of the dandified artist of good taste. Was not Whistler, after all, somewhat too exquisite, had he not cultivated taste to the loss of this sturdy capacity for truth?

'I want to look through the keyhole.'

This was what Degas said when showing you one of those drawings of women in the bath, in which with unsentimental eye he had depicted exactly what he saw with realism and even with brutality. He meant that he wished to avoid the conventional pose as a writer would avoid a conventional phrase, to see nature as nature was when the artist was not before it. 'Why do you make women ugly?' Degas had been asked by an inquiring lady at the dinner table. 'Because, Madam, women usually are ugly.'

It was of course not a view that would be acceptable in England. 'If I sent that to the Royal Academy would they show me the door?' inquired the Frenchman curiously, referring to a very uncompromising pastel of this kind.

Sickert admitted that that would be likely. 'I suspected as much. They don't admit cynicism in art.' It was stimulating to put one's cynical wit into one's pictures instead of keeping it in a separate compartment as Whistler had done. The words of the Butterfly stripped away all pretensions; yet the Butterfly's paintings gingerly clothed the reality with a veil of mist. It was better, thought Sickert, to see Mornington Crescent in all the veracity of its ugliness, to investigate 'through the keyhole' the sordid décor of back rooms, and to find in the depiction of fat naked women the same detached interest that Degas had found.

Thus he too was to carry on the continental tradition of the century – the search for a new sensation in what was outwardly or superficially unprepossessing – together with the conviction that modern man (and woman) can best be studied in their haunts of pleasure. To him the Bedford Palace of Varieties provided the same stimulus as the Moulin Rouge had given to Toulouse-Lautrec and the Opéra to Degas.

\*

It was second-hand to George Moore, but he determined to make the best of this insular artistic world, and of the lights of the New English. He represented now, in some curious way, the elderly, even, though it is a hard word to use of one so consistently would-be romantic, the stodgy aspect of Edwardian culture. He was resigned to being comfortable. It was obvious enough that he thought his world a second-best – that he looked on the New English Art Club and its outstanding figures as but a pale reflexion of the brilliant French culture that he had known, though even that seemed to him to have come to an end. 'Impossible to doubt any longer that the great French renaissance of the beginning of the century [he wrote in 1893] has worn itself out, that the last leaves are falling, and that probably a long period of winter rest is preparing.' Since Manet died the sun had ceased to shine. In his quarters at 121 Ebury Street, a street with that muted dreariness, that hopeless shabbiness which made it like the setting of a realistic novel, whose characteristic noises were the cries of children playing on the pavements and the distant rumble of trains going to and from Victoria Station, he settled down like an aesthetic Mrs Gummidge, perpetually thinking of the 'old 'un', to the last stage of reminiscence. From the 'Young Man', full of audacious thoughts, the hero of gallant adventures, he had evolved into the carpet-slippered philosopher, meditating over times gone by.

There was, in George Moore, the same unsettlement, produced by Paris, as in Whistler. It was the fount of his ideas: though ties of language and of race drew him away and prevented his making it a material anchorage. At the same time he was subtly dissociated from 'insular affairs'. His return to Ireland, at the time of the Boer War, served to show how little possible it was for him to enter into the spirit which animated his native land. Among people passionately in earnest, he was not so or at any rate not about the same things, and the result except for the production of an amusing account of the country was failure.

The Irish fervour it is true was concerned with literature and to that extent it seemed eminently reasonable that he should join with kindred spirits, Edward Martyn, William Butler Yeats, and Lady Gregory in the foundation of a means of upholding and developing the national genius. The trouble was they were not kindred spirits exactly; moreover that this literary genius was linked inextricably with a cause, a national, a political cause, and was therefore to one brought up in the principles of art for art's sake, to that extent incomprehensible. George Moore was after all an absentee landowner, which made it double impossible for him to take the side of the people. The peasantry, in whom so many found mystical virtues, for him did not count. The politicians seemed to him to be immensely serious about something which no cultivated cosmopolitan could take seriously. He was full of gibes against Catholicism. There was no point indeed at which he was entirely in harmony with even the most brilliant of his fellow countrymen.

It is true that he advocated the revival of the Gaelic tongue.

English, he theorized, was worn out. 'From universal use and journalism the English language in fifty years will be as corrupt as the Latin of the eighth century.' Walter Pater, 'England's last great writer', had said that he used to write in English as in a learned tongue. All the more reason why the Irish should develop their own means of artistic expression. 'There is no such thing,' said Moore, 'as a beautiful unknown page of literature ... were a great work written in Irish to-morrow, in a few years it would have travelled all over Europe.' This was very well, but then, when it came to the point, he could not help seeing a comic side to the Gaelic League, and laughing immoderately at the 'Irish streaming like porter through Hyde's long black moustache'.

To simple, earnest, wealthy Edward Martyn, who combined so strangely the extreme of austerity and an interest in culture, who had a Degas in his castle in Galway and who had the greatest fear of any offence against faith and morals, Moore was at once a friend and a torment. In him, Moore held up to ridicule all that puritanical fervour which underlay the National Theatre and the revival of church music.

The severe romantic figure of William Butler Yeats, a kind of Irish Pre-Raphaelite, disdaining the corruption of civilization, leading a return to nature, appeared similarly as material for fun. But in the brilliant city of Dublin where every wit was another wit's butt the exchange was not at all one-sided. It was possible to make much merriment about the supposedly mythical nature of George Moore's love affairs, of his ingenuous remark that having no children of his own, he had arranged to have his brother's children taught Gaelic, of the oddities of his person which were at least as pronounced as those he maliciously described in others. In short, the time Moore spent in Ireland was one of intellectual slapstick, from which he retired, having been elbowed out of a movement with which he had no genuine sympathy and with a corresponding return of that 'Anglo-Saxon' character which he was ever ready to resuscitate at need.

He settled down cosily in Ebury Street to the old task of writing aesthetic prose, though his popular esteem rested less on this than on his powers of conversation; to the cultivation of a small inner circle of friends; and to a position among the New English painters in which he was able to indulge his delight in reminiscence and to feel that he was at the centre of something roughly corresponding to the old Parisian circle.

There was for example Wilson Steer, 'whom I had the wit to pick out as the only painter in London who could fill the blank that Manet's death had made in my life.'

Whether Manet ever listened to Moore we have now no means of knowing but undoubtedly Steer was a good listener – one who cared to say very little himself and was content to let the voices of others drone on while he relapsed at ease. Only rarely would he write a letter or express an opinion. Never did he exert himself to rage against the Royal Academy and his contribution to argument was the briefest occasional word.

He appears before us as a truly Edwardian figure. There is something secure, safe, and well-regulated about his existence – an easy detachment from the complications and problems of the world. He sits at home with his hands crossed over his stomach and a cat at his side, both screened from draughts, in a room glittering with decorous objects, Chelsea china, Japanese prints, brass Persian salvers kept in beautiful order by the old nurse who is also his housekeeper.

It is typical of him that he paints not in some vast ramshackle studio but in the intimate surroundings of a drawing-room. Typical also that his life is strictly regulated and that the periods of his annual 'outing' – that is to say devoted to painting in the open air – remain constant. In spite of the appearance of ease all his time is given up to the painting of pictures.

Another friend is the great drawing-master Henry Tonks, 'a herring-gutted fellow with a high bridge on his nose', says Moore. This tall spare man with the Roman nose, grim mouth and cool blue eyes, was, with Steer, Moore's closest friend, certainly one of his best listeners. Although he had been a surgeon and still at the age of thirty was demonstrator in Anatomy to the London Hospital Medical School, art had always been a religion with him; and the knowledge of anatomy he gained in the hospital made him a useful assistant to Fred Brown at the Slade School, of which eventually he became the revered tyrant.

He had the qualities of a good schoolmaster – he possessed an awe-inspiring manner and exterior, combined with earnestness and tempered by a measure of kindliness – a mixture which had the effect of keying up his pupils to a pitch of effort which was the result both of fear and affection. There were those who found it difficult to meet that cold blue eye, which seemed to diagnose like that of the doctor he was intended to be, and to search out talent and incompetence with the authority of medical science; though, unlike the doctor, he had no use for hopeless cases and gave his principal attention to the healthy and brilliant. 'Can you sew?' Such a question uttered sarcastically by the stern Dantesque figure was calculated to make the female aspirant burst into tears, as also the silent and contemptuous withdrawal from the proximity of any too assertive and talkative young man, to deflate vanity. But it was observed that the devotion of his women students was in no way lessened by his occasional sharp cruelty, that young men strained the harder to draw well. Discipline, order, reason – these were the main of his tenets. By the use of intelligence and exactness anyone could learn to draw, it being of course understood that a superlative gift was a different matter altogether. It was an outlook produced equally by the anatomical school and the ancestral tradition of the Birmingham brass foundry. By its means Henry Tonks ruled the Slade School with a pencil of iron.

And yet behind this daunting exterior there seemed to be diffidence and uncertainty – the uncertainty of one who had ventured into the artistic life at a somewhat advanced age and moreover from a sphere where such a thing was unusual and even a source of grief and disquiet. 'Harry can't paint,' said that inventive industrialist and local worthy, Edmund Tonks, his father, and though one might not take much notice of such a remark it was discouraging. He had emerged from provincial darkness into a world of dazzling light and its light, wonderful as it was, was still mysterious and strange. There was in it some revelation, if one could find the means of getting at it – for want of which there remained a lurking unease. George Moore, analysing his friends at his elderly leisure, fastened upon this. 'Never was there a man so anxious to learn ... He read everything that was written about drawing; he thought about drawing, praying that the secret might be vouchsafed to him ...' The clavicle and the tibia he knew, but art was beyond explanation.

By natural taste he inclined towards the poetical and the faithful detail of the Pre-Raphaelite illustrators of the sixties. And yet he found himself in a circle which had discarded or chose to look down on these qualities – among people who talked continually of the virtues of the French or were in themselves habituated to the French idiom. There was Moore ever ready to expatiate on the Impressionists, who, though he now was prepared to say that art in France had come to an end, still asserted the superiority that had been. There was D. S. MacColl, the 'Ruskin of the Impressionists' as Will Rothenstein termed him, consistent and tenacious in advocacy, a formidable opponent in controversy, Steer, very English in person and temperament but an enthusiast for Monet and Degas, and trained in sympathy with them. With Moore, and Steer, too, Tonks's intimacy was of that kind which is sometimes found among settled bachelors – an intimacy in which there were no secrets, in which petty tyrannies and minute rebellions resolved themselves by settled habit into an acceptance of a mental life in common.

In Ebury Street the indeterminate character of the Edwardian Age made itself felt – in the Slade School and the New English Art Club. Artists were not quite French, and not quite English. Perhaps the secret was gone from the world, perhaps in this easy self-indulgent period there was neither the strength of external stimulus nor the inward conviction that made for great art. So they may have thought in moments of depression. It induced 'this anxious feeling', a continuous anxiety about 'tones' and 'values', a preoccupation with accuracy of outline and proportion, a keen consciousness of mistakes and the possibility of making them, a fretful recourse to the plumb-line – but it did not supply that contact with reality that had somehow, unaccountably, got lost.

Of that sense of reality Sickert had most. There was evident in him a dissatisfaction with the existing state of things, which expressed itself in several ways. He grew out of the habit of conversation in the Ebury Street circle. He was sufficient of a pupil of Whistler to have a profound contempt for an author's views on painting, although he had adopted the practice of the Master in putting his own views into words. Whistler had thought Moore absurd – and so did Sickert, and when in the conversations in Ebury Street he found himself described with patronizing friendliness and a complete lack of reticence he was angry as well.

In Degas still he had a rock, an unfailing touchstone, contact with which restored his confidence and refreshed his spirit. But to live always in Dieppe, in spite of the friendships made there, no longer seemed enough now that he was approaching middle age. Being a man of international background he felt the need of immersing himself in the life of a capital city and in 1905 he returned more definitely to London than before. Yet the fixed, easy propriety of Edwardian life was not for him. He turned instinctively not to Chelsea with its old world charm but to the North London of which he had pleasant early recollections, which provided a view, more squalid and to him more entertaining, of the life of the people. He took a studio at No. 19 Fitzroy Street.

That district was now to become to London what Montparnasse was to Paris. It had, it is true, always possessed an affiliation with the arts. The great Constable had given lustre to Charlotte Street and his studio was occupied with reverence by one painter after another. The region also possessed many memories of the Rossetti family; but in the twentieth century it had acquired a new personality.

The echoing stone-paved halls were like those of decayed palaces, whose emptiness testified to an indifference on the part of the owner (if they had one) as to who should inhabit them. The massive front doors, each with an array of bells that did not ring, were studded with knockers whose hollow and portentous sound brought no hope of answer. The pattern of names and duty visiting cards testified to the coming and going of who knows how many birds of passage; though the big rooms with their windows and skylights, looking out on many a dedalian tangle of brick walls and mysterious workshops, admitted freely that precious artist's material – light.

The district was, as an artist would always like a district to be, of a mixed population. Jewish tailors, Swiss waiters, Italian cabinet-makers, here lived and plied their crafts. At a handy continental bookshop one could buy the latest issue of the *Nouvelles Littéraires* or *Action Française*. It was foreign and yet of an anglicized foreignness; and the substratum was the life of the native London poor. The side streets, with their dusky brick turned to pale gold slabs in the hazy sunshine, were interestingly poised between drabness and romance.

All this Sickert loved, and the forgotten streets drowsing in genial squalor but touched with ducal magnificence which spread out to the north and east and are comprised in the manorial word, Bloomsbury. From this area, planned in so stately a fashion in the eighteenth century by the Dukes of Bedford, whose marriages and associations are commemorated in the names of streets, one proceeded by an easy transition to Camden Town, Islington, and Clerkenwell. In dreary Mornington Crescent, in Augustus Street near the Caledonian Market, Sickert worked happily and with a positive inspiration derived from his surroundings; and he lunched for preference at grim and grimy Euston Station.

The choice of habitat might seem eccentric were it not so evidently related to the school of thought in which he had grown up. Degas had explained or indicated to him the peculiar and rarified pleasures of cynicism in painting; and it was possible to take this pleasure without illusion in places as well as people, in the shabby surroundings of a railway terminus as well as the human form unidealized.

This sophisticated comment, however, was not especially

profitable. The gods of the Music Hall were unpalatable to those who still preferred Olympus. It is typical of Sickert's patrician contempt for convention that for a long time he held no exhibitions in London and continued to sell his pictures (for extremely small sums) in France. Indeed his fastidiousness was a queer compound. He was a recluse like Degas, yet restless, a collector of places to live in, a hermit of twenty different addresses. He had Whistler's taste for dressing up, but not as a settled dandyism, something rather in the nature of quick-change, reminiscent of the stage, and becoming in later life almost a mania. Withal he looked for some concerted effort, in spite of the extreme individualism of his behaviour and opinions. At the Fitzroy studio he organized 'Saturday or Sunday afternoons' where artists came to show their pictures and their friends to see them, from which enterprise the 'Camden Town' group and eventually the still extant London group emerged, both seeking to find a new impetus which would escape from the blind alley into which Impressionism had apparently led.

There is a photograph of the selection jury of the New English Art Club taken in 1904 which gives an interesting and characteristic group of the period. Some of the members are still living. They are all looking at the picture which an attendant holds up for their inspection. The tall figure of Henry Tonks, with a stern correctness of white collar and a lock of hair drooping over the brow in Edwardian style, gazes sombrely over the shoulder of a young bearded man whose dress is in vigorous contrast with the conventional attire of those around him. His black hat is gaily tilted. He wears a rough jersey, a light coat with velvet collar and, with his hands tucked in the front pockets of his cord trousers, and a pipe in his mouth, he seems to assert the individuality of a new generation. Tonks's most brilliant pupil at the Slade School is he, already regarded as outstanding. His name is Augustus John. D. S. MacColl, painter as well as critic, stands by his side; next to him is the Edwardian figure of Wilson Steer, while sitting near to him is Will (now Sir William) Rothenstein. Between them is another man in early middle age, whose top hat perhaps it is that rests on the table, who has, with his butterfly collar and carefully rolled tie a precise air and also a look of intellectual earnestness which especially catches the attention. It is to be his part to complete or to bring to a final state, the aesthetic movement in Britain, to foster that process of evolution which links the aesthete of the nineties with the intellectual of more recent times. His name is Roger Fry.

# VI

# THRESHOLD OF A NEW AGE

MUCH has been written about the great political families of
Britain – the dynasties which even as far back as Anglo-Saxon
times, though more particularly since the sixteenth and
seventeenth centuries, have had and continued to have a
stake in the management of the country. The Cecils and the
Churchills serve as examples of the family which has become
a part of the national fabric. The average middle-class group
has pursued a less settled and traditional course, though the
Victorian age created a severe middle-class code exerted
through the family and often becoming a despotism which
in turn produced an opposite reaction. The culture of the
late nineteenth and early twentieth centuries was strongly
influenced by this feeling of revolt. Strict control, the in-
culcation of the most emphatic principles of duty, self-
sacrifice, and social responsibility; the pain and bewilderment
of the child and the youth, oppressed by a discipline which
ran counter to their instinctive desires; the subsequent discovery or creation of a scheme of things to which this
discipline did not apply; these have been the constant themes
of novelists and reformers.

King Edward, himself, to some extent, represents the
reaction. His mature personality took a different course from
that prescribed by his austere Victorian upbringing. Among
his subjects the development took various forms. The outstanding Edwardian novel (it may so be called for its revised
edition appeared in 1906), Samuel Butler's *The Way of All*

*Flesh*, was a deliberate attack on the family, a cynical reversion of the whole Victorian creed. The history of Roger Fry reflects this trend of the times.

The Frys, too, were a dynasty – a dynasty of the Quaker and merchant class. There were eight generations before him. The puritanical character of the family had been affirmed by constant Quaker intermarriage. The parents of Roger Fry, Edward Fry and Mariabella, daughter of Thomas Hodgkin, were Quakers both. Their second son, Roger was born in 1866.

It was not necessarily the Quaker element in him that made Edward Fry 'alarming'. That seems to have come from some special quality inherent in the Victorian system. 'My father was always cross,' said Henry Tonks, who was closely contemporary with Roger Fry. These Victorian parents were 'Manicheans'. The whole universe to them was a war of good and evil. They saw evil to be warred against in everything, even in the most trifling things. They discovered it with exasperation and horror in themselves and in those closest to them. They became afraid and their fear made them angry. The anger they vented on the young was a gesture against evil, which must be crushed at its very beginning.

It was natural to associate evil with pleasure – and even what they themselves wished for most was suspect in that it pleased them. Thus Edward Fry had a natural bent for scientific learning but either through his own fears or through the inevitable discouragement of a natural bent he took to the law instead, for which he had no love at all.

A small boy in the seventies (he appears in a photograph of 1872 with a rather puzzled dubious expression, wearing the vaguely military suit of the period) Roger Fry found himself in a world full of stern and infuriated giants. There loomed up the red Dundreary whiskers, the upraised cane of Mr Sneyd flogging the boys at his private school at Sunninghill; the sweeping beard and shaggy eyebrows of Canon Wilson, the devout and earnest head of Clifton School to which he went in 1881.

Clifton was a new public school. It had, therefore, in full measure, all the main traits of the Victorian system of education. It was religious in tone, strenuous in sports, insistent on a belief in existing institutions. It turned its pupils into a definite mould.

To Roger Fry it was an extension of domestic discipline which he resented. He had already some indistinct yearnings towards beauty. The colour of the red oriental poppies in the garden at home was one of his early passions; but there was no one to sympathize with or to encourage his bent; and this being so it was natural enough that he should dislike the system which was not merely indifferent but crushed such symptoms as idle and offensive. He became, as a result of his education, an enemy of the public school 'and all those imperialistic and patriotic emotions which it enshrined'.

He began to try his hand at painting in Cambridge, going, on leaving Clifton, as an exhibitioner to King's College. Here, at least, there were men who had some understanding of the importance of things that school despised. He became the friend of Lowes Dickinson, a young fellow of King's, through whom he was enlightened on the beauty of the ancient world as Oscar Wilde had been through Mahaffy. He went to meetings of the Fine Art Society in the rooms of Sidney Colvin, the Slade Professor, who had not escaped the lash of Whistler's tongue. His enthusiasms at this time were for the early English water-colourists and the Pre-Raphaelites. Like Ruskin before him he was delighted with the picturesque drawings of continental churches by Samuel Prout, the landscapes of David Roberts. At the Manchester Exhibition of 1887 he was impressed also by Ford Madox Brown, by some of the paintings of Millais; but possibly the greatest experience of his university days was his acquaintance with John Henry Middleton – Slade Professor in 1886. Middleton was a connoisseur and a traveller. He had been a friend of Rossetti in his early days. He had roamed far and wide, in the near East, in Africa, and America. His rooms were full of choice works of art – early Flemish and Italian paintings, tiles, pottery, fabrics which seemed somehow to hint at a new world to discover, a revelation of art that had not yet been made.

But was a university a suitable environment for a young man who wanted to be a painter? Roger Fry took first class honours in the Tripos. From an academic point of view this was a brilliant conclusion to his period of training though as a student of painting it could not be said that his training had begun. He had no experience of figure drawing and he lived in a circle where the study of the nude seemed a distressing necessity even if it could be said to be a necessity at all, where the sensuousness of art was so much frowned on that even to read Rossetti's poems was considered a sinful indulgence. Still if it had to be, if he were really determined, his parents thought, at least the most respectable practitioner should be consulted, just as in law or medicine one would consult a man of substance and repute. Consequently they approached the Royal Academician, Briton Rivière, and for a while Roger Fry worked with Francis Bate.

But something was wrong; perhaps the restrictions of the family circle, the conventional nature of his studies, the need to see more, to find out something that England could not provide, or at any rate had not provided. By 1891 he had severed all these home ties and was travelling about Italy. In Rome he discovered the greatness of Raphael, in Florence Botticelli's *Primavera* 'as splendid as to be expected', and the magnificence of Michelangelo's Chapel of the Medici. From Italy he went to Paris to work in the now usual fashion at Julian's, and returning to London he settled in Chelsea and resumed his earnest endeavours to paint.

He was at this time still painting in the manner of the early English water-colour painters. He seemed to his contemporaries shy and afraid of life. His ideas were still in the melting-pot though he found much comfort in the society of his neighbours in Chelsea, Charles Ricketts and Charles Shannon.

That curious parallel between English and French characters in the later nineteenth century, whether due to deliberate imitation or to the spirit of the times, is observable between these two, Ricketts and Shannon, and the brothers de Goncourt. The two Englishmen, in exactly the same way as their French counterparts, lived the aesthetic life – even as it might be put, with the characteristic inversion of the eighteen-nineties – the Life Aesthetic. They had been apprenticed together to a wood engraver. They found a community of interests which led them to set up a joint household and a partnership not only in the practice of art but in the cultivation of the most delicate and refined appreciation, which continued throughout life. Like the de Goncourt they weighed each sensation, and distilled it until it became as a fine perfume surrounding an existence to which music, literature, and painting all contributed. Like the de Goncourt they had a passion for eighteenth-century France, for the art of Japan. Ricketts, a small delicately made man with a head of fine tow-coloured hair 'like a dandelion puff', was the leader of the two, 'the noble and generous Ricketts' as Bernard Shaw described him, 'who always dealt *"en grand seigneur"*, a natural aristocrat and a loyal and devoted artist.' 'A house where you will never be bored', so Oscar Wilde had commented on their house in the Vale, Chelsea. Here it was that Roger Fry sat at Ricketts' feet, realized afresh in less shadowy outline than before the values to which he aspired.

The rectitude of this life appealed to him. It was separated from the vulgarities and complexities of ordinary existence. It was not merely devoted to art, it recognized that art was a system of values which had nothing to do with or at least transcended common experience. Among these works of beauty in which they had, as it were, barricaded themselves, the Tanagra statuettes, the drawings by Hokusai, by early Italian masters, there was, if one could find it, some universal key to the secret which all works of art had in common.

By the end of the century his search was already enticing him into writing and away from painting, in which it seemed, indeed, he had been intended neither by nature nor his early training to excel. As the centre of the serious artistic life of the day, he sent his pictures to the New English Art Club. He sought, for he was as anxious in this matter as Tonks, to find some definite indication that he was on the right lines from his colleagues. 'Steer has been round and I think he likes my work more than before but it is difficult to know what he thinks.' Such is one note of his, illuminating both as to himself and Wilson Steer. Perhaps a sense of dissatisfaction with his own efforts coloured the views he now began to express more distinctly as to the shortcomings of the art of the time. In the capacity of art critic he praised Steer, Conder, Sickert, Shannon, and Rothenstein but it was a modified praise, relative only to his condemnation of the academicians, Sir Edward Poynter, Frederick Goodall, and the Hon. John Collier, the famous exponent of the 'problem' picture. He was bleakly convinced that nothing done in England was of any particular value. These provincial 'impressionists' were all very well – but on the other hand how meagre really was their equipment, how poor their emotional and intellectual condition. Sargent he attacked in 1900 as a superficial painter – not even to be compared in degree with true artists but as one practising some other and vulgar occupation.

Bound to support the New English painters because they were the only active movers against the Victorianism he disliked so much and for various reasons, he could not feel at one with them. He saw clearly, perhaps too clearly, their limitations. He fretted at the difficulties he himself encountered in the art of painting; and this self-criticism seemed to become transferred into a wider deprecation. To express this discontent, to find the meaning, the secret and underlying meaning which eluded him and others, he began to write. He sent an article on Impressionism in 1893 to the *Fortnightly Review*, and before the new century began he was the regular critic of the *Athenaeum*.

Colouring his outlook was a combination of factors – the native Puritanism of his family which did in fact lead him to seek something pure, some principle uncorrupted and untarnished by worldly contacts; the philosophic and intellectual training of the university which led him to value erudition, and implanted in him the habit of the scholar and the scientist rather than the craftsman; their revolt against the Philistinism of the middle class and the intense and narrow Victorian nationalism. All these factors made him into the aesthete rather than the creator; were indeed a rearrangement of the qualities which had formed Ruskin and Pater before him; although, unlike Ruskin, he had no underlying motive of social reform and, unlike Pater, had a specialist rather than a poetical appreciation. He could speak as an 'expert', skilled in the intricacies of dates, periods, and styles. He was able to pronounce with conviction that 'Lady Wantage's Adam and Eve is not, we think, Bronzino, as stated, but by some Parmese artist, probably Mazzuola Bedoli, working under the influence of Parmegiano.' To see pictures, in Florence and Rome, Berlin and Dresden, Amsterdam and Madrid became his work and the continual examination of masterpieces in Europe caused him to refer ever more critically to the current production in his native land. There were a few, a very few occasions on which he could give praise. It was bestowed on the consummate ability of Augustus John – 'we hardly dare confess how high the hopes of Mr John's picture which his paintings have led us to form.' Thus he wrote in an account of the New English Art Club exhibition in 1904. But, on other occasions, and they were the more frequent, it became a duty, a severe and responsible duty, to condemn. It was, for example, necessary to dethrone Sargent, to explain how different the superficial animation of his portraits was from the profound life imparted by the great masters, to point out not merely a difference in the degree of ability but positively a difference in kind – that Sargent provided not one type of art but a clever commodity which was not art at all.

Such views were not popular, nor indeed did Fry win acceptance either in official circles or from the public at large. Of his great predecessors, Ruskin had been Slade Professor by general acclaim; but in 1904 Fry failed to secure that appointment. Pater had been a Fellow of an Oxford College, but Fry had no academic status; and in 1905 he failed to become the Director of the National Gallery.

'Doesn't anyone know you?'

In an interview with some Tadpole or Taper at Whitehall this was the question he was asked and as he was apparently unable to affirm this knowledge on the part of anyone who was sufficiently Anyone, official interest waned. It was natural enough in these circumstances that the art expert should seek a new and more encouraging field of activity. He had bought pictures for the American millionaire Pierpont Morgan, and being invited by him to go to New York, Roger Fry accepted.

The millionaire tends in these days to arouse that mixture of discomfort and amusement which might be caused by some freak of nature. Not only is there a monstrous disproportion between his worldly goods and those of the mass of men – there is a wild rate of increase in his wealth, against which eventually he seems to struggle in vain. He reverses a natural process. He must find means not of acquiring the wherewithal to live but of reducing the vast accumulations which mount up of their own accord and imprison him with their many responsibilities. Pierpont Morgan was the arch type of millionaire. His appearance was that of Capital as depicted in fiery socialist caricature. The top hat, the frock coat, the vast, bulbous nose, due to some constitutional defect and yet seeming to mock the frugal visages of other men, were the symbols of a financial uniqueness. He had the power and prodigality of a great pioneer, indeed he was the nearest modern approach to the bold and ruthless ruler of a city state at the time of the Italian Renaissance who had an equal enjoyment of art and domination. The only difference was that the millionaire had no more interest in a living artist than in any other of his numberless hirelings and that his immense and necessary prodigality was devoted to anything of value and not what pleased him. He was a 'cheque book collector' who could plunder whole countries with his pen. 'I'll take this at the price you paid for it plus fifteen per cent. How much did you pay?' Together he and Fry went to Italy – a triumphal progress, for to the Italians the American millionaire was a god-like creature to be approached with veneration. At Siena they took up the cathedral floor to show him the mosaics, a privilege which had not been granted to the Queen of Italy.

They returned to America loaded with statuary and ceilings, with majolica and paintings, with a million dollars' worth of plunder. There was a certain satisfaction for Fry in the beauty of these things, in the pictures he was able to buy for the Metropolitan Museum, Goyas, Guardis, Murillos, often 'at ridiculously low prices'. But America puzzled him. It seemed to him hospitable and yet fierce and cruel. It was barbarous and yet not original. There seemed to be no standard of values on which one could rely. There was a mixture of credulity and suspicion. There were 'nameless horrors of modern art'. Perhaps he missed or shrank from, with that characteristic shrinking from life which acquaintances in England had noted in him, the intense drama and activity of existence in America and exaggerated its shortcomings of taste with too great a fastidiousness.

There is something marvellously discrepant too in the relation between him and Morgan – between the ascetic figure worn and pale and the harsh and jovial Maecenas, with the opulent bottle nose. It was scarcely a relation likely to continue for very long; and in 1910 his relations with Morgan and the Metropolitan were abruptly severed. He returned to Britain, with the matter rankling in his mind; with the gloom too of domestic worry, for his wife, whom he had married in 1896, who had long been ill, in this year went into an asylum.

And yet his travels had been of value to him, had their own formative effect. All the treasures of the world had been laid before his eyes, treasures of East and West, of Christians, Moslems, Buddhists, of times recent and remote. To him had come the necessity of handling, comparing and estimating their worth. Of art of every kind he had seen, in quantity infinitely more than Ruskin, art of which Pater, shut up in his intellectual seclusion, had never dreamed. Why were these precious but so various objects, of like value; why were they all good? Clearly it had nothing to do with the period when they were produced, because they were of many periods; or of the religion of their producers because they were of several religions; or the story or the message conveyed, for a Mohammedan rug told no story and a Ming vase conveyed no message. There was a quality in them which was art and art alone. It was a quality not to be found in Britain; but it was to be found in some French artists. The key that unlocked all aesthetic doors was certainly to be found in the studio of the long-despised Paul Cézanne.

\*

There was an essential difference between the Impressionists and those who followed them and who have been styled, in a fashion descriptive of that fact but otherwise without meaning at all, as 'Post-Impressionists'. It was a difference not easy to understand while they lived because the three principal 'Post-Impressionists', Paul Cézanne, Vincent Van Gogh and Paul Gauguin, were all very closely bound up either with Impressionism as a movement or else with individual representatives of it. At the time they appeared to be obscure people of very doubtful talent who were simply the hangers-on of men established and unquestionable in brilliance. Cézanne had contributed to the first Impressionist exhibition of 1874 and had by his well-meant efforts done much to bring odium upon it. Degas was convinced he was no painter and it was a view which all the friends of Degas continued to hold. In the year of that famous exhibition Paul Gauguin was a young stockbroker of twenty-six, respectably married to a Danish girl, with a taste for buying pictures and some humble and amateur desires of painting on his own account. A meeting with Pissarro quickened Gauguin's enthusiasm and caused him to frequent the Nouvelle Athènes and to copy the Impressionist manner. Vincent Van Gogh was a little later on the scene. He came to Paris in 1886 at the age of thirty-three and stayed at first with his brother Theo. As the latter dealt in Impressionist works at the Goupil Gallery, Vincent acquired an eager interest in them and even made the by then belated discovery of the Japanese print.

The personal connexion existing between them has been much exaggerated. Cézanne's acquaintance with Gauguin and Van Gogh was never more than casual. 'He paints like a madman,' he said, outraged, of Van Gogh. Very brief trial in the South of France in the course of one famous summer convinced both Van Gogh and Gauguin that they were not destined to be the joint founders of an ideal community of artists.

Yet there are several things which they had in common, which mark an abrupt divergence from the Impressionist tradition. In each of them there is an absence of that dandyism which had been one of the essential traits of the nineteenth-century artist, the dandyism not merely of clothes but of attitude.

Dandyism was no trivial thing. It was a sign of a firmly established outlook. It was more than being well-dressed or fastidiously dressed, it was an urbane code of manners. It was wit. It was the capacity to pose amusingly in order to express a conviction instead of delivering a prosy sermon, a solemn harangue. It was the aristocratic lightness of touch, the perfection of culture's etiquette. And as such it disappeared with the advent of these new men. In its disappearance is to be read the difference between them and the artists from whom they had learnt, with whom they have been associated. The new men had, of course, many points in which they were unlike each other – but most significant points in common.

For example, there is the rejection of the city; the rejection of 'urbanity' itself. Manet and Degas were closely bound up with the capital, still more so Toulouse-Lautrec. How opposite to them is Gauguin! The restlessness of the sea was in his blood. He had been in the merchant navy at the age of seventeen, had served, while in the twenties, on a cruiser during the Franco-Prussian war. He returned from active service (as men have done since) to find his family house and its contents destroyed by German bombardment.

Ten years (1872–83) cover the period of Gauguin's stay in Paris, during which he appeared to be a respectable and prosperous young business man. He was, even so, not such a well-ranged individual as this might suggest. He made money by the gamble of stocks and shares and, as his interest in art grew, so he chafed the more at middle-class domesticity represented by his Lutheran wife from Copenhagen. The plunge into the artist's life at the age of thirty-five was carried out with a characteristic severance of ties. He disposed of all he had and departed for Rouen, whence his wife, hoping to lure him back into gainful employment, persuaded him to go to Copenhagen.

It might have been expected that this would not do. By 1885 Gauguin was back in Paris, in effect separated for ever from his wife and all respectable ties. Yet he did not settle down to paint. '*On peint si bien aux Batignolles,*' said Renoir, expressing his wonderment that anyone should need any other inspiration than Paris could give. Yet Gauguin, in spite of this gentle word of advice, now began his strangely intricate saga. He went first to Pont-Aven in Brittany, which occupied a year. He went in 1887 with a sailor friend to Panama, breaking both the outward and return voyage at Martinique. He returned to Paris in 1888, but once more went off to Pont-Aven. Thence he went to Arles, and made his famous stay with Vincent van Gogh. He returned to Brittany. He appeared once more in Paris. Once more the pull of the sea exerted itself and by 1891 he was in Tahiti. It was only the first of his visits. He made a flamboyant reappearance in Paris but the attraction of the South Seas was not to be resisted. In 1895 he was back in Tahiti. His final move was to the Marquesas where he died in 1903.

In Paul Cézanne there was, if not such an adventurous spirit, an equal hatred of organized society. He desired absolute seclusion – not the primeval seclusion of Papeete but, at least, the provincial quietude of Aix, Provence and the Midi. The South of France, where he had been born, was more satisfying to him than any other place. Gauguin escaped from his 'struggle with fools' by a prolonged voyage, dis-appointing inasmuch as he found more fools on the other side of the world. Cézanne escaped by a determined isolation – an avoidance of human contacts expressed in his cele-brated remark: 'No one is going to get their hooks into me.'

Vincent van Gogh was as obsessed with the idea of the simple life as Gauguin himself. He had some vague scheme of a Utopian community of artists, by which he induced Gauguin to join him at Arles. Prior to that he had been as much a wanderer as any. He had reached Paris by way of Antwerp and England. He had a few years of intense industry in the South of France. There followed a sojourn in asylums and it was under the care of the sympathetic Dr Gachet that he shot himself at Auvers in 1890.

With this desire for escape, for isolation, came other notable changes. They were very serious these men, with the seriousness that goes so naturally with simplicity. Wit and scholarship were outside their scope, something even to be suspected. This earnestness with Van Gogh takes on an almost religious character. It was his great ambition to do good. He felt vaguely, as he had felt in early life when preaching to the poverty-stricken Belgian miners of Le Borinage, that he must imitate Christ, living in poverty and without earthly goods, stooping to give compassion and help to the lowliest and most fallible of God's creatures, paint in a kind of religious frenzy almost as an act of worship. In the letters in which he poured out his suffering soul to his brother, there was a sort of clumsy strength; but never was there the slightest gleam of humour, the slightest relaxation of a deadly earnestness.

The intense aristocratic pride of a Degas in his mastery is replaced in Cézanne by a profound humility. He envied the accomplished and sentimental Bouguereau, the general laugh-ing-stock of sophisticated spirits. He fretted at his inability to be brilliant, to 'realize' what he was trying to do. He had a pathetic desire for formal honours and certificates of merit, for a ribbon to put in his coat.

Gauguin was somewhat more complex. He had the simplicity of the sailor with a sardonic streak which grew from or was aroused by his hatred of the middle class and all its works. The fact remains that he was able to live in the most primitive conditions and found in the attendance of a native girl an entirely satisfactory substitute for what he termed 'that detestable institution, marriage'.

The correctness of a Baudelaire or a Manet is emphatically missing in their appearance. Gauguin, with his great beak of a nose, in his rough fisherman's jersey and his carved clogs, or in such a barbarous caricature of Western splendour as some Polynesian chief would wear for a ceremonial occasion with a walking stick carved with indecent figures, was a sort of wild man, 'a wolf', as Degas said. Van Gogh, with his head close cropped, his ear lobe slashed, a wild glare in his green eyes, a coarse and untidy reddish beard growing on his chin, had about him the look of a peasant touched by lunacy or genius. Cézanne in the rough clothes of a farmer, with his bowler hat, and a curious look of furtiveness and guilt in his sidelong glance, shuffling on foot to his lonely studio with his satchels and canvas, was pursued by the jeers of children. Conventional refinement was lacking in all three.

As clearly as it is written in their appearance conventional refinement was lacking in their painting. They called a halt to that cult of delicate sensations which had for so many years been all important. That, in painting, had been translated into a shimmer of atmosphere, into a delicate observation of the effects of light. In literature there had been a corresponding shimmer of moods, an effect obtained by suggestion rather than statement. The tendency was found in all the arts, including music. Debussy, in his *L'Après-midi d'un Faune*, borrowed the title and interpreted the allusiveness of the French poet Mallarmé's best-known poem. But these new men instinctively sought for what was massive and rough-hewn, for what was elemental and even elementary. They had as strong a desire to discard from their art the accretions of the past, as they had in their lives to disclaim all connexion with normal society. Although Gauguin had enjoyed the intimacy of the Nouvelle Athènes, it was from the great but neglected Puvis de Chavannes that he drew his real inspiration. In Puvis' wall paintings, in the severe figures placed in stately groups, immune from the trivial accidents of light and shade, he saw the permanence of a primitive community. It was a like, heroic world, more barbarous but therefore the nearer to the mainspring of life that he imagined in the paradises of Oceania.

Van Gogh felt the need for a direct, a blurting sincerity. What he meant must be made plain, underlined, exaggerated with a savage anxiety. Subtlety or the art of suggestion was beyond him. The paint must be slashed on, wildly, emotionally, directed only by his intense will that what he was painting should live as the person or landscape before him lived.

Cézanne was the subtlest of the three. He had been, of them all, the earliest and closest follower of the original Impressionists. He was also the most typically French: a characteristic which showed itself in a greater reverence for the past and for the classic models to be found in the museums. But he too had the same urge to make what was solid and durable, to depend not merely on the transitory play of colour but on the rock of form. In his humble fashion he was ready to start in the simplest possible way, just like a learner in an art school, with a few apples on a plate and a napkin draped in careless folds. An apple was after all a coloured solid and by the minute and patient observation of its rounded surface, noting the changes of colour with the incidence of light on each segment of the curve, it was possible to arrive at the secret of form in other solids, in a man or a mountain. There was in this business of beginning at the very beginning a sort of ascetic self-discipline, a mortification of the flesh and its vanities.

In one respect the 'Post-Impressionists' were like their Impressionist predecessors. They were divorced from the middle-class world. The difference was that artists had previously adopted an aristocratic attitude. The new men were if anything, proletarian. They put aside all graces and luxuries. The world of the opera and the ballet, of polite society, was not for them. Theirs was a world of peasants and savages.

Van Gogh died in 1890, Gauguin in 1903, Cézanne in 1906.

They were still derided or ignored even in France; although in so complex a fashion do artistic generations overlap, that by the beginning of the new century various young men were already taking note of them and preparing the way for developments which have only recently created a general stir. They had little sympathy from the older generation of painters.

Degas' aversion to Cézanne was notorious. Whistler emulating him had said that if a child painted in that way its mother should put it across her knee and spank it. Walter Sickert had been approached by Gauguin while he was still in the 'bank' and (though he later somewhat modified his opinion) had been unable to resist the cutting word of advice which doubtless the 'Butterfly' himself would have given: 'Better stick to the "bank".'

On Roger Fry the impression was far different. In 1906, he saw and was convinced of the superlative genius of Cézanne, as to which he had previously been sceptical. Here, it seemed, was that long-expected revelation, the only stimulus that could reform and stiffen this smug and flabby Edwardian period. His instinctive puritanism responded to the renunciation which he found in the Frenchman, the refusal to be beguiled by what was superficially pleasing, the rejection of all enjoyments, even those most usual to a painter, the stern devotion to what he considered a duty even if the rest of the world considered it simple monomania. The rough-hewn character of these novel pictures was in itself a sign of sterling worth, like the plain manners of a Quaker merchant as opposed to the insincere courtesies of some over-fine gentleman; and with acquaintance they yielded in the same way more lasting and satisfactory relationship.

The roughness, the primitive nature of the work of these uncouth painters was even one which promised a refinement all the greater because it was austere. Beneath the lack of finish, the 'incompetence' as it was termed by the unimaginative virtuosos, Fry perceived an unyielding effort to arrive at truth, an unswerving honesty which pursued art alone and in itself. It seemed a quality all the more precious in an age which was all 'finish', in which great and simple purposes seemed entirely to have disappeared. Unlike highly cultivated philosophers before him Fry was not greatly attracted by the return to the simple life of which the Post-Impressionists offered a new example. Their unusual personalities, the curious details of their lives might seem of paramount interest to the public, always avid of such curiosities, but he rejected all this as irrelevant. His theory depended on such rejections. The importance of the simple life as led by the Post-Impressionists was, according to him, that it was an exclusion of life. Art was divested of all that was superfluous – the necessity of 'telling a story', descriptive detail, incident, pyschology, all things human except those which served as a pretext merely for the expression of form. At all events this was so with Cézanne. Perhaps Van Gogh and Gauguin retained something too much of human and non-aesthetic weakness, were interested either in the peculiarities of faces or in the cloudy mysteries of human fate; but Cézanne, in the often told tale, after a hundred portrait sittings declared himself 'not displeased with the shirt front' – in which remark he clearly proclaimed his indifference to the likeness and his equal regard for a piece of fabric as for an eye or a nose.

And here surely, thought Roger Fry, was the key, the talisman which explained the affinity between all great works – French or Persian, Italian or Japanese, ancient or modern. Form in itself, pure and uncorrupted by the myriad accidents and associations of life – 'more profound and more significant spiritually than any of the emotions which had to do with life'.

Such was Roger Fry's conclusion. It was the doctrine of Art for Art's sake brought up to date. There was the characteristic reversal of importance as between nature and art. 'It might even be,' he wrote, 'that we should justify actual life by its relation to the imaginative, justify nature by its likeness to art. I mean this, that since the imaginative life comes in the course of time to represent more or less what mankind feels to be the completed expression of its own nature, the freest use of its innate capacities, the actual life may be explained and justified by its approximation here and there, however partially and inadequately, to that freer and fuller life.' This, after all, was a more philosophic rendering of Whistler's witticisms, repeated by Wilde with so many variations, concerning the imitation of art by nature, though he was influenced also by Reynolds and his typically eighteenth-century view of the necessity of artifice. The insistence on form in the abstract was entirely harmonious with Pater's saying that the arts aspire to the condition of music; and in the rejection of popular elements, in the choice of a hard and narrow path of appreciation, in the insistence on the value of an entirely personal experience – the 'little sensation' – Roger Fry was at one with the established aristocratic contempt for the Philistine.

At the same time the pervading literary strain which had now touched, now departed from, the sister art since the days of Gautier and Baudelaire, the idea that in rejecting morality art must seek inspiration from what was morbid and sordid or even merely hedonistic, was purged. The completeness of the new Art for Art depended on its being armed at all points against these intruding factors. Not only morality but representation itself was proscribed.

The full development of these thoughts in Roger Fry's mind, their amazingly lucid and persuasive exposition, was later in date than the end of King Edward's reign. It might be said that he was then still on the threshold of discovery; but towards it he was already bending. He had never been greatly in sympathy with the British Impressionists, and he resigned with relief in 1908 from the jury of the New English Art Club. It seemed to him as if he had set behind him small and parochial entanglements; was positively beginning a new life.

And in 1910 he went to Paris to choose pictures for an exhibition that would introduce the new art to Britain. Two exhibitions were held – the first at Brighton, the second at the Grafton Galleries in London. The effect of the latter was extraordinary.

It contained a number of paintings by Manet including the *Bar of the Folies-Bergère*: twenty-one by Cézanne, forty-one by Gauguin, twenty-one by Van Gogh, two landscapes by Georges Seurat, a somewhat isolated master (whose work had completely baffled George Moore when he saw it in Paris).

There was also a certain proportion of works by living men – mainly of the group called 'Les Fauves' – or wild men. Their leader was Henri Matisse. They were much influenced by Van Gogh and painted with the brightest colours and with slashing, summary outlines. It was all quite new to Britain. With magnificent inaccuracy George Moore had mixed up Cézanne with Van Gogh in a lecture on Impressionism given at Dublin in 1906, referred to 'Cézanne's crazy cornfields, peopled with violet reapers'. The reaction was prompt and decisive. The cry of outrage was once more raised. Political firebrand, poet, and diarist, Wilfrid Blunt called the exhibition 'an extremely bad joke or a swindle'. Little Charles Ricketts gasped in horror. 'Why talk of the sincerity of all this rubbish.' 'Idleness and impotent stupidity, a pornographic show', 'the gross puerility which scrawls indecencies on the walls of a privy'. 'This art,' said the critic of The Times, 'stops where a child would begin.' 'Like Anarchism in politics, it is a rejection of all that civilization has done, the good with the bad.' Desmond MacCarthy, the writer, helped Roger Fry to organize the exhibition. He noted with interest the violence of criticism to which it gave rise among visitors. Said Fry himself, 'There has been nothing like this outbreak of militant Philistinism since Whistler's day'.

The curious thing was that the Philistines of the old type were not the most angry of all. The British 'impressionists' and their critic supporters were so; even though they had accepted the French movement immediately preceding that now put before their eyes, even though they accepted Manet himself, and subscribed to an aesthetic doctrine which was modified but not in essence changed. A native conservatism appeared in their desire to preserve a revolt as an institution. D. S. MacColl, surveying the situation, remarked that though we had been intelligent enough to accept Manet and Degas, that was no reason to throw all barriers down. To welcome a second revolt was unprincipled. In the criticism of the Post-Impressionists there was not only a hatred of change. There was also a conviction that these violent canvases were an evolutionary step downwards. They were the work of uncultured and unskilful men. How could this represent an improvement on the efforts of those who possessed both culture and skill? Impossible, thought Henry Tonks, whose tidy, anxious world seemed tumbling about his ears; on whom the dogmas of Fry had an even more powerful effect than the pictures of Cézanne, becoming, as time went on, an obsession, a fascinated revulsion in which there was possibly even a measure of thwarted agreement.

To Walter Sickert, who wrote in the spirit of a lively man of the world, Cézanne was 'immensely overrated'. The pupil of Whistler and Degas, the author of so much witty comment on contemporary life in paint, anxious as he was to give an impression of scrupulous fairness, could not be expected to be very enthusiastic over 'a couple of unhappy looking apples on a shaky saucer'.

George Moore took the whole thing rather less seriously. He told Tonks that children always devoured their parents; that therefore one movement in art must replace another inevitably, so why worry; but Tonks and many others continued to worry a great deal. And principally they worried about the completeness of Fry's theory. It impaled them, so to speak, wriggling violently, on the sharp point of a reasoning which they could not easily refute and yet which all their instincts denied.

A period was over. A new period was to begin.

# Conclusion

WHAT was the result of the aesthetic 'adventure'? As the economists of the early nineteenth century had made political economy into a science with its own laws and invented the 'economic man', so now the cultivation of 'Art for Art's sake' had produced 'the aesthetic man'.

The 'aesthetic man' recognized no duties, pursued no interests, save those of art, just as the 'economic man' was actuated solely by profit.

He was indifferent to religion, morality, education, political principle or social improvement.

He was an unexpected abnormality arising from the system of the division of labour, a form of over-specialization.

Thus the aesthetic movement was fundamentally selfish. Perhaps it was necessarily so. Only, it seemed, by a determined egotism could the precious grain of beauty be separated from the common substance in which it lay concealed.

It was opposed and offensive to Victorian idealism. The essence of that idealism was social service. Ruskin attacked the economies of his day because it was intolerable to him that the motive of gain should be made all important. It was with a similar motive that he attacked a self-sufficient art. William Morris, believing that everyone had the capacity of an artist, that all happy work was a form of art, could not but be antagonistic to the mystic cult of irresponsible 'genius'.

It had some of the character of a witty play, a comedy performed by highly accomplished actors who wrote (very brilliantly) their own words; who also created situations, merely by virtue of their personality, in which there was a comedy they had not intended or foreseen. It is this quality which Max Beerbohm, so elegantly a part of and yet so detached from the eighteen-nineties, has preserved, in Post-Victorian retrospect, in drawings which distil the humour incidental to the rarified existence of genius, implicit in the meeting of the gay Whistler and the solemn Carlyle, in Wilde's ecstatic explanation of Botticelli to American mining camps, in Verlaine's Sunday walks, as French master, with his pupils at an English school.

The movement was never popular in Britain. It was mainly foreign in origin and though it had a profound effect in a limited circle it was uneasily placed between the prejudice of idealist and Philistine alike.

Great thoughts, great emotions were lacking. They were indeed deliberately avoided. To the prophet and reformer there succeeded the wit and the outcast, and the exhortations of the preacher were followed by the mockery of the *enfant terrible*. As far as this cleared minds of cant it had its use; but the clearance of cant involved a danger of loss of proportion. The nineties, in which aestheticism reached its height, grow smaller as this proportion readjusts itself.

'With a few pounds more weight,' said George Moore, 'Whistler would have been the equal of Velasquez.'

'Fellow artists to the weighing scales,' observed Whistler, nettled. Yet it was perhaps those few pounds that he needed. Weight is the element lacking in the period, though of good, of exquisite art the aesthetic development of the century provides so many examples.

Whistler, in the suit against Ruskin, made on behalf of art a declaration of independence. Wilde, in more unfortunate fashion, attempted to demonstrate that ethics and beauty had no connexion. Roger Fry placed round the visual arts the barriers of a rigid system.

In some respects it is not a very edifying story. There was much that was unhappy in the long-drawn struggle against society or for a liberty more complete than it would allow. Whistler at the end of it was an embittered old man perpetually engaged in trifling disputes; Wilde, an ex-convict, incapable of writing; Swinburne, a character reformed and made meaningless. Among many others the search for sensation at all costs was a self-imposed penance, producing squalor and suffering.

The aesthetic movement was never popular in Britain. The denial of moral purpose, the compression of what has to be said into an exact form, the greater importance given to form than to matter, were alien to its complex and romantic genius. In literature, the effect of Art for Art's sake was severely limited, although in France it has coloured all modern poetry and influenced most writers of note. Nor, in painting, was the effect very different. A hybrid school developed which, whatever its merits, could not compare with the French art from which it was derived.

There was in total result a grain of beauty, impossible to weigh and estimate against the insignificant expenditure of lives.

# SOURCES AND ACKNOWLEDGEMENTS

THE sequence of original works which express the nature and spirit of the aesthetic movement, both in France and Britain, is amply referred to in the course of the text and need not be repeated here.

A general scholarly survey is provided by Dr Farmer's *Le Mouvement Esthétique et Décadent en Angleterre*. Mr Holbrook Jackson's celebrated *The Eighteen Nineties* is a standard work of reference. Sir William Rothenstein's *Men and Memories* contains much relevant matter. Biographies consulted include: *The Life of Whistler* and *The Whistler Journal* by Joseph and Elizabeth Robins Pennell and *Whistler* by James Laver; *The Life of Swinburne* by Edmund Gosse; *The Life of Walter Pater* by Thomas Wright and also *Pater* in the English Men of Letters series by A. C. Benson; *The Life of George Moore* by Joseph Hone; *The Life of Oscar Wilde* by Frank Harris; *Oscar Wilde and the Yellow Nineties* by Frances Winwar and various biographical studies including *Aspects of Wilde* by Vincent O'Sullivan and *Oscar Wilde – A Summing Up* by Lord Alfred Douglas; *Aubrey Beardsley, the Man and His Work* by Haldane Macfall and *Aubrey Beardsley* by Robert Ross; *The Life of Francis Thompson* by Everard Meynell; *The Life of Walter Sickert* by Robert Emmons; *Charles Ricketts, R.A.*, by T. Sturge Moore; *The Life of Henry Tonks* by Joseph Hone; *The Life of Roger Fry* by Virginia Woolf; *The Tribulations of a Baronet* (Sir W. Eden) by Sir Timothy Eden.

Much information concerning Simeon Solomon is given in *Five Years Dead* by Bernard Falk. Interesting sidelights on Whistler and Swinburne are contained in *Whistler the Friend* by E. R. Pennell and *Swinburne as I Knew Him* by Coulson Kernahan. *Edward Martyn and the Irish Revival* is valuable for George Moore's Irish period.

*The Memoirs of Thomas Armstrong* are valuable for the student life of du Maurier, Whistler, and Poynter. *A Comedy of Masques*, semi-autobiographical novel by Ernest Dowson, provides a useful account of artistic life in London in the late nineteenth century.

*Bad Companions* by William Roughead gives an account of the Queen *v.* Boulton and Others trial, referred to. *Oscar Wilde Three Times Tried* in the Famous Old Bailey Trials of the Nineteenth Century gives a detailed reporting of the Wilde case.

## SOURCES AND ACKNOWLEDGEMENTS

Of many works on French art and the Anglo-French connexion in art it is possible to mention only a few. George Moore's *Modern Painting* and D. S. MacColl's *Nineteenth Century Painting* and *Confessions of a Keeper* are relevant. R. H. Wilenski's *Modern French Painters* give a useful account of the French background. *Vision and Design* by Roger Fry should also be referred to.

# INDEX

263